Software Testing Foundations

About the Authors

Andreas Spillner is a professor of Computer Science in the Department of Electrical Engineering and Computer Science at Bremen University of Applied Sciences. For more than 10 years, he was president of the German Special Interest Group in Software Testing, Analysis, and Verification of the German Society for Informatics. He is a member of the German Testing Board. His work emphasis is on software, quality assurance, testing, and object-oriented system development.

Tilo Linz is CEO of imbus AG, a leading service company for software testing in Germany. He is president of the German Testing Board and was president of the ISTQB from 2002 to 2005. His work emphasis is on consulting and coaching projects on software quality management, and optimizing software development and testing processes.

Hans Schaefer is an independent consultant in software testing in Norway. He is president of the Norwegian Testing Board. He has been consulting and teaching software testing methods since 1984. He organizes the Norwegian Special Interest Group in Software Testing for Western Norway. His work emphasis is on consulting, teaching, and coaching test process improvement and test design techniques, as well as reviews.

Andreas Spillner · Tilo Linz · Hans Schaefer

Software Testing Foundations

A Study Guide for the Certified Tester Exam

- Foundation Level
- ISTQB compliant

2nd Edition

Andreas Spillner
spillner@informatik.hs-bremen.de

Tilo Linz
tilo.linz@imbus.de

Hans Schaefer
hans.schaefer@ieee.org

Editor: Jimi DeRouen
Copyeditor: Joan Dixon
Layout and Type: Josef Hegele
Cover Design: Helmut Kraus, www.exclam.de
Printer: Malloy, Ann Arbor, MI
Printed in the U.S.A.

ISBN: 978-1-933952-08-6

2nd Edition
© 2007 by Rocky Nook Inc.
26 West Mission Street Ste 3
Santa Barbara, CA 93101

www.rockynook.com

This 2nd English book edition conforms to the 3rd German edition
"Basiswissen Softwaretest – Aus- und Weiterbildung zum Certified
Tester – Foundation Level nach ISTQB-Standard" (dpunkt.verlag GmbH,
ISBN 3-89864-358-1), which was reprinted in 2006.

Library of Congress catalog application submitted.

Distributed by O'Reilly Media
1005 Gravenstein Highway North
Sebastopol, CA 95472

Foreword to the First Edition
by Rex Black

I've been in the software and systems engineering business for over twenty years, with most of that time spent as a tester. In the 1980s, when I shifted my career emphasis from programming and system administration to testing, the resources were pretty limited. There were a few books by testing pioneers such as Boris Beizer, Bill Hetzel, Glenford Myers, and Bill Perry. Some of these books were – and remain – good resources. Someone new to the field could cover the entire software and systems testing library in a few months of reading.

Not any more. Now we have dozens and dozens of books out there on testing. You can read a book on testing specific kinds of applications, like Web applications and embedded applications. You can read a book on testing in formal settings and informal settings. You can even read a book or two on test management.

However, every professional needs to start somewhere. Every profession needs its foundation. The profession of software and systems testing needs books that provide the basic techniques, tools, and concepts. This is one such book.

This book will provide you with a solid practical foundation for your work and study of testing. Software and system testing suffers from a serious gap between best practices and common practices. If you're someone who is making a living from doing testing but haven't gotten around to reading a book, why not start with this one?

The authors wrote this book using the International Software Test Qualification Board's Foundation Level Syllabus as an outline. So, if you're pursuing test certification, I recommend this book. You can get certified according to the Foundation Level Syllabus by taking an exam offered through a recognized National Board. Such National Boards include the American Testing Board, the Indian Test Board, and the Israeli Test Certification Board, to name three such boards that I serve on.

This book would also make a fine textbook for a college course. If you're a professor looking for a good testing textbook, both you and your students may find this book a good choice.

This book should prove especially useful to you if you work on inhouse system development. The discussion on the role, techniques, and importance of requirements specification and acceptance testing in such environments is excellent. Of course, we don't always find ourselves working in organizations that have the overall system lifecycle process maturity that underpins this book. However, assuming that the testing process is part of a larger set of mature, well-managed development, maintenance, and deployment processes is a smart way to keep the book from spiraling into a complex discussion on how testing can adapt to dysfunctional organizations.

One problem we face in the testing profession is the lack of a universally-accepted glossary. That leads to a lot of discussion and confusion. The authors deal with that by providing definitions for their terms, based on the International Software Testing Qualification Board's glossary. I found a lot that I liked in this book. It provides a good description of what software and systems testing is. It explains not just the best practices and techniques, also the whys and hows of these techniques.

If you've read my books, *Critical Testing Processes* and *Managing the Testing Process*, you know that I like case studies and examples. If you've taken my training courses, you've worked through exercises based on real-world examples. This book uses a well-described, practical, true-to-life running case study to illustrate the key points. That helps bring the material to life and make it clear.

I also liked the survey of the commonly-used and commonly-useful black box and white box techniques. The authors also provide good brief discussions of some of the more unusual – but sometimes useful – techniques, too. If you're an analyst or test manager, this should help you understand the essential techniques of test design.

There's also a good survey of test automation tools and techniques. The authors give a balanced perspective that neither bashes nor boosts the tools. With so much hype and confusion surrounding this topic – and, sadly, so many failed attempts at test automation – the authors' dispassionate approach, with plenty of cautionary notes, is refreshing.

Finally, it's nice to see a test book that includes a broad, helpful discussion of test management. Other than my own two books, this topic hasn't gotten much attention. If you're a tester or QA analyst who needs to understand the management perspective, this book should help.

As you can see, this book introduces many topics in the field of software and system testing. In spite of that, this is a relatively short book, which makes it more approachable for busy test professionals. As a writer, I know it's hard to write books that are both comprehensive and brief. The authors have struck a good balance in the level of detail they provide, focusing on the needs of the target audience. This book will provide a solid foundation for you when you read more advanced books on specific topics like test management, test design, test automation, or testing particular kinds of applications.

Bulverde, Texas, June 2004

Rex Black, President of the ISTQB

Contents

Foreword

In the foreword to the German first edition of *Software Testing Foundations*, we asked if more books on software testing were needed. Since both the first and second German editions quickly sold out, we consider the answer to our question to be a resounding "Yes!". The German second edition was translated to English and this English edition also sold out surprisingly fast.

There has only been one internationally recognized syllabus published since 2005 for the ISTQB® Certified Tester, Foundation Level, and the two existing compatible syllabi by the Information Systems Examinations Board (ISEB) [URL: ISEB] and the German Testing Board (GTB) have been combined and updated.

The current syllabus

This second English edition of *Software Testing Foundations* conforms to the International Software Testing Qualifications Board Foundation Level Syllabus (ISTQB) [URL: ISTQB], which was published in July 2005. The book includes additions to the syllabus with respect to the two earlier versions.

Found in the syllabus, and therefore also in this second English edition, is some new content (such as the test first approach and risk-based testing), and you will find that the formulation of learning objectives is the basis for a new learning dimension. Explicit learning objectives help the reader to remain oriented. These learning objectives also clarify the knowledge and the depth of knowledge that is expected from an ISTQB Certified Tester, Foundation Level. This means, for example, that at the lowest level of the learning objectives the glossary definitions of all marked key terms of the syllabus are relevant for the examination.

What is new in the new ISTQB Syllabus?

"The terms are no longer defined in the new ISTQB Foundation Level Syllabus, but can be found in the ISTQB Glossary of Testing Terms [URL: ISTQB] and its national equivalents. The new ISTQB Foundation Level Syllabus, on the other hand, provides a detailed explanation of Best Practices of Software Testing, not relying on outside sources such as national standards. Analogous to the Advanced Level, the content relevant for the examination (i.e., test management) has now been structured in the same way for the Foundation Level. Thus, the Foundation Level creates the basis for the additional knowledge required for the Advanced Level" (Horst Pohlmann, German Testing Board, Working Party Foundation Level).

Certification

The education and certification for the Certified Tester have been very well received worldwide. At the end of 2006, there are already more than 40,000 certified testers (i.e., those who passed the exams organized worldwide by several national testing boards) [URL: ISTQB]. Approximately Eighty percent of the examined people passed the exam and received the certificate. The official exam questions are currently being updated so they match the new ISTQB Syllabus. New examinations are now run only based on the most current syllabus. Several companies have been accredited to hold training seminars for the Certified Tester examination. Thus, qualified training is available in Europe, the USA, and India.

ISTQB members

Currently, the following countries have national testing boards in the ISTQB: Australia/New Zealand, Austria, Bangladesh, Brazil, Canada, China, Denmark, England, Finland, France, Germany, India, Israel, Japan, Korea, Netherlands/Belgium, Norway, Poland, Portugal, Russia, Spain, Sweden, Switzerland, Turkey, the United States, and the Ukraine. There are also testing boards for Latin America and South East Europe.

In response to the international interest in software testing and Certified Tester education, we also published a Dutch edition of *Software Testing Foundations* in 2004. Translations into Polish and Romanian are currently under way. At the 2nd level, there are currently two schemes and two syllabi: ASQF/iSQI Advanced Level (developed by the German Testing Board) and ISEB Practitioner Level (developed by the UK Board). Both are recognized by ISTQB as professional qualifications for testers, as they have gained a respect in the testing community over many years. ISTQB intends to have these two 2nd level schemes integrated into a single unified 2nd level "ISTQB Advanced Level" qualification, which should supersede both existing schemes. Seminars for advanced topics (i.e., test management, test methods) are already being offered and these seminars are well attended. We are currently busy writing the literature to match this syllabus. The German book "Praxiswissen Softwaretest – Testmanagement" was recently published and covers parts of the syllabus for these

The next qualification level

topics. In spring 2007 there will also be an English edition of the book »Software Testing Practice – Test Management«. Books about »Test Design« and the topics for the yet to be defined Expert Level shall follow.

Use at universities and colleges

We are pleased to note that this book has been adopted at universities and colleges, and lectures with attached examinations are being offered at the technical universities of Munich and Darmstadt, the University of Dortmund, the universities of applied science in Cologne and Bremen, as well as the University of Iceland in Reykjavik, and the University of Graz, Austria. Students of these classes were able to take the exam for the Certified Tester, Foundation Level.

We want to thank our readers for their helpful comments, which have contributed to corrections and clarifications in the first and second German editions of this book. We would like to extend a further thank you to our colleagues in the GTB and ISTQB, without whose great work there would be no Certified Tester scheme. We especially want to thank Horst Pohlmann for his excellent contributions when composing the syllabi, examination questions, and the Certified Tester glossary.

Thank you notes

We want to cordially thank Martin Pol for his translation of the book to Dutch. Rex Black has also given us many valuable comments, as well as his foreword for the first English edition.

Andreas Spillner, Tilo Linz and Hans Schaefer
Bremen, Möhrendorf, and Valestrandsfossen,
December 2006

1 Introduction

Software has found an enormous dissemination in the past years. There are few machines or facilities left today that are not controlled by software or at least include software. In automobiles, for example, from the engine to the transmission and up to the brakes, more and more functions are controlled by microprocessors and their software. Thus, software is crucial to the functionality of devices and industry. Likewise, the smooth operation of an enterprise or organization depends largely on the reliability of the software systems used for supporting the business processes or particular tasks. The speed at which an insurance company is able to introduce a new product, or even a new rate, most likely depends on how quickly the IT systems can be adjusted or extended.

Within both sectors (embedded and commercial software systems), the quality of software has become the most important factor in determining the success of products or enterprises.

High dependence on the correct functioning of the software

Many enterprises have recognized this dependence on software and strive for improved quality of their software systems and software engineering (or development) processes. One way to achieve this goal is systematic evaluation and testing of the developed software. In some cases, appropriate testing procedures have found their way into the daily practice of software development. However, in many sectors, there remains a significant need to become educated in regard to evaluation and testing procedures.

With this book, we offer basic knowledge that helps to achieve structured and systematic evaluation and testing. Implementation of these evaluation and testing procedures should contribute to an improved quality of the software being developed. This book is written in such a way that it does not presume previous knowledge of software quality assurance. It is designed as a textbook and is meant for self-study. A single, continuous case example is included which will help explain every shown topic and its practical solution.

Basic knowledge for structured evaluation and testing

We want to appeal to the software testers in software and industry enterprises who strive for a well-founded, basic knowledge of the principles behind software testing. We also address programmers and developers who are already practicing testing tasks or will do so in the future. The book will help project managers and team leaders to improve the effectiveness and efficiency of software tests. Even those in related disciplines close to IT jobs, as well as other employees who are involved in the process of acceptance, introduction, and further development of IT applications, will find this book helpful for their daily tasks.

Evaluation and testing procedures have a high cost in practice (expenditures in this sector are estimated to be 25 % to 50 % of the software development time and cost [Koomen 99]). Yet, there are few universities, colleges, or vocational schools in the sector of computer science that offer courses that intensively teach this topic. This book is of value to both students and teachers, as it provides the material for a basic course.

Lifelong learning is indispensable, especially in the IT industry, therefore many companies offer further education to their employees. The general recognition of a course certificate is, however, only possible if the contents of the course and the examination are defined and followed up by an independent body.

Certification program for software testers

In 1998, the *Information Systems Examinations Board* [URL: ISEB] of the *British Computer Society* [URL: BCS] [URL: ISEB] started such a certification scheme.

International initiative

Similar to the British example, other countries took up these activities and established country specific *Testing Boards* in order to make it possible to run training and examination in the language of the respective country. These national boards cooperate in the *International Software Testing Qualifications Board* [URL: ISTQB].

The current structure of the ISTQB is shown in figure 1-1.

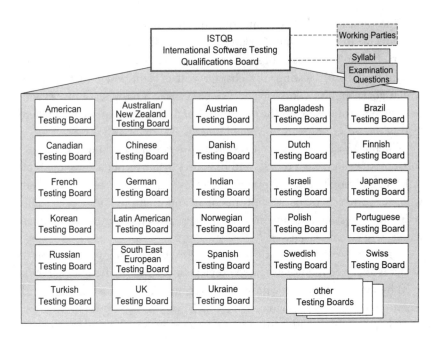

The *International Software Testing Qualifications Board* coordinates the national initiatives and provides the uniformity and comparability of the teaching and exam contents in the countries involved.

They are responsible for issuing and maintaining curricula in their country language and for organizing and executing examinations in their countries. They assess the seminars offered in their countries according to defined criteria and accredit training providers. The testing boards thus guarantee a standard of high quality of the seminars. After passing an exam, the seminar participants receive an internationally recognized qualification certificate.

National Testing Boards

The *ISTQB Certified Tester* Qualification scheme has three steps [URL: ISTQB]. The basics are described in the curriculum (syllabus) for the *Foundation Level*. Building on this is the *Advanced Level* certificate, showing a deeper knowledge of testing. The third level, for the *Expert Level* certificate, is currently being developed.

The content of this book corresponds to the requirements of the ISTQB *Foundation Certificate*. The knowledge needed for the exams can be acquired by self-study. The book can also be used to extend knowledge after, or parallel to, participation in a course.

Chapter overview basics

The topics of this book, and thus the rough structure of the course contents for the *Foundation Certificate,* are described below.

In chapter 2, the basics of software testing are discussed. In addition to the motivation for testing, the chapter will explain when to test, with which goals, and how intensively. The concept of a basic test process will be shown. It will deal with the psychological difficulties experienced when testing one's own software, and the blindness for one's own errors.

Testing in the software life cycle

Chapter 3 discusses which test activities should be done during the software development process, and how they relate to other development tasks. In addition to the different →test levels and →test phases, it will deal with the differences between functional and nonfunctional tests. The economy of testing and how to test changes, as well as testing in maintenance, will also be discussed.

Static test

Chapter 4 discusses static methods, i.e., procedures where the test object is analyzed but not executed. Reviews and static analyses are already used by many enterprises with positive results. The various methods and techniques will be described.

Dynamic test

Chapter 5 deals with testing in a narrower sense. The classification of dynamic testing into *black box* and *white box* techniques will be discussed. Various test techniques are explained in detail with the help of a continuous example. Illustrated at the end of the chapter is the reasonable usage of exploratory and intuitive testing, which may be used in addition to the other techniques.

Test management

Chapter 6 shows which aspects should be considered in test management, how systematic incident handling appears, and some basics about establishing sufficient →configuration management.

Test tools

Testing of software without the support of appropriate tools is very labor and time intensive. The seventh and last chapter of this book introduces different classes of tools for supporting testing, and hints for tool selection and implementation.

Notes to the subject matter and for the exam are in the appendix

The appendix offers notes and additional information on the subject matter and the exam to the Certified Tester. Further appendices of this book contain explanations to the test plan according to [IEEE 829-1983], exemplary exercises, a glossary, and the list of literature. The technical terms are marked with an appropriate hint when they appear for the first time in the text. The hint points to a detailed definition in the glossary. Text passages that go beyond the material of the syllabus are marked as *excursions.*

2 The Basics of Software Testing

This chapter will explain some basic facts of software testing, covering every-thing that is required for understanding the following chapters. Important phrases and essential vocabulary will be explained by using an example application. This example appears frequently to illustrate and clarify the sub-ject matter throughout the book. In the following section this example will be introduced. The fundamental test process and the single activities of testing will be illustrated. Psychological problems will be discussed.

The procedures for testing software presented in this book are mainly illus-trated by one general example. The fundamental scenario is described as follows:

A car manufacturer develops a new electronic sales support system called *VirtualShowRoom* (VSR). The final version of this software system is supposed to be installed at every car dealer worldwide. Any customer who is interested in buying a new car will be able to configure their favorite model (model, type, color, extras, etc.), with or without the guidance of a salesperson.

*Case study
"VirtualShowRoom" – VSR*

The system shows possible models and combinations of extra equipment, and instantly calculates the accurate price of the configured car. This functionality will be implemented by a subsystem called *DreamCar*.

If the customer has made up their mind, they will be able to calculate the most suitable payment (*EasyFinance*) as well as to place the order online (*Just-InTime*). Of course, they will get the possibility to sign up for the appropriate insurance (*NoRisk*). Personal information and contract data about the customer is managed by the *ContractBase* subsystem.

Figure 2-1 shows the general architecture of this software system. Every sub-system will be designed and developed by separate developer teams. Altogether about 50 developers and additional employees from the respective user depart-ments are involved in working on this project. External software companies will also participate.

Before shipping the VSR-System, it must be tested thoroughly. The project members who have been assigned to test the software apply different techniques and procedures. This book contains the basic knowledge for those techniques and procedures of software testing.

Figure 2–1
Architecture
of the VSR-System

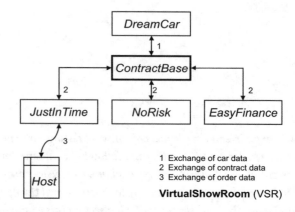

2.1   Terms and Motivation

Requirements

During the construction of an industry product, the parts and the final product are usually tested to check if they fulfill the given →requirements. It must be determined whether the product solves the required task. There may be differences between the requirements and the implemented product. If the product exhibits problems, necessary corrections must be made in the production process and/or in the construction.

Software is immaterial

What generally counts for the production of industry products is also appropriate to the production or development of software. However, testing (or evaluation) of partial products and the final product respectively is more difficult, because a software product is not a physical product. A direct examination is not possible. The only way to directly examine the product is by reading the development documents very carefully.

The dynamic behavior of the software, however, cannot be checked this way. It must be done through →testing, where the tested software will be executed on a computer. Its behavior must be compared to the given requirements. Thus, the testing of software is a very important and difficult task in the software development process. It contributes to reducing the →risk of use of the software, because bugs can be found by testing. Testing and its documentation are sometimes also required by the contract, or in legal or industrial standards.

To identify and repair possible faults before delivery, the VSR-System from the case example must be tested intensively before it is used. For example, if the system executes order transactions incorrectly, this could result in frustration for the customer and a serious financial or image loss to the dealer and the car manufacturer. Anyway, not finding the bugs holds a high risk when using the system.

Example

2.1.1   Error and Bug Terminology

When do we have a behavior of the system which does not conform to requirements? A situation can be classified as incorrect only after we know what the expected correct situation is supposed to look like. Thus, a →failure is a nonfulfillment of a given requirement; a discrepancy between the →actual result or behavior (identified while executing the test) and the →expected result or behavior (defined in the specifications or requirements). A failure is present if a warrantable (user) expectation is not fulfilled adequately. Examples of failures are products that are too hard to use or too slow, but still fulfill the functional requirements.

What is an error, failure, or fault?

In contrast to physical systems, software failures do not occur because of aging or abrasion. They occur because of →faults in the software. Every →fault (or →defect or →bug) in the software is present since it was developed or changed. Yet, the fault materializes only when executing the software, becoming visible as a failure.

Causal chain

To describe the event when a user experiences a problem, [IEEE 610.12] uses the term failure. However, other terms like "problem" or "incident" are often used. During testing or use of the software, the failure becomes visible to the →tester or user; for example, an output is wrong or the application crashes.

Failures

We must differentiate between the occurrence of a failure and its cause. A failure has its roots in a fault in the software. This fault is also called a defect or internal error. Programmer slang for this term is a "bug". An example might be wrongly programmed or forgotten code in the application.

Faults

It is possible that a fault is hidden by one or more other faults in different parts of the application (→defect masking). In that case, a failure only occurs after the masking defects have been corrected. This demonstrates that corrections can have side effects.

Defect masking

One problem is that a fault can cause none, one, or many failures for any number of users, and that the fault and the corresponding failure are arbitrarily far away from each other. A particularly dangerous example is some small corruption of stored data, which may be found a long time after it first occurred.

The cause of a fault or defect is an error or mistake by a person. For example, wrong programming by the developer, or a misunderstanding of the commands in a programming language. However, faults may even be caused by environmental conditions, like radiation, magnetism, etc., that introduce hardware problems. This last factor is, however, not further discussed in this book.

More detailed descriptions of the terms within the domain of testing are given in the following paragraphs.

2.1.2   Testing Terms

Testing is not debugging

To be able to correct a defect or bug, it must be localized in the software. Initially, we only know the effect of a defect but not the precise location in the software. The localization and the correction of defects are the job of the software developer and are called →debugging. Repairing a defect generally increases the →quality of the product, provided that in most cases no new defects are introduced. Debugging is often equated with testing, but testing and debugging are totally different activities.

Debugging is the task of localizing and correcting faults. The goal of testing is the (more or less systematic) detection of failures (that indicate the presence of defects).

A test is a sample examination

Every execution (even using more or less random samples) of a test object, in order to examine it, is testing. The conditions for the test must be defined. The actual and the expected behaviors of the test object must be compared[1].

Testing software has different purposes:

▓ Executing a program in order to find failures
▓ Executing a program in order to measure quality
▓ Executing a program in order to provide confidence[2]
▓ Analyzing a program or its documentation in order to prevent defects

The whole process of systematically executing programs to demonstrate the correct implementation of the requirements, to increase confidence, and to detect failures is called test. In addition, a test includes static meth-

---

1.   It is not possible to prove correct implementation of the requirements. We can only reduce the risk of serious bugs remaining through testing.
2.   If a thorough test finds little or no failures, confidence in the product will increase.

ods, i.e., static analysis of software products using tools, as well as document reviews (see chapter 4).

Besides the execution of the test object with →test data, the planning, design, implementation, and analysis of the test (→test management) are also part of the →test process. A →test run or →test suite consists of the execution of one or more →test cases. A test case contains defined test conditions (mostly the requirements for execution), the inputs, and the expected outputs or the expected behavior of the test object. A test case should have a high probability of revealing previously unknown faults [Myers 79].

Several test cases can often be combined to create →test scenarios, whereby the result of one test case is used as the starting point for the next test case. For example, a test scenario for a database application can contain one test case which writes a date into the database; another test case which manipulates that date; and a third test case which reads the manipulated date out of the database and deletes it. Then all three test cases will be executed, one after another, all in a row.

At present, there is no known bug free software system, and there will not be in the near future if the system has nontrivial complexity. Often the reason for a fault is that certain exceptional cases were not considered during development as well as during testing of the software. Such faults could be the incorrectly calculated leap year, or the not considered boundary condition for the timely response, or the needed resources. On the other hand there are many software systems in many different fields that operate reliably, day in and out.

No complex software system is bug free

Even if all the executed test cases do not reveal any further failures, we cannot conclude with complete safety (except for very small programs) that there do not exist further faults.

Absolute correctness cannot be achieved with testing

There are many confusing terms for different kinds of software testing tasks. Some will be explained later within the description of the different →test levels (see chapter 3). This excursion is supposed to explain some of the different terms. It is helpful to differentiate these categories of testing terms:

Excursion: Naming of tests

1. →**Test objective or test type:** Calling a kind of test by its purpose (e.g., →load test).
2. →**Test technique:** The test is named using the name of the technique used for the specification or execution of the test (e.g., →business-process-based test or →boundary value test).
3. **Test object:** The test is named after the kind of the test object to be tested (e.g., GUI test or DB test (data base test)).

4. **Testing level:** The test is named after the level or phase of the underlying life cycle model (e.g., →system test).
5. **Test person:** The test is named after the person subgroup executing the tests (e.g., developer test, →user acceptance test).
6. **Test extent:** The test is named after the level of extent (e.g., partial →regression test).

Thus, not every term means a new or different kind of testing. In fact, only one of the aspects is pushed to the fore. It depends on the perspective we use when we look at the actual test.

2.1.3   Software Quality

Testing of software contributes to improvement of →software quality. This is done through identifying defects and their subsequent correction by debugging. But testing is also measurement of software quality. If the test cases are a reasonable sample of software use, quality experienced by the user should not be too different from quality experienced during testing.

But software quality entails more than just the elimination of failures that occurred during the testing. According to the ISO/IEC-Standard 9126-1 [ISO 9126] the following factors belong to software quality: →functionality, →reliability, usability, →efficiency, →maintainability, and portability.

All these factors, or →quality characteristics (also: →quality attribute), have to be considered while testing in order to judge the overall quality of a software product. It should be defined in advance which quality level the test object is supposed to show for each characteristic. The achievement of these requirements must then be examined with capable tests.

Example
VirtualShowRoom

In the example of the VSR-System, the customer must define which of the quality characteristics are most important. Those have to be implemented and examined in the system. The characteristics of functionality, reliability, and usability are very important for the car manufacturer. The system must reliably provide the required functionality. Beyond that, it must be easy to use so that the different car dealers can use it without any problems in everyday life. These quality characteristics should be especially well tested in the product.

Functionality

We discuss the individual quality characteristics of ISO/IEC-Standard 9126-1 [ISO 9126] in the following section. Functionality contains all characteristics which describe the required capabilities of the system. The capabilities are usually described by a specific input/output behavior and/or an appropriate reaction to an input. The goal of the test is to prove that every single required capability in the system was implemented in the specified way. According to ISO/IEC-Standard 9126-1, the functionality characteristic contains the subcharacteristics: adequacy, interoperability, correctness, and security.

An appropriate solution is achieved if all required capabilities exist in the system and they work adequately. Thereby it is clearly important to pay attention to, and thus to examine during testing the correct or specified outputs or effects that the system generates.

Software systems must interoperate with other systems, or at least with the operating system (unless the operating system is the test object itself). Interoperability describes the cooperation between the system to be tested and the previously existing system. Trouble with this cooperation should be detected by the test.

One area of functionality is the fulfillment of application specific standards, agreements, or legal requirements and similar regulations. Many applications give a high importance to the aspects of access security and data security. It must be proven that unauthorized access to applications and data, both accidentally and intentionally, will be prevented. *Security*

Reliability describes the ability of a system to keep functioning under specific use over a specific period. In the standard, the quality characteristic is split into maturity, →fault tolerance, and recoverability. *Reliability*

Maturity means how often a failure of the software occurs as a result of defects in the software.

Fault tolerance is the capability of the software product to maintain a specified level of performance, or to recover from faults in cases of software faults, or of infringement of its specified interface.

Recoverability is the capability of the software product to reestablish a specified level of performance and recover the data directly affected in the case of a failure. Following a failure, a software product will sometimes be "down" for a certain period of time, the length of which is assessed by its recoverability. The ease of recovery and the work required should also be assessed.

Usability is very important for interactive software systems. Users will not accept a system that is hard to use. How significant is the effort that is required for the usage of the software for the different user groups? Understandability, ease of learning, operability, and attractiveness, as well as compliance to standards, conventions, style guides or user interface regu- *Usability*

Efficiency

lations are partial aspects of usability. These quality characteristics are examined in →nonfunctional tests (see chapter 3).

The test for efficiency measures the required time and consumption of resources for the fulfillment of tasks. Resources may include other software products, the software and hardware configuration of the system, and materials (e.g., print paper, network, and storage).

Changeability and portability

Software systems are often used over a long period on varied platforms (operating system and hardware). Therefore, the last two quality criteria are very important: maintainability and portability.

Subcharacteristics of maintainability are analyzability, changeability, stability against side effects, testability, and compliance to standards.

Maintainability

Adaptability, ease of installation, conformity, and interchangeability have to be considered for the portability of software systems. Many of the aspects of maintainability and portability can only be examined by →static analysis (see section 4.2).

Portability

A software system cannot fulfill every quality characteristic equally well. Sometimes it is possible that a fulfillment of one characteristic results in a conflict with another one. For example, a highly efficient software system can become hard to port, because the developers usually use special characteristics (or features) of the chosen platform to improve the efficiency, which in turn affects the portability in a negative way.

Prioritize quality characteristics

Quality characteristics must therefore be prioritized. This definition also acts as a guide for the test to determine the examination's intensity for the different quality characteristics. The next chapter will discuss the amount of work that is involved in these sorts of tests.

2.1.4   Test Effort

Complete testing is not possible

Testing cannot prove the absence of faults. In order to do this, a test would need to execute a program in every possible way with every possible data value. In practice, a →complete or exhaustive test is not feasible. Such a test contains the combination of all possible inputs under consideration of all different conditions that have an influence on the system. Through the multiple combinatorial possibilities, the outcome of this is an almost infinite number of tests. Such a "testing" for all combinations is not possible.

Example

This circumstance is illustrated by an example of →control flow based testing [Myers 79]:

A small program with an easy control flow will be tested. The program consists of four links (IF-instructions) that are partially nested. The appropriate control flow graph of the program is shown in figure 2-2. Between Point A and B is a loop, with a return from Point B to Point A. If the program is supposed to be fully tested in relation to the different control flow based possibilities, every possible combination of links must be executed.

At a loop limit of maximum 20 cycles and considering that all links are independent, the outcome is the following calculation:

$$5^{20} + 5^{19} + 5^{18} + \ldots + 5^1$$

Whereby 5 is the number of possible ways within the loop. 5^1 test cases result through the execution of every single possible way within the loop, but in each case without return to the loop starting point. If executed test cases result in one single return to the loop stating point, then $5*5 = 5^2$ different possibilities of executions must be considered, and so on. To that effect the total result of this calculation is about 100 quadrillion different sequences of the program.

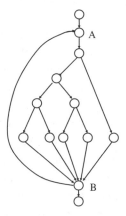

Figure 2–2
Control flow graph
of a small program

Assuming that the test is done manually and a test case, like [Myers 79] describes, takes 5 minutes to specify, to execute, and to be analyzed, the time for this test would be one billion years. If we would take five microseconds instead of five minutes, because the test mainly runs automatically, it would still last 19 years.

Thus, in practice it is not possible to test even a small program exhaustively. It is only possible to consider a part of all imaginable test cases. But even so, testing still takes a lot of the development effort. However, a generalization of the extent of the →test effort is difficult, because it depends very much on the character of the project. In the following, some example

Test effort between
25% and 50%

data from projects of one large German software company are shown. They should shed light on the spectrum of different testing efforts relative to the total budget of the development.

- For some major projects with more than ten person-years' effort, coding and testing together used 40%, and a further 8% was used for the integration. At test intensive projects (e.g., year 2000 bug), the testing effort increased to as much as 80% of the total budget.
- In one project, the testing effort was 1.2 times as high as the coding effort, with 2/3 of the test effort consisting of →component testing.
- At another project of the software company, the system test cost was 51.9% of the project resources.

Test effort is often shown by the proportion between the number of testers and the number of developers. The proportion varies from 1 tester per 10 developers up to 3 testers per developer. Conclusion: test efforts or the budget spent for testing vary enormously.

Faults can cause high costs   But is this high testing effort affordable and justifiable? The counter question from Jerry Weinberg is: "Compared to what?" [DeMarco 93]. His question refers to the risks of faulty software systems. The risk is calculated as the probability of occurrence and the expected amount of loss. Faults that were not found during testing can cause high costs when the software is used. The German Newspaper *Frankfurter Allgemeine Zeitung* from the 17th January 2002 had an article with the topic "IT system breakdowns cost many millions". One hour system breakdown in the stock exchange is estimated to cost $7.8 million. When →safety critical systems fail, it is possible that the lives and health of people are in danger.

Since a full test is not possible, the testing effort must have an appropriate relation to the attainable result. "Testing should continue as long as costs of finding and correcting a defect[3] are lower than the costs of failure in operation" [Koomen 99]. Thus, the test effort is always dependent on an estimation of the application risk.

Example of a high risk   In case of the VSR-System, the prospective customer shall configure their favorite
in case of a failure   car model on the display. If the system calculates a wrong price, the customer can insist on that price. In a later stage of the VSR-System the company plans to offer a web based sales portal. In that case, a wrong price can lead to thousands of cars

---

3.   The cost must include all aspects of a failure, even the possible cost of bad publicity, litigation, etc., and not just the cost of correction, retesting and distribution.

being sold for an incorrect price. The total loss can amount to millions, depending on how much the price was miscalculated by the VSR-System for each car. The legal view is that a valid sales contract with the listed price is initiated by the online order.

Systems with high risks must be tested more thoroughly than systems that do not generate a big loss in case of a failure. The risk assessment must be done for the individual system parts, or even for single error possibilities. In the case of a high risk for failures by a system or subsystem, there must be a greater testing effort than for less critical (sub)systems. International standards for production of safety critical systems use this approach to require that different test techniques be applied for software of different integrity levels.

For a producer of a computer game, an erroneous saving of game scores can mean a very high risk, because the customers will not trust the defective game. This leads to high losses of sales, maybe even for all games produced by the company.

Thus, it must be decided for every software program how intensively and thoroughly it shall be tested. This decision must be made based upon the expected risk of failure of the application. Since a complete test is not possible, how the limited test resources are used is very important. In order to get a satisfying result, the tests must be designed and executed in a structured and systematic way. In this way, it is possible to find many faults with an appropriate effort and avoid unnecessary tests that would not find more faults or give more information about system quality.

Define test intensity and test extent in dependence to the risk

There exist many different methods and procedures for testing software. Every method intensively considers and examines particular aspects of the test object. Thus, the focus of examination for the control flow based test techniques is the program flow. In case of the →data flow test techniques, the examination focuses on the usage and flow of data. Every test technique has its strengths and weaknesses in finding different kinds of faults. There is no test technique which is equally well suited for all aspects. Therefore a combination of different test techniques is always necessary to detect failures with different causes.

Select adequate test procedures

During the test execution phase the test object is checked to determine if it works as required by the →specifications. It is also important – and thus naturally examined while testing – that the test object does not execute functions that go beyond the requirements. The product should only provide functions that are required.

Test of extra functionality

→Test case explosion

The testing effort can grow large. Test managers have the dilemma that the possible test cases and test case variants quickly become hundreds or thousands of tests. This problem is also described with the term combinatorial explosion.

Besides the necessary restriction in the number of test cases, the test manager normally has to struggle with another problem; the lack of resources.

Limited resources

Every software development project has restricted resources. Often, there will be changes in resource estimation and use during the process. This can easily start a fight for resources. The complexity of the development task is underestimated, the development team is delayed, the customer pushes for an earlier release, and the project leader wants to deliver "something" as soon as possible. The test manager normally has the worst position in this "game". Often there is only a small time window just before delivery for testing and very few testers available to run the test. At that point, it is certain that the test manager does not have the time and resources for executing "astronomically" many test cases.

However, it is expected from the test manager that they deliver trustworthy results, and makes sure that the software is sufficiently tested. Only if the test manager has a well-planned, efficient strategy, do they have the chance to fulfill this challenge successfully. A fundamental test process is required. Besides the adherence to a fundamental test process, further →quality assurance activities must be accomplished, for example →reviews (see chapter 4).

The next section describes a fundamental test process typically used for the development and examination of systems like the VSR-System.

2.2   The Fundamental Test Process

Excursion:
Life cycle models

In order to accomplish a structured and controllable software development effort, software development models and →development processes are used. There are many different models: examples are the Waterfall-model [Boehm 73, 81], the V-model [Boehm 79], [IEEE/IEC 12207], the German V-model (V-model – Development Standard for IT Systems of the Federal Republic of Germany ("Vorgehensmodell des Bundes und der Länder") [URL: V-model XT]), the Spiral Model, different incremental or evolutionary models, and the "agile" or "light weight" methods like XP (Extreme Programming), which are popular nowadays [Beck 00]. For the development of object-oriented software systems, the Rational Unified Process [Jacobson 99] is discussed.

All these models define a systematic way to achieve an orderly way of working during the project. In most cases, phases and design steps are defined. They have to be completed with a result in the form of a document. A phase completion, often termed as a →milestone, is achieved when the required documents are completed and conform to the given quality criteria. Usually, →roles dedicated to specific tasks in software development are defined. These tasks have to be accomplished by the project staff. Sometimes, in addition to the models, the techniques and processes to be used in the particular phases are described. With the aid of models, a detailed planning of the resources (time, personnel, infrastructure etc.) can be performed. In a project, the development models define the collective and mandatory tasks to be accomplished by everyone involved, and their chronological sequence.

Testing appears in each of these life cycle models, but with very different meanings and different extent. In the following, some models will be briefly discussed from the view of testing.

The first fundamental model was the Waterfall-model (see figure 2-3, shown with the originally defined levels [Royce 70][4]). It is impressively simple and very well known. Only when one development level is completed will the next one be initiated. Only between adjacent levels are there feedback loops that allow, if necessary, required revisions in the previous level. The crucial disadvantage of this model is that testing is understood as a "one time" action at the end of the project just before the release to operation. The test is seen as a "final inspection", an analogy to a manufacturing inspection before handing over the product to the customer.

Waterfall-model: Testing as "final inspection"

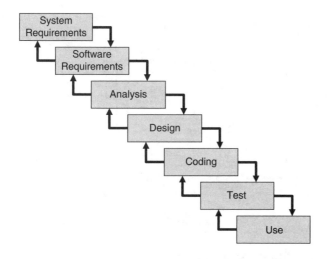

Figure 2–3
Waterfall-model

An enhancement of the Waterfall-model is the general V-model ([Boehm 79], [IEEE/ IEC 12207]), where the constructive activities are separated from the examination

General V-model

---

4.   Royce did not call his model Waterfall-model, and he said in his paper: "Unfortunately, for the process illustrated, the design iterations are never confined to the successive steps."

activities (see chapter 3, figure 3-1). The model has the form of a "V". The construction activities, from requirements definition to implementation, are found on the downward branch of the "V". The test execution activities on the ascending branch are ordered into test levels, and matched to the appropriate abstraction level on the opposite side's construction activity.

The general V-model is very common and frequently in practice.

The description of tasks in the process models discussed above is not sufficient as an instruction on how to perform structured tests in software projects. In addition to the embedding of testing in the whole development process, a more detailed process for the testing tasks themselves is needed (see figure 2-4). This means that the "content" of the development task testing must be split into smaller subtasks, as follows: →test planning and control, test analysis and design, test implementation and execution, evaluation of test →exit criteria and reporting, and test closure activities. Although logically sequential, the activities in the test process may overlap or take place concurrently. These subtasks form a fundamental test process and are described in more detail in the following sections.

Figure 2–4
Fundamental test process

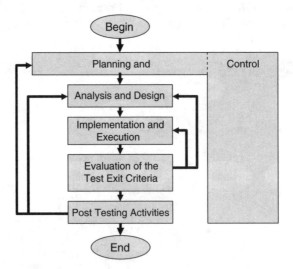

2.2.1   Test Planning and Control

Execution of such a substantial task as testing must not take place without a plan. Planning of the test process starts at the beginning of the software development project. As with all planning, during the course of the project the previous plans must be regularly checked, updated, and adjusted.

The mission and objectives of testing must be defined and agreed upon. Necessary resources for the test process should be estimated. Which employees are needed, for the execution of which tasks and when? How much time is needed, and which equipment and utilities must be available? These questions and many more must be answered during planning and the result should be documented in the →test plan (see chapter 6). Necessary training of the employees should be provided. An organization a organizational structure with the appropriate test management must be arranged or adjusted if necessary.

Planning of the resources

Test control is the monitoring of the test activities and comparing what actually happens during the project with the plan, reporting status of deviations from the plan, and taking any actions to meet the mission and objectives in the new situation. The test plan must be continuously updated, taking into account the feedback from monitoring and control.

Part of the test management tasks is administrating and maintaining the test process, the →test infrastructure, and the →testware. Progress tracking can be based on the appropriate reporting from the employees, as well as data automatically generated from tools. Agreements on this point must be made early.

The main task of planning is to determine the →test strategy (see section 6.4). Since an exhaustive test is not possible, priorities must be set based on risk assessment. The test activities must be distributed to the individual subsystems, depending on the expected risk and the severity of failure effects. Critical subsystems must get greater attention, thus being tested more intensively. Less critical subsystems get less extensive testing. If no negative effects are expected in case of a failure, testing could even be skipped on some parts. However, this decision must be made with great care. The goal of the test strategy is the optimal distribution of the tests to the "right" parts of the software system.

Determination of the test strategy

The VSR-System consists of the following subsystems:

Example of a test strategy

- *DreamCar* allows the individual configuration of a car and its extra equipment
- *ContractBase* manages all customer information and contract data
- *JustInTime* implements the ability to place online orders (within the first expansion stage by the dealer)
- *EasyFinance* calculates an optimal method of financing for the customer
- *NoRisk* provides the ability to purchase appropriate insurance

Naturally, the 5 subsystems should not be tested with identical intensity. The result of a discussion with the VSR-System client is that incorrect behavior of the subsystems *DreamCar* and *ContractBase* will have the most harmful effects. Because of this, the test strategy dictates that these two subsystems must be tested more intensively.

The possibility to place orders online, provided by the subsystem *JustInTime*, is found to be less critical because the order can, in the worst case, still be passed on in other ways (e.g., fax). But it is important that the order data must not be altered or get lost in the subsystem *JustInTime*. Thus, this aspect should be tested more intensively.

For the other two subsystems *NoRisk* and *EasyFinance*, the test strategy defines that all of their main functions (computing a tariff, recording and placing contracts, saving and printing contracts, etc.) have to be tested. Because of time constraints, it is not possible to cover all conceivable contract variants for the financing and insurance of a car. Thus, it is decided to concentrate the test around the most commonly occurring tariff combinations. Combinations that occur less frequently get a lower priority (see sections 2.4 and 6.4). These first thoughts about the test strategy for the VSR-System make clear that a definition of the intensity of testing is reasonable for whole subsystems, as well as for single aspects of a system.

Define test intensity for subsystems and individual aspects

The intensity of testing depends very much on which test techniques are used and the →test coverage that must be achieved. The test coverage serves as a test exit criterion. Besides →coverage criteria, which refer to the source code (for example statement coverage, see section 5.2), it is possible to define the fulfillment of the customer requirements as an exit criterion. It may be demanded that all functions must be tested at least once or, for example, that at least 70% of the possible transactions in a system are executed once. Of course, the definitions of the exit criteria, and thus the intensity of the tests, should be done with consideration of the risk. Once all test exit criteria are defined their values are appraised after executing the test cases to decide if the test process can be finished.

Prioritization of the tests

Because software projects are often run under severe time pressure, it is reasonable to appropriately consider the time aspect during planning. The prioritization of tests guarantees that the critical software parts are tested first, in case time constraints do not allow executing all the planned tests (see section 6.4).

Tool support

If the necessary tool support (see chapter 7) does not exist, selection and acquisition of tools must be initiated early. Existing tools must be evaluated for use in the actual situation. It also needs to be checked if these tools are current. If parts of the test infrastructure have to be developed, this should be started immediately. →Test harnesses (or →test beds), where subsystems can be executed in isolation, must in most cases be programmed by the developing or testing organization. They must be created soon enough to be ready after programming the respective test objects. If frameworks are applied, like Junit [URL: xunit], their usage in the project must be checked and announced early.

2.2.2   Test Analysis and Design

The first task is to review the →test basis, i.e., the specification of what should be tested. The specification may not be concrete or clear enough to develop test cases. As an example, a requirement is so imprecise in defining the expected output or the expected behavior of the system that no test cases can be specified. The →testability of the requirement is insufficient, therefore rework of the requirements has to be done. Determining the →preconditions and requirements to test case design should be based on an analysis of the requirements, the expected behavior, and the structure of the test object.

The test strategy determined in the test plan defines which test techniques shall be used. The test strategy may be further detailed in this step, however the most important task is to develop test cases. Appropriate test cases are then developed using the test techniques specified in the test plan, as well as techniques chosen based on an analysis of possible complexity in the test object.

The specification of the test cases takes place in two steps. →Logical test cases have to be defined first. After that, the logical test cases can be translated into concrete, physical test cases, meaning the actual inputs are chosen (→concrete test cases). Also, the opposite sequence is possible: from the concrete to the general logical test case. This procedure must be used if a test object is specified insufficiently and test specification is done in a rather experimental way (→exploratory testing, see section 5.3). The development of physical test cases, however, is part of the next phase, test implementation.

Logical and concrete test cases

The test basis guides the selection of logical test cases with each test technique. The test cases can be determined from the test object's specification (→black box test design technique), or be created by analyzing the source code (→white box test design technique). It becomes clear that the →test case specification can take place at totally different times during the software development process, depending on the chosen test techniques determined in the test strategy. The process models shown at the beginning of section 2.2 represent just the test execution phases. Test planning, analysis, and design tasks can and should take place in parallel to earlier development activities.

For each test case the initial situation (precondition) must be described. It must be clear which environmental conditions are needed for the test, and which must be fulfilled. Furthermore, it must be defined in advance which results and behavior are expected. The results include outputs, changes to global (persistent) data and states, and any other consequences of the test case.

To define the expected results, the tester must obtain the information from some adequate source. In this context, this is often called an oracle, or →test oracle. A test oracle is a mechanism for predicting the expected results. The specification can serve as a test oracle. Here are two possibilities:

- The tester derives the expected data from the input data by calculation or analysis, based on the specification of the test object.
- If functions that do the reverse action are available, they can be run after the test and then the result is verified against the old input. An example of this scenario is encryption and decryption.

See also chapter 5 for more information about predicting the expected results.

Test cases for expected and unexpected inputs

Test cases can be differentiated by two criteria:

- First are test cases for examining the specified behavior, output, and reaction. Included here are test cases that examine the specified handling of exception and error cases. But it is often difficult to create the necessary conditions for the execution of these test cases (e.g., capacity overload of a network connection).
- Next are test cases for examining the reaction of test objects to invalid and unexpected inputs or conditions, which have no specified →exception handling.

Examples of test cases

The following example is intended to clarify the differences between logical and concrete (physical) test cases.

A company orders an application that is supposed to calculate the Christmas bonus of the employees depending on the length of their company affiliation. In the description of the requirements the following is found: "Employees with a company affiliation of more than three years, get 50% of their monthly salary as Christmas bonus. Employees that have been working more than five years in the company get 75%. With an affiliation greater than eight years, a 100% bonus will be given".

This text shows the following cases for the bonus depending on the affiliation:

Company affiliation <= 3   results in a bonus = 0%
3 < company affiliation <= 5   results in a bonus = 50%
5 < company affiliation <= 8   results in a bonus = 75%
Company affiliation > 8   results in a bonus = 100%

Based on this it is possible to create the following logical test cases (see table 2-1).

Test case number	Input x (company affiliation)	Expected result (bonus in %)
1	X <= 3	0
2	3 < x <= 5	50
3	5 < x <=8	75
4	X > 8	100

Table 2–1

Table with logical test cases

To execute the test cases, the logical test cases must be converted into concrete test cases, i.e., concrete input data must be defined (see table 2-2). Special initial situations or conditions are not given for these test cases.

Test case number	Input x (company affiliation)	Expected result (bonus in %)
1	2	0
2	4	50
3	7	75
4	12	100

Table 2–2

Table with concrete test cases

The chosen inputs in these examples are merely supposed to show the differences between the logical and concrete test cases. Any explicit test technique to create these test cases was not used. Furthermore, we do not claim that the four test cases adequately examine the bonus calculation. For example, there are no test cases for the treatment of invalid inputs (e.g., a negative company affiliation). More detailed information about creating systematic test cases with appropriate test techniques can be found in chapter 5.

In parallel to the described test case specification, it is important to decide on and prepare the test infrastructure and the necessary environment to execute the test object. In order to prevent delays during test execution, the test infrastructure should already be assembled, integrated, and verified as far as possible at this time.

2.2.3   Test Implementation and Execution[5]

Test implementation and execution are the activities where test conditions and logical test cases are transformed into concrete test cases, all the details of the environment are set up to support the test execution activity, and the tests are executed and logged.

When the testing process has advanced and more is known about the technical implementation, the concrete, physical test cases will be developed from the logical ones. These test cases can then be used without further modifications or additions for executing the test. To state this in more detail: the preconditions and input values will then be used.

Test case execution   In addition to defining test cases one must describe how the tests will be executed. The priority of the test cases (see section 6.2), decided during test planning, must be taken into account. Only if the test developer executes the tests himself, additional, detailed description may not be necessary.

The test cases should also be grouped into test suites for efficient test execution and easier overview.

Test harness   In many cases specific test harnesses, →drivers, →simulators, etc., must be programmed, built, acquired, or set up as part of the test implementation. Because failures may also be caused by faults in the test harness, the correct functioning of the test environment must be checked.

When all preparatory tasks for the test have been accomplished, test execution can start immediately after programming and delivery of the subsystems to testing. Test execution may be done manually or with tools using the prepared sequences and scenarios.

Checking for completeness   First, the parts to be tested are checked for completeness. The test object is installed in the available test environment and tested for its ability to start and do the main processing.

Examination of the main functions   It is recommended to start test execution with the examination of the test object's main functionality. If failures or →deviations from the expected result show up at this time, it is foolish to continue testing. The failures or deviations should be corrected first. After passing this test, all

---

5.   In other literature, test implementation is often called test preparation, and test execution is often defined as a work phase by itself.

additional items are tested. Such a sequence should be defined in the test strategy.

The test execution must be exactly and completely logged. This includes logging which testing activities have been carried out, i.e., logging every test case run, logging its results (success or failure) for later analysis. On one hand, the test execution must be comprehensible to people not directly involved, for example the customer, on the basis of these →test logs. On the other hand, it must be provable that the planned test strategy was actually executed. The test log must document who tested which parts, when, how intensively, and with which results.

Tests without a protocol are of no value

Besides the test object, quite a number of documents and information belong to each test execution: test environment, input data, test logs, etc. The information belonging to a test case or test run must be maintained in such a way that it is possible to easily repeat the test later with the same input data and conditions. In some cases it must also be possible to audit the test. The testware must be taken under configuration management (see also section 6.7).

Reproducibility is important

If during test execution a difference shows up between expected and actual results, it must be decided, when evaluating the test logs, if it really is a failure. If this is the case, the failure must be documented and a first, rough analysis of possible causes must be made. This analysis may require the tester to specify and execute additional test cases.

Failure found?

The cause can be an erroneous or inexact test specification, problems with the test infrastructure or the test case, or an incorrect test execution. It must be examined carefully which of all these possibilities applies. Nothing is more detrimental to the credibility of a tester than a reported assumed failure whose cause actually is a test problem. But the fear of this possibility should not result in potential failures not being reported, i.e., the testers starting to self-censor their results. This could be fatal in almost the same manner.

In addition to reporting discrepancies, test coverage should be measured (see section 2.2.4) and if necessary the use of time should be logged. The appropriate tools for this purpose should be used (see chapter 7).

Invoking →incident management: based on the →severity of a failure (see section 6.6.3) the priority of fault correction must be decided. After the correction, it must be examined whether the fault has really been corrected and that no new faults have been introduced (see section 3.7.4). New testing activities result from the action taken for each incident, e.g., re-execution of a test that previously failed in order to confirm a defect fix,

Correction may lead to new faults

execution of a corrected test, and/or regression tests. If necessary new test cases must be specified to examine the modified or new source code. It would be convenient to correct faults and retest corrections individually, in order to avoid unwanted interactions of the changes. In practice this is not often possible due to the extra cost for every installation of changed software into the test environment. To report every failure individually to the developer and to continue testing only after the fault is corrected leads to an unjustifiable level of effort. Several faults should be corrected as a group and then the program should be resubmitted to testing with a new version state.

The most important test cases first

In many projects, there is not enough time to execute all specified test cases. When that happens, a reasonable selection of test cases must be made to make sure that as many critical failures as possible are detected. Even with a limited number of executed test cases the most critical parts of the system under test must be demonstrated. Therefore, test cases should be prioritized. In case of a premature stop of the tests, the best possible result should be achieved. This is called →risk-based testing (see section 6.4.3).

Furthermore, giving priority has the advantage that important test cases are executed first, and thus important problems are found and corrected early. An equal distribution of the limited test resources on all test objects of the project is not reasonable. Critical and uncritical program parts are then tested with the same intensity. Critical parts would then be tested insufficiently and resources would be wasted on uncritical parts for no reason.

2.2.4   Evaluation of the Test Exit Criteria and Reporting

End of test?

This is the activity where the test object is assessed against set objectives, the test exit criteria[6] specified earlier. This may result in normal termination of the tests if all criteria are met, or it may be decided that additional test cases should be run, or that the criteria had an unreasonably high level. It must be decided if the test exit criteria defined in the test plan are fulfilled. Considering the risk, an adequate exit criterion must be determined for each used test technique. For example, it could be specified that a test is sufficient if 80 % of the statements of the test object were executed during test execution. This would not be considered a strong test criterion. Appro-

---

6.   Also called test completion criteria.

priate tools should be used to collect such measures, or →metrics, in order to decide the end of the test (see section 7.1.4).

If at least one test exit criterion is not fulfilled after executing all tests, further tests must be executed. Attention should be paid to ensure that the new test cases lead to fulfilling the respective exit criteria. Otherwise, the extra test cases just result in additional work but no improvement concerning the test result.

A closer analysis of the problem can also show that the necessary effort to fulfill the exit criteria is not appropriate. In that situation, further tests are then canceled. Such a decision must, naturally, consider the associated risk. An example of such a case may be the treatment of an exceptional situation. With the available test environment it may not be possible to introduce or simulate this exceptional situation. The appropriate source code for treating the exceptional situation cannot then be executed and tested. In such cases, other examination procedures should be used, for example static analysis (see section 4.2).

Is further effort justifiable?

A further case of nonfulfillment of test exit criteria may occur if the specified criterion is impossible to fulfill in the concrete case. If, for example, the test object contains →dead code, then this cannot be executed. Thus, 100 % statement coverage is not possible, as this would also include the unreachable (dead) code. Even this possibility must be considered in order to avoid further senseless tests in relation to the criterion.

Dead code

An impossible criterion is often a hint to possible inconsistency in or impreciseness of the requirements or specifications. In the given example, it certainly makes sense to investigate why the program contains inexecutable instructions. Doing this allows further faults to be found so their effects can be avoided in advance.

If further tests are planned, the test process must be resumed, and it must be decided at which point the test process will be reentered. Sometimes it is even necessary to revise the test plan because additional resources are needed. It is also possible that the test specifications must be amended in order to fulfill the required exit criterion.

In addition to test coverage criteria, other criteria can be used to define the test end. Another possible criterion is the failure rate, or the →defect detection percentage (DDP). Figure 2-5 shows the average number of new failures per testing hour over ten weeks. In the first week, there was an average of two new failures per testing hour. In the tenth week, it is less than one failure per two hours. If the failure rate falls below a given threshold (e.g., less than one failure per testing hour), it will be assumed that more testing is not justified and the test can be ended.

Further criteria
for the determination
of the test's end

Figure 2–5
Failure rate

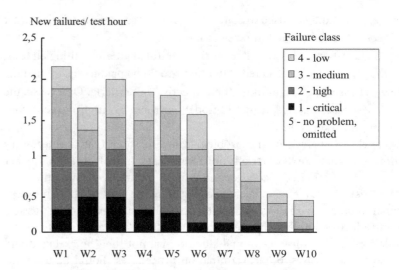

When doing this it must be considered that some failures can have very different effects. A classification and differentiation of failures, according to the impact to the stakeholders, i.e., failure severity, is therefore reasonable and should generally be considered (see section 6.6.3).

Consider several test cycles

The failures found during the test must be repaired according to their severity, after which a new test becomes necessary. Cycles often result if further failures occur during the test of modifications. These failures need to be isolated and corrected and a new test cycle is necessary. Not planning such correction cycles, by assuming that no failures will occur while testing, is unrealistic. Because it can be assumed that testing finds failures, additional faults must be removed and tested in a further →test cycle. If this cycle is ignored, then project delays will become the standard. The required effort for defect correction and the following cycles is difficult to calculate. Historical data from previous, similar projects can help. The project plan has to provide for the appropriate time buffers and personnel resources.

Exit criteria in practice:
Time and costs

In practice, the end of a test is often defined by factors that have no direct connection to the test: time and costs. If these factors lead to stopping the test activities, it is because not enough resources were provided in the project plan or the effort for an adequate test was underestimated.

Successful testing saves costs

Even if more resources than planned were used in testing, it nevertheless results in savings due to elimination of faults in the software. Faults delivered in the product mostly cause higher costs when found during operation rather than during testing (see section 6.3.1).

When the test criteria are fulfilled or their nonfulfillment is clarified, a →test summary report should be written for the stakeholders. In lower level tests (component tests) this may just take the form of a message to the project manager about meeting the exit criteria. In higher-level tests (integration tests, system tests) there may be a formal report.

Test summary report

2.2.5   Test Closure Activities

These activities, which should be executed during this final phase in the test process, are often left out. The experience gathered during the test work should be analyzed and made available for further projects. Of interest are deviations between planning and execution for the different activities, as well as the assumed causes. For example, the following data should be recorded: When was the software system released? When was the test finished or terminated? When was a milestone reached or a maintenance release completed?

Important information for evaluation can be extracted by asking the following questions:

- Which planned results are achieved – if at all?
- Which unexpected events happened (reasons and how they were circumvented)?
- Are there open →change requests? Why were they not implemented?
- How good was user acceptance after deploying the system?

The evaluation of the test process, i.e., a critical evaluation of the executed tasks in the test process, taking into account the spent resources and the achieved results, will probably show possibilities for improvement. If these findings are used in subsequent projects, continuous process improvement is achieved. Detailed hints for analysis and improvement of the test processes can be found in [Pol 98] and [Black 03].

A further finishing activity is the "conservation" of the testware for the future. Software systems are used for a long time. During this time, failures not found during testing will occur. Additionally, customers require changes. Both of these occurrences lead to new versions of the program, and the changed program must be tested. A major part of this test effort during →maintenance can be saved if the testware (test cases, test logs, test infrastructure, tools, etc.) is still available. The testware should be delivered to the organization responsible for maintenance. It can then be adapted instead of being constructed from scratch, and can also be successfully used for projects having similar requirements, after adaptation.

2.3   The Psychology of Testing

Errare humanum est

People make mistakes, but they do not like to admit them! One goal of testing software is uncovering discrepancies between the software and the specifications, or customer needs. The failures found must be reported to the developers. This chapter describes how psychological problems can be handled.

The tasks of developing software are often seen as constructive actions. The tasks of examining documents and software are seen as destructive actions. Just out of this perception there are already differences in the involved peoples' attitude to their job. But these differences are not justifiable, because "testing is an extremely creative and intellectual challenging task" [Myers 79, p.15].

Developer test

"Can the developer test his own program?" is an important and frequently asked question. A universally valid answer does not exist. If the tester is also the author of the program, they must examine their own work very critically. Only a few people are able to keep the necessary distance to the self-created product. Who really likes to prove their own errors? Rather, there is the interest to show that their own source code works well.

The big weakness of developer tests is that every developer who has to test his or her own program parts will tend to be too optimistic. There is the danger of forgetting reasonable test cases because the developer is more interested in programming than in testing, or only tests superficially.

Blindness to one's own errors

If the developer implements a fundamental design error, for example if they misunderstood the conceptual formulation, then it is possible that she will not find this using their own tests. The proper test case will not even come to mind. One possibility to decrease this problem of "blindness to their own errors" is to work together in pairs and let the programs be tested by a colleague.

On the other hand, it is an advantage to have a good knowledge of one's own test object. It is not necessary to learn the test object and thus time is saved. Management has to decide when it is an advantage to save time, even with the disadvantage of blindness for ones own errors. The decision must be made depending on the criticality of the test object and the associated failure risk.

An independent testing team tends to increase the quality and comprehensiveness of the tests. The tester can look at the test object without bias. It is not "their" product and possible assumptions and misunderstandings of the developer are not necessarily the assumptions and misunderstandings of the tester. The tester must acquire the necessary knowledge of the test object in order to create test cases, with a corresponding cost in time. But the tester comes along with a deeper testing knowledge, which a developer does not have or must first acquire (or rather should have acquired before, because the necessary time is often not available at present). *Independent testing team*

It is the job of the tester to report the failures and discrepancies observed to the author and/or to the management. The manner of this reporting can contribute to cooperation between developers and testers, or have a negative influence on the important communication of these two groups. To prove other peoples' errors is not an easy job and requires diplomacy and tact. *Reporting of failures*

There is often the problem that failures found during testing are not reproducible for the developers in the development environment. Besides the detailed description of failures, the test environment must also be documented in detail in order to be able to trace any differences in the environments, which can be the cause for the different behavior.

It must be defined in advance what constitutes a failure or discrepancy. If it is not clearly visible from the requirements or specifications, the customer, or management, is asked to make a decision. A discussion between the involved staff, developer, and tester as to whether this is a fault or not does not help. Also, the often heard reaction of developers against any critique: "It's not a bug, it's a feature!" is not very helpful.

Mutual knowledge of their respective tasks encourages cooperation between tester and developer. Developers should know the basics of testing and testers should have a basic knowledge of software development. This eases the understanding of the mutual tasks and problems. *Mutual comprehension*

The illustrated conflicts between developer and tester exist in a similar way at the management level. The test manager must report the →test results to the project manager, and is thus often the messenger bringing bad news. The project manager then has the task to decide whether there still is a chance to meet the deadline and possibly deliver software with known problems, or if the delivery must be delayed and additional time should be used for corrections. This decision must be made according to the severity of the failures and the possibility to work around the faults in the software.

2.4   General Principles of Testing

During the last 40 years, several principles for testing have become accepted as general rules for test work.

Principle 1:

Testing shows the presence of defects, not their absence

Testing can show that the product fails, i.e., that there are defects. Testing cannot prove that a program is defect free. Appropriate testing reduces the probability that hidden defects are present in the test object. Even if no failures are found during testing, this is no proof that there are no defects.

Principle 2:

Exhaustive testing is not possible

An exhaustive test where all values possible for all inputs and their combinations are run, combined with taking into account all different preconditions, is impossible. Software, in normal practice, would require an "astronomically" high number of test cases. Because of this, every test is always just a sample. The test effort must therefore be controlled, taking into account risk and priorities.

Principle 3:

Testing activities should start as early as possible

Testing activities should start as early as possible in the software lifecycle and should focus on defined goals. This contributes to finding defects early.

Principle 4:

Defects tend to cluster together

Often, most defects are found in just a few parts of the test object. Defects are not evenly distributed, but cluster together. Thus if many defects are detected in one place, there are normally more defects nearby. During testing one must react flexibly to this principle.

Principle 5:

The pesticide paradox

If the same tests are repeated over and over again, they tend to loose their effectiveness. Previously undetected defects are not discovered. Thus, in order to maintain the effectiveness of tests and to fight this "pesticide paradox", new and modified test cases should be developed. Parts of the software that until now were not tested, or previously unused input combinations will then be executed, and more defects may be found.

Principle 6:

Test is context dependent

Testing must be adapted to the risks inherent in the use and environment of the application. Therefore, no two systems should be tested in the exactly same way. For every software system the test exit criteria, etc., should be decided upon individually, depending on its usage environment. Safety critical systems require different tests than e-commerce applications.

Principle 7:

The fallacy of assuming that no failures means a useful system

Finding failures and repairing defects does not guarantee that the system as a whole meets user expectations and needs. Early involvement of the users in the development process and the use of prototypes are preventive measures intended to avoid problems.

2.5 Summary

Technical terms in the domain of software testing are often defined and used very differently, which can result in misunderstandings. The knowledge of standards (e.g., [BS 7925-1], [IEEE 610.12], [ISO 9126]) and the terminology defined in them is, therefore, an important part of the education of the Certified Tester. The glossary in the appendix of this book compiles the relevant terms.

- Tests are important tasks for quality assurance in software development. The international standard ISO 9126-1 [ISO 9126] defines appropriate quality characteristics

- The fundamental test process consists of the phases planning and control, analysis and design, implementation and execution, evaluation of the test exit criteria and reporting, and test closure activities. The test can be finished when the exit criteria are fulfilled.

- A test case consists of input, expected results, and the list of defined preconditions under which the test case must run, as well as the specified →postconditions. When the test case is executed, the test object shows a behavior. If the expected result and actual result are different, there is a failure. The expected results should be defined before test execution and during test specification (using a test oracle).

- People make mistakes, but they do not like to admit them! Because of this, psychological aspects play an important role in testing.

- The seven principles for testing must always be kept in mind during testing.

3   Testing in the Software Lifecycle

This chapter explains the role of testing in the entire life cycle of a software system, using the general "V-model" as a reference. Furthermore, we look at →test levels and the →test methods that are used during the development process.

Each project in software development should be approached using a life cycle model (see [IEEE/IEC 12207]) that has been chosen in advance. Some important models have been presented and explained in section 2.2. Each of these models implies certain views on software testing. From the viewpoint of testing, the general V-model according to [Boehm 79] plays an especially important role here.

In Boehm's model, the testing activities play an equally important role in development and programming. This has had a lasting influence on the appreciation of software testing. Not only every tester, but every developer as well, should know this general V-model and the views on testing implied there. Even if a different development model is used on a project, the principles presented in the following sections can be transferred and applied.

The role of testing within lifecycle models

3.1   The General V-Model

The main idea behind the general V-model is that development tasks and testing tasks are corresponding activities of equal importance. The two branches of the letter "V" symbolize this.

The left branch represents the development process. During the development process the system is gradually being designed, and then programming is the final step. The right branch represents the integration and testing process, in which the program elements are successively being assembled to form bigger subsystems (integration), and where their functionality is tested.

→Integration and Testing end upon completion of the acceptance test of the entire system developed according to this process.

Figure 3-1 shows such a V-model.[7]

Figure 3–1
General V-model

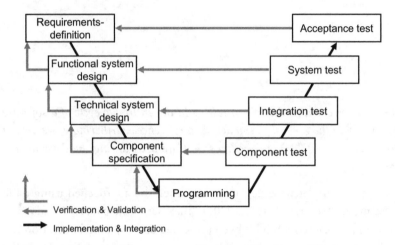

The constructive activities of the left branch are the activities we know from the Waterfall-model:

■ **Requirements specification:** The needs and requirements of the customer or the future system user are gathered, specified, and finally approved. Thus, the purpose of the system and the desired characteristics and features are defined.

■ **Functional system design:** The requirements are mapped onto functions and dialogues of the new system.

■ **Technical system design:** The implementation of the system is designed. This includes the definition of interfaces to the system environment and the decomposition of the system into smaller understandable subsystems (system architecture). Each subsystem can then be developed independently.

■ **Component specification:** Each subsystem, including its task, behavior, inner structure, and interfaces to other subsystems, is defined.

■ **Programming:** Each specified component (module, unit, class) is implemented in a programming language.

---

7.   The V-model is used in many different versions. The name and the number of levels vary according to literature source or the interpretation of the enterprise that uses it.

As one progresses through these construction levels, the software system is described in more and more detail. If mistakes are made during this construction, usually, the easiest way to find them is to look for them on the level of abstraction on which they are produced. Thus, the right branch of the V-model defines a corresponding test level for each construction level.

- **Component test** (see section 3.2) verifies whether each software →component performs correctly according to its specification.
- →**Integration test** (see section 3.3) checks if groups of components collaborate in the way that is specified by the technical system design.
- **System test** (see section 3.4) verifies whether the system as a whole meets the specified requirements.
- →**Acceptance test** (see section 3.5) checks if the system meets the requirements, as specified in the contract, from the customers point of view.

Within each test level, it must be checked whether the outcomes of development meet the specified requirements, or those requirements that are relevant on this specific level of abstraction. This process of checking the development results according to their original requirements is called →validation.

During validation[8] the tester judges whether a product (or a part of the product) solves its task, and therefore if this product is suitable for its intended use.

Are we building the right system?

In addition to validation testing, the V-model also requires verification[9] testing.

Unlike validation, →verification refers to only one single phase of the development process. Verification shall assure that the outcome of a particular development phase has been achieved correctly and completely, according to its specification (the input documents for that development level).

That means, it is examined as to whether specifications are correctly implemented and whether the product meets its specification, but not whether the resulting product is suitable for its intended use.

Are we building the system right?

In reality, every test includes both aspects; but the validation aspect increases from lower to higher levels of testing. To summarize, we again

---

8. To validate: to affirm, to declare as valid, to check if something is valid.
9. To verify: to prove, to inspect.

list the most important characteristics and ideas behind the general V-model:

Characteristics of the general V-model

▦ Implementation activities and testing activities are separated, but are equally important (left side / right side).
▦ The "V" illustrates the testing aspects of Verification and Validation.
▦ We distinguish between different test levels where each test level is testing "against" its corresponding development level.

The V-model may give the impression that testing starts relatively late, after the system's implementation, but this is not the case. The tests on the right branch of the model shall be interpreted as the levels of test execution.

Test preparation (test planning and control, and test analysis and design) starts earlier and is performed in parallel to the development phases on the left branch[10].

The differentiation of test levels in the V-model is more than a temporal subdivision of testing activities. It is rather a process of defining abstraction levels in testing. These levels are technically very different, have different objectives, and thus imply different methods and tools, and require personnel with different knowledge.

The exact contents and the process for each test level are explained in the following chapters.

3.2   Component Test

3.2.1   Explanation of Terms

Within the first test level (component testing), the software units that had been implemented just prior to the programming phase are tested systematically for the first time.

Depending on the programming language that the developers used, these software units may be referred to as a number of different things, e.g., modules, units, programs, or functions. In object-oriented programming, they are called classes. The respective tests, therefore, are called →module, →unit, program, or →class tests.

---

10. The so-called "W"-model [Spillner 00] is a more detailed model that explicitly shows this parallelism of development and testing.

Generally, we speak of software units or components. The testing of a single software component is therefore called component testing.

Component and component test

3.2.2 Test Objects

The main attribute of component testing is the following: the software components are tested individually and isolated from all other software components of the system. The isolation is necessary to prevent external influences on components. If testing detects a problem, it is definitely a problem originating from the component under test itself.

The component under test can also be assembled from various smaller components. However, it is crucial that the tester focuses on internal aspects and behavior of the component. Component testing is not about testing the interaction with neighbor components. That is the task of integration testing.

The component test checks aspects internal to the component

3.2.3 Test Environment

Component testing as the lowest test level deals with test objects coming "directly from the developer's desk". It is obvious that in this test level, testing is performed in close cooperation with development.

In the VSR subsystem *DreamCar*, the specification for calculating the price of the vehicle states the following:

Example:
Testing of a class method

- The starting point is `baseprice` minus `discount`, where `baseprice` is the basic price of the vehicle and `discount` is the discount to this price granted by the dealer.
- A `specialprice` for a special model and the price for extra equipment items `extraprice` shall be added.
- If three or more extra equipment items (which are not part of the special model chosen) are chosen (extras), there is a discount of 10 percent on these particular items only. If five or more special equipment items are chosen, this discount is increased to 15 percent.
- The discount that is granted by the dealer applies only to the `baseprice`, whereas the discount on special items applies to the special items only. These discounts cannot be added.

The following C++-function calculates the total price[11]:

```
double calculate_price
    (double baseprice, double specialprice,
    double extraprice, int extras, double discount)
{
    double addon_discount;
    double result;

    if (extras >= 3) addon_discount = 10;
    else if (extras >= 5) addon_discount = 15;
    else addon_discount = 0;

    if (discount > addon_discount)
        addon_discount = discount;
    result = baseprice/100.0*(100-discount)
    + specialprice
    + extraprice/100.0*(100-addon_discount);

    return result;

}
```

In order to test the price calculation, the tester uses the corresponding class interface; they call the function calculate_price() with appropriate parameters and data. Then they record the function's reaction to the function call. That means reading and recording the return value of the previous function call. For that, a →test driver is necessary. A test driver is a program that calls the component under test (e.g., calculate_price()) and then receives the test object's reaction.

For the test object calculate_price(), a very simple test driver could look like this:

```
bool test_calculate_price() {
double price;
bool test_ok = TRUE;

// testcase 01
price = calculate_price(10000.00,2000.00,1000.00,3,0);
test_ok = test_ok && (abs (price-12900.00) < 0.01);[12]
```

---

11. Actually, there is a defect in this program: Discount calculation for more than 5 is never reachable. The defect is used when explaining the use of white box analysis in chapter 5.

12. Floating point numbers should not be directly compared, as there may be imprecise rounding. As the result for price can be less than 12900.00, the absolute value of the difference of "price" and 12900.00 must be evaluated.

```
// testcase 02
price = calculate_price(25500.00,3450.00,6000.00,6,0);
test_ok = test_ok && (abs (price-34050.00) < 0.01);

// testcase ...

// test result
return test_ok;

}
```

The above test driver is programmed in a very simple way. Some useful extensions could be, for example, a facility to record the test data and the results, including date and time of the test, or a function that reads test cases from a file or a database.

In order to write test drivers, programming skills and knowledge of the component begin tested are necessary. The test object's program code (in the example, a class function) must be available and understood by the tester, so that the call of the test object can be correctly programmed in the test driver. To write a suitable test driver, the tester must know the programming language and suitable programming tools must be at hand.

This is why the developers themselves usually perform the component testing. Although this is truly a component test, it may also be referred to as a developer test. The disadvantages of a programmer testing his own program have already been discussed in section 2.3.

Often, component testing is confused with "debugging". But debugging is not testing. Debugging is finding the cause of failures and removing them, while testing is the systematic approach for finding failures.

Hint

The use of generic test drivers can help to simplify the component test, because the costly programming of various test drivers for each single component is not necessary anymore. Generic test drivers are available on the market (e.g., [URL: xunit]) or are to be produced for a specific project. Generic test drivers make testing easier if testing is performed by team colleagues[13] who are not familiar with the particular component and the programming environment. The test driver should, for example, provide a command interface and comfortable mechanisms for handling the test data and

---

13. Sometimes, two programmers work together, each of them testing the components that their colleague has developed. This is called "buddy testing" or "code swaps". Some "pair programming" usage shares this meaning, as well.

for recording and analyzing the tests. All test data and test protocols will be structured in a very similar way. An analysis of the tests across several components is then possible.

3.2.4   Test Objectives

The test level component test is not only characterized by the kind of test objects and the testing environment; the tester also pursues test objectives that are specific for this phase.

Testing the functionality

The most important task of component testing is to guarantee that the particular test object executes its entire functionality correctly and completely, as required by the specification (see →functional testing).

Here, functionality means the input/output behavior of the test object. In order to check the correctness and completeness of the implementation, the component is tested with a series of test cases, where each test case covers a particular input/output combination (partial functionality).

Example:
Testing the VSR price calculation

The test cases for the price calculation of the "CarConfigurator" in the previous example very clearly shows how the examination of the input/output behavior works. Each test case calls the test object with a particular combination of data, in this example, the price for the vehicle in combination with a different set of extra equipment items. It is then examined whether the test object, given this input data, calculates the correct price.

Test case 2, for example, checks the partial functionality of "discount in the case of five or more special equipment items". If test case 2 is executed, we can see that the test object calculates an incorrect total price. Test case 2 produces a failure. The test object does not completely fulfill the requirements as stated by its specification.

Typical software defects found during functional component testing are wrong calculations and missing or wrongly chosen program paths (e.g., special cases that were forgotten or misinterpreted).

Later, when the whole system is integrated, each software component must cooperate with many neighboring components and must have the ability to exchange data with them. The possibility that a component will be called (or used) in a way that is not in accordance with its specification must be taken into account. In such cases of component misuse, the component that is called should not suspend its service or cause the whole system to crash. Rather, it should be able to handle the error situation in a reasonable and robust way.

This is why testing for →robustness is another very important aspect of the component test. The way to do this resembles the functional tests. However, function calls and test data are used that are either known to be wrong or at least are special cases not mentioned in the specification. Such test cases are also called →negative tests. The component's reaction should be an appropriate exception handling. If there is no such exception handling, wrong inputs can trigger domain faults like division by zero or access through a null pointer. Such faults could lead to a program crash.

Testing robustness

In the price calculation example, such negative tests are function calls with negative values, values that are far too large, or are wrong data types ("char" instead of "int" etc.)[14]:

Example:
Negative Test

```
// testcase 20
price = calculate_price(-1000.00,0.00,0.00,0,0);
test_ok = test_ok && (ERR_CODE == INVALID_PRICE);

// testcase 30
price = calculate_price("abc",0.00,0.00,0,0);
test_ok = test_ok && (ERR_CODE == INVALID_ARGUMENT);
```

Some interesting aspects become clear:

Excursion

- There are at least as many reasonable negative tests as positive ones.
- The test driver must be extended in order to be able to evaluate the test object's exception handling.
- The test object's exception handling (the analysis of ERR_CODE in the previous example) requires additional functionality. Often more than 50% of a program's code deals with exception handling. Robustness has its cost.

Component testing should not only check functionality and robustness. All the component's characteristics that have a crucial influence on its quality and that cannot be tested in higher test levels (or only with a much higher expense) should be checked during component testing. This may refer to nonfunctional characteristics like efficiency and maintainability.

Efficiency states how efficiently the component uses computer resources. Here we have various aspects such as use of memory, computing time, disk or network access time, and the time required to execute the

Efficiency test

---

14. Depending on the compiler, data type errors can already be detected during the compiling process.

component's functions and algorithms. In contrast to most other nonfunctional tests, a test object's efficiency can be exactly measured during the test. This is done by exactly measuring suitable criteria (i.e., memory usage in kilobytes, response times in milliseconds). Efficiency tests are seldom done for all the components of a system. Efficiency must be verified only in efficiency-critical parts of the system or if efficiency requirements are stated by specifications. This happens, for example, in testing embedded software, where only limited hardware resources are available. Another example is the case of realtime systems, where given timing constraints must be guaranteed.

Maintainability test

Maintainability means all the characteristics of a program that have an influence on how easy or how difficult it is to change the program or to continue developing it. Here, it is crucial that the developer fully understand the program and its context. This includes the developer of the original program who is asked to continue development after months or years, as well as the programmer who takes over responsibility for the code that someone else has written. Thus, the following aspects are most important for testing maintainability: code structure, modularity, and quality of the comments in the code, adherence to standards, understandability, and currency of the documentation, etc.

Example:
Code that is hard to maintain

The code that is shown in the example `calculate_price()` shows some deficits. There are no comments, numeric constants are not defined but are just written into the code. If such a value must be changed at a later time, it is not clear whether and where this value occurs in other parts of the system, nor is it clear how to find and change it.

Of course, such characteristics cannot be tested by dynamic tests (see chapter 5). Analysis of the program text and the specifications is necessary. →Static test, and especially reviews (see section 4.1), are the correct means for that purpose. Because the characteristics of a single component are examined, it is best to include such analyses in the component test.

3.2.5 Test Strategy

As we explained earlier, component testing is very closely related to development. The tester usually has access to the source code, which makes component testing the domain of white box testing (see section 5.2).

The tester can design test cases using their knowledge about the component's program structures, its functions, and variables. Access to the program code can also be helpful for executing the tests. With the help of special tools (→debugger, see section 7.1.4), it is possible to observe program variables during test execution. This helps in checking for correct or incorrect behavior of the component. The internal state of a component can be observed but can also be manipulated with the debugger. This is especially useful for robustness tests, because the tester is able to trigger special exceptional situations.

White box test

Analyzing the code of `calculate_price()`, the following command can be recognized as a line that is relevant for testing:

Example:
Code as basis for testing

```
if (discount > addon_discount )
    addon_discount = discount;
```

Additional test cases that lead to fulfilling the condition (`discount > addon_discount`) can easily be derived from the code. The specification of the price calculation contains no information whatsoever on this situation; the implemented functionality is not supposed to be there.

In reality however, component testing is often done as a pure "black box" test, which means that the inner structure of the code is not used to design test cases[15]. On the one hand, real software systems consist of hundreds or thousands of elementary components, therefore anaysis of the code for designing test cases is probably only feasible with very few selected components. On the other hand the elementary components will later be integrated to larger units. Often, the tester can only see these larger units as units that can be tested, even in component testing. Then again, these units are already too large to make observations and interventions on the code level with reasonable effort. Therefore, when planning integration and testing, the question must be answered whether to test elementary parts or only larger units in the component test.

A modern approach in component testing, popular in incremental development, is to prepare and automate test cases before coding. This is called →test-first programming or test-driven development. This

Test-driven development

---

15. That is a big mistake, because that leaves untested a sizeable percentage of the code – often as much as 60–80%. This untested code is, of course, a perfect hiding place for bugs.

approach is highly iterative. Pieces of code are repeatedly tested and improved until the component passes all its tests (see [Link 03]).

3.3   Integration Test

3.3.1   Explanation of Terms

After the component test, the second test level in the V-model is the integration test. Integration testing supposes that the test objects subjected to it (i.e., components) have already been tested. Defects should, if possible, already have been corrected.

Integration

Groups of these components are composed to form larger structural units and subsystems. This connecting of components is called integration and is done by developers, testers, or special integration teams.

Integration test

After assembling the components, it must be confirmed through testing that all components collaborate correctly. Therefore, the goal of this integration testing is to expose faults in the interfaces and in the interaction between integrated components.

Why is integration testing necessary, if each individual component has already been tested? The following example illustrates the problem:

Example:
Integration test
VSR-DreamCar

The VSR subsystem *DreamCar* (see figure 2-1) consists of several elementary components.

Figure 3–2
Structure of the subsystem
VSR-DreamCar

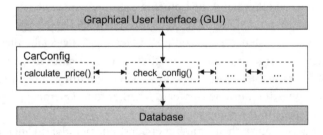

One element is the class CarConfig with the methods calculate_price(), check_config() and other methods. check_config() retrieves all the vehicle data from a database and presents them to the user through a graphical user interface (GUI). From the user's point of view, this looks like figure 3-3.

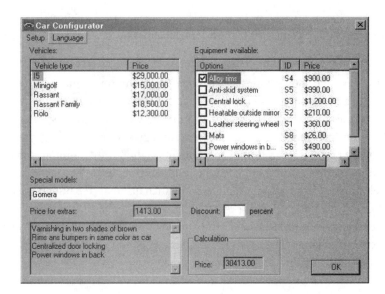

Figure 3–3
User Interface VSR-DreamCar

When the user has chosen the configuration of a car, check_config() executes a plausibility check of the configuration (base model of the vehicle, special equipment, list of further extra items) and then calculates the price. In this example (see figure 3-3), the total resulting from the vehicle that was chosen, the special model, and the extra equipment should be $ 29,000 + $ 1,413 + $ 900 = $ 31,313. However, the price indicated is only $ 30,413. Obviously, in the current program version, one can choose accessories (e.g., alloy rims) without paying for them. Somewhere on the way from the GUI to calculate_price() the calculation misses the fact that alloy rims were chosen.

If the test protocols of the previous component tests show that the fault is neither in the function calculate_price() nor in check_config(), the cause of the problem could be a faulty data transmission between the GUI and check_config() or between check_config() and calculate_price().

Even if a complete component test had been executed earlier, such interface problems can still occur. That is why integration testing is necessary as a further test level. Its task is to find collaboration and interoperability problems and isolate their causes.

The integration of the single components to the subsystem *DreamCar* is just the beginning of the integration test in the project VSR. The other subsystems of the VSR (see chapter 2, figure 2-1) must also be integrated. Then, the subsystems must be connected to each other. *DreamCar* has to be connected to the subsystem *ContractBase*, which is connected to the subsystems *JustInTime* (order management),

Example:
VSR integration test

NoRisk (vehicle insurance) and *EasyFinance* (financing). In one of the last steps of integration, VSR is connected to the external mainframe in the computing center of the enterprise.

Integration testing in the large

As the example shows, interfaces to the system environment, i.e., external systems, are also subject to integration and integration testing. If interfaces to external software systems are examined, we sometimes speak of a →"system integration test", "higher level integration test", or "integration test in the large" (integration of components is then "integration test in the small", sometimes called →"component integration test"). The fact that the development team has only "one half" of such an interface under its control constitutes a special risk. The "other half" of the interface is determined by an external system. It must be taken as it is, but it is subject to unexpected change. A passed integration test is no guarantee for flawless functioning at this point for all future time.

3.3.2 Test Objects

Assembled components

In the course of integration, the single components are assembled step by step and will result in larger units (see section 3.3.5). Ideally, there should be an integration test after each of these steps. Every subsystem generated in this manner can later be the basis for the integration of even larger units. Such composed units might be objects of the integration test at a later time.

External systems or off-the-shelf products

In reality, a software system is seldom developed from scratch. Usually, an existing system is changed, extended, or linked to other systems. Furthermore, many system components are commercial →off-the-shelf software products (COTS); for example, the database in *DreamCar*. In the component test, such existing or standard components are probably not tested. In the integration test, however, these system components must be taken into account and their collaboration with other components must be examined.

3.3.3 Test Environment

As with component testing, test drivers are also needed in the integration test. They send test data to the test objects, and they receive and log the results. Because the test objects are assembled components that have no interfaces to the "outside", other than their constituting components, it is obvious and sensible to reuse the test drivers that were used earlier for component testing.

If the component test was well organized, then one or more test drivers should be available. It is preferable to use one generic test driver for all components, or at least test drivers that were designed with a common architecture and are compatible to each other. In this case, the testers can reuse these test drivers without much effort.

Reuse of the testing environment

In a poorly organized component test, there may be test drivers for only a few of the components. Their user interface may also be completely different, which will create trouble: The tester now (during integration testing in a much later stage of the project) must put much effort into the creation, change, or repair of the test environment. This means that valuable time needed for testing is lost.

During integration testing, additional tools, called monitors, are required. →Monitors are programs that read and log data traffic between components. Monitors for standard protocols (e.g., network protocols) are commercially available. Special monitors must be developed for the observation of project specific component interfaces.

Need for monitors

3.3.4   Test Objectives

The test objective of the test level "integration test" is to reveal interface and cooperation problems, as well as conflicts between integrated parts. Problems can arise even when an attempt is made to integrate two single components. Linking components together might not work because, for example, their interface formats may not be compatible to each other, because some files are missing, or because the developers have split the system into completely different components than were in the original design (see static testing, section 4.2).

Wrong interface formats

The harder to find problems, though, are due to the execution of the connected program parts. These can only be found by dynamic testing. These are faults in the data exchange or in the communication between the components. The following types of faults can roughly be distinguished:

Typical faults in data exchange

- A component transmits syntactically wrong or no data. The receiving component cannot operate or crashes (functional fault in a component, incompatible interface formats, protocol faults).
- The communication works but the involved components interpret the received data in a different way (functional fault of a component; contradicting or misinterpreted specifications).

▨ Data is transmitted correctly but is transmitted at the wrong time, or is late (timing problem), or the intervals between the transmissions are too short (throughput, load, or capacity problem).

Example: Integration problems in VSR

According to the above mentioned failure types, the following interface failures could occur during the VSR integration test:

▨ In the GUI of the *DreamCar*, selected extra equipment items are not passed on to check_config(). Therefore, the price and the data of the order would be wrong.
▨ In *DreamCar*, a certain code number (e.g., 442 for metallic blue) represents the color of the car. In the order management system running on the external mainframe, however, the code numbers are interpreted differently (there, 442 probably represents red). A correct order from the VSR would lead to delivery of a wrong product.
▨ The mainframe computer confirms an order after checking whether delivery would be possible. In some cases, this examination takes so long that the "VSR" assumes a transmission failure and aborts the order. A customer who has carefully chosen their car would not be able to order it.

None of these failures could be found in the component test, because the resulting failures occur only when there is interaction between two software components.

In addition to testing functionality, nonfunctional tests may also be executed during integration testing, if such attributes are important or are considered at risk. These may include testing performance and capacity of interfaces.

Can the component test be omitted?

Is it possible to do without the component test and execute all the test cases after integration is finished? Of course, it is possible to do so, and we have seen this done, but only at the risk of great disadvantages:

▨ Most of the failures that will occur in a test designed like this are caused by functional faults within the individual components. An implicit component test is therefore carried out, but in an environment that is not suitable and that makes it harder to access the individual components.
▨ Because there is no suitable access to the individual component some failures cannot be provoked and many faults, therefore, cannot be found.
▨ If a failure occurs in the test, it can be difficult or impossible to locate its origin and to isolate its cause (see section 3.2.4).

The cost of trying to save effort by cutting the component test is identifying fewer of the existing faults and having more difficulty in diagnosis, thus spending more rather then less effort. The combination of a component test and a subsequent integration test is most often more effective and efficient.

3.3.5   Integration Strategies

In which order should the components be integrated in order to execute the necessary testing as quickly and easily as possible? How do we get the greatest possible efficiency of testing? Efficiency is the relation between the cost of testing (expense of testing personnel and the usage of tools, etc.), and the benefit of testing (number and severity of the problems revealed). It is the test manager's task to figure this out and to choose and implement an optimal integration strategy for the project.

In practice, there is the difficulty that the different software components are completed at different times. These can be weeks or even months apart. The project manager and the test manager cannot allow the testers to do nothing while waiting until the development of all the components is finished and they are ready to be integrated.

Components are completed at different times

An obvious ad hoc strategy to quickly solve this problem is to integrate the components in the order in which they are ready. This means, as soon as a component has passed the component test, it is checked whether it fits with another already tested component, or if it fits into a partially integrated subsystem. If so, both parts are integrated and the integration test between both of them is executed. However, integration test planning should attempt to organize the delivery of components to correspond risk, system architecture, etc.

In the project VSR, the central subsystem *ContractBase* turns out to be more complex than expected. The completion of it is delayed for several weeks because the work on it is much more costly than originally expected. In order not to lose even more time, the project manager decides to start the tests with the available components *DreamCar* and *NoRisk*. These do not have a common interface but they exchange data through *ContractBase*. In order to calculate the price of the insurance, *NoRisk* needs to know which type of vehicle was chosen, because this determines the parameters of the insurance. As a temporary replacement for *ContractBase*, a →stub is programmed. This stub receives simple car configuration data from *DreamCar*, then determines the vehicle type code from these data and passes it on to *NoRisk*. Furthermore, the stub makes it possible to put in dif-

Example:
Strategy of integration in the VSR project

ferent relevant data about the customer. *NoRisk* calculates the insurance price from these data and indicates it in a window for checking. The price and other data are then saved in a test log. The stub serves as provisional replacement for the yet missing subsystem *ContractBase*.

This example makes clear that the earlier the integration test is started (in order to save time), the more effort is necessary for programming of stubs. The test manager has to choose her integration strategy for optimizing both factors (time saving vs. cost for the testing environment).

Constraints for integration   Which strategy is optimal (most time-saving and least costly) depends on the individual circumstances in each project. The following items must be analyzed:

- The **system architecture** determines how many and which components the entire system consists of and in which way they depend on each other.
- The **project plan** determines at what time during the course of the project single parts of the system are developed and when they should be ready for testing. However, when determining the order of implementation, the tester or test manager should be consulted.
- The **test plan** determines which aspects of the system are to be tested, how intensely this will be done, and on which test level this has to happen.

Discuss the integration strategy   The test manager, taking into account these general constraints, has to design a viable integration strategy. As the integration strategy depends on delivery dates, the test manager should consult with the project manager in writing regarding the project plan. The order of implementation of the components should be suitable for integration testing.

When making plans, the test manager can follow these generic integration strategies:

Basic integration strategies
- **Top-down integration:** The test starts with the top level component of the system that calls other components but is not called itself (except for a call from the operating system). Stubs replace all subordinate components. Successively, integration proceeds with lower level components. The higher level that has already been tested serves as test driver.
  - Advantage: Test drivers are not needed or only simple ones are required, because the higher-level components that

have already been tested serve as main part of the test environment.

- Disadvantage: Lower level components not yet integrated must be replaced by stubs. This can be very costly.

Bottom-up integration: The test starts with the elementary system components that do not call further components, except for functions of the operating system. Larger subsystems are assembled from the tested components and then these integrated parts are tested.

- Advantage: No stubs are needed.
- Disadvantage: Higher-level components must be simulated by test drivers.

Ad hoc integration: The components are being integrated in the (casual) order in which they are finished.

- Advantage: This saves time, because every component is integrated as early as possible into its environment.
- Disadvantage: Stubs as well as test drivers are required.

Backbone integration strategy
A skeleton or backbone is built into which components are gradually integrated [Beizer 90].

- Advantage: Components can be integrated in any order.
- Disadvantage: Labor intensive skeleton or backbone is required.

Top-down or Bottom-up integration in their pure form can only be applied to program systems that are structured in a strictly hierarchical way; in reality, this rarely occurs. This is the reason why a more or less individualized mix of the above mentioned integration strategies[16] may be chosen.

Any non-incremental integration – also called → "big bang" – should be avoided. Big bang integration means waiting with the integration until all software elements are developed and then throwing everything together in one step. This typically happens due to the lack of an integration strategy. In the worst cases, even component testing is skipped. The disadvantages of this are obvious:

Avoid the big bang!

---

16. Special integration strategies can be followed for object-oriented, distributed, and real-time systems (see [Winter 98], [Bashir 99], [Binder 99]).

- The time leading up to the big bang is lost time that could have been spent testing. As testing always suffers from lack of time, not a single day that could be used for testing should be wasted.
- All the failures will occur at the same time. It will be difficult, if not impossible, to get the system to run at all. And it will be very difficult and time-consuming to localize and correct defects.

3.4 System Test

3.4.1 Explanation of Terms

After the integration test is completed, the next test level is the system test. System testing checks if the integrated product meets the specified requirements. Why is this still necessary after the component and integration tests? The reasons for this are as follows:

Reasons for system test

- In the lower test levels, the testing was done against technical specifications, i.e., from the technical perspective of the software producer. The system test, though, looks at the system from the perspective of the customer and the future user[17]. The testers validate whether the requirements are completely and appropriately met.
- Many functions and system characteristics result from the interaction of all system components, consequently, they are only visible on the level of the entire system and can only be observed and tested there.

Example:
VSR-System tests

The main purpose of the VSR-System is to make ordering a car as easy as possible. While ordering a car, the user implements all the components of a VSR-System: the car is configured (*DreamCar*); financing and insurance are calculated (*Easy-Finance, NoRisk*); the order is transmitted to production (*JustInTime*); and the contracts are archived (*ContactBase*). The system suits its purpose only when all of these system functions and all of the components collaborate correctly. The system test determines whether this is the case.

---

17. The customer (who has ordered and paid for the system) and the user (who uses the system) can be different groups of people or organizations with their own specific interests and requirements of the system.

3.4.2   Test Object and Test Environment

After the completion of the integration test, the software system is completely assembled and the system test looks at the system as a whole. This is done in an environment as similar as possible to the intended operational environment.

Instead of test drivers and stubs, the hardware and software products that are used later should be installed on the test platform (hardware, system software, device driver software, networks, external systems, etc.). Figure 3-4 shows an example of a VSR-System test environment.

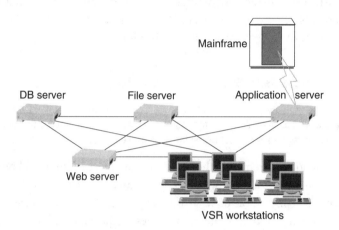

Figure 3–4
Example of a system test environment

In an attempt to save costs and effort, one mistake is commonly made: Instead of testing the system in a separate environment, the system test is run in the customer's operational environment. This is not beneficial because of the following reasons:

The system test requires a separate test environment

- During system testing it is likely failures will occur, and damage to the customer's operational environment can result. Expensive system crashes and data loss in the production system can occur.
- The testers have only limited or no control over parameter settings and configuration of the operational environment. The test conditions can gradually change because the other systems in the customer's environment are running simultaneously with the test. The system tests that have been executed cannot be reproduced or can only be reproduced with difficulty (see section 3.7.4).

The effort of an adequate system test must not be underestimated, especially because of the complex testing environment. [Bourne 97] states the

System test effort is often underestimated

experience that at the beginning of the system test, only half of the testing and quality control work have been done (especially when a client/server-system is developed, as in the current example).

3.4.3 Test Objectives

As described above, it is the goal of the system test to validate whether the complete system meets the specified functional and nonfunctional requirements (see sections 3.7.1 and 3.7.2), and how well it does that. Failures from incorrect, incomplete, or inconsistent implementation of requirements should be detected. And requirements that are undocumented or have been forgotten should be identified.

3.4.4 Problems in System Test Practice

Excursion

In (too) many projects, the written documentation of the requirements is very incomplete or does not exist at all. Then, the testers face the problem that it is not clear what represents the system's correct behavior. This makes it hard to find defects.

Unclear system requirements

If there are no requirements, then all behaviors of a system would be valid, and assessment would be impossible. Of course, the user or the customer has a certain conception of what they expect of "their" software system. Thus, there *must be* requirements. Yet, these requirements are not written down anywhere, they only exist in the minds of a few people who are involved in the project. The testers then have the undesirable role of gathering information about the required behavior after the fact. One possible method to cope with such a situation is exploratory testing (see section 5.3 and for more detailed discussion [Black 02]).

Missed decisions

While the testers identify the original requirements, they will discover that different people have completely different views and ideas on the same subject. This is not surprising as the requirements have never been documented, reviewed, or released during the course of the project. As a consequence, those responsible for the system test not only must gather information on the requirements; they also must enforce decision-making that should have been done many months earlier. This gathering of information may be very costly and time consuming. The finalization of the tests and the release of the completed system will surely be delayed.

Projects may fail

If the requirements are not specified at the outset of a project, of course the developers do not have clear objectives. Thus, it is not very likely that the developed system will meet the implicit requirements of the customer. Nobody can seriously expect that it is possible to develop a usable system given these conditions. In such projects, the only thing that the system test can probably do is to announce the collapse of the project.

3.5   Acceptance Test

All the test levels described thus far represent testing activities that are run while still under the producer's responsibility. They are executed before the software is presented to the customer or the user.

But, before installing and using the software in real life, another test level must be executed: the so-called acceptance test. Here, the focus is on the customer's perspective and judgment. This is especially important if the software was developed customer specific. The acceptance test might be the only test the customer is actually involved in or which they can understand. The customer may even be completely responsible for the acceptance test!

Acceptance tests can even be executed within lower test levels or distributed over several test levels:

- A commercial off-the-shelf software product may be acceptance tested when it is installed or integrated.
- Acceptance testing of a component's usability may be done during component testing.
- Acceptance testing of new functionality may come before system testing (using a prototype).

Typical forms of acceptance testing include the following:

1. Testing to determine if the contract has been met
2. User acceptance testing
3. Operational (acceptance) testing
4. Field test (alpha and beta testing)

The extent of acceptance testing will vary considerably. It is dependent upon application risk. If the software is developed as customer specific, the risk is high and a full acceptance test as outlined above is necessary. The other extreme is an acquisition of a standard product that has been used for a long time in a similar environment. In that case, the acceptance test will consist of installing the system and maybe running a few representa-

How much
acceptance testing?

tive →use cases. If the system is expected to cooperate with other systems in a new way, at least the interoperation should be tested.

3.5.1 Testing for Acceptance According to the Contract

If customer specific software was developed, the customer (in cooperation with the vendor) will perform acceptance testing according to the contract. On the basis of the results of these acceptance tests the customer considers whether the ordered software system is free of (major) deficiencies and whether the development contract or the service defined by the contract has been accomplished. In the case of internal software development, this can be a more or less formal contract between the user department and the IT-department of the same enterprise.

Acceptance criteria

The test criteria are the acceptance criteria determined in the development contract. Therefore, these criteria must be formulated clearly and explicitly. Also, any regulations that must be adhered to, such as governmental, legal, or safety regulations, are to be addressed here.

In practice, the software producer will have checked these criteria within his own system test. For the acceptance test, it is then enough to rerun the test cases which are relevant for acceptance, demonstrating to the customer that the acceptance criteria of the contract have been met.

As the supplier may have misunderstood the acceptance criteria, it is crucially important that the acceptance test cases be designed by, or at least thoroughly reviewed by the customer.

Acceptance test at the customer's site

In contrast to system testing which takes place in the environment of the producer, acceptance testing is run in the customer's actual operational environment[18]. Due to these different testing environments, a test case that worked correctly during the system test may now suddenly fail. The final acceptance test also checks the delivery and installation procedures. The acceptance environment should be as similar as possible to the later operational environment. But a test in the operational environment itself should be avoided to avoid the risk of damage to other running software systems.

For determining acceptance criteria and acceptance test cases the same methods as discussed earlier in the system test can be used. For

---

18. Sometimes acceptance test consists of two runs: the first within system test environment; the second within customers environment.

administrative IT-systems, business transactions with time constraints or periodic transactions (like a billing period), must be considered.

3.5.2   Testing for User Acceptance

Another aspect concerning acceptance as the last phase of validation is the test for user acceptance. Such a test is especially recommended if the customer and the user are different individuals.

In the example of the VSR, the responsible customer is a car manufacturer. But the system will be used by the car manufacturer's dealers. The system's end users will be the employees of these dealers and their customers who want to purchase cars. In addition some clerks in the company's headquarter will work with the system, e.g., to put, new price lists into the system.	*Example:* *Different user groups*

Different user groups usually have completely different expectations of the new system. And if only one user group rejects the system because it finds it too awkward, this can lead to trouble with the introduction of the system. This may happen even if the system is completely OK from the technical or functional point of view. Thus, it is necessary to organize a user acceptance test for each user group. The customer usually organizes these tests, selecting test cases based on business processes and typical use scenarios.

Every user group should be included in the acceptance

But if major user acceptance problems are detected during acceptance testing, it is often too late to implement more than cosmetic measures. In order to prevent such disasters, it is advisable to allow a number of representatives from the future users to examine prototypes of the system at an early stage of the project.

Present prototypes to the users early

3.5.3   Operational (Acceptance) Testing

Operational (acceptance) testing assures the acceptance of the system by the system administrators. It may include the testing of backup/restore cycles, disaster recovery, user management, maintenance tasks, and checks of security vulnerabilities.

3.5.4   Field Testing

If the software is supposed to run in many different operational environments, it is very expensive or even impossible for the software producer to create a test environment for each of them during system testing. In such cases, after the system test, the software producer may choose to carry out a →field test. The objective of the field test is to identify influences from users' environments that are not entirely known or that are not specified, and to eliminate them if necessary.

Testing done by representative customers

Therefore, the producer delivers stable prerelease versions of the software to preselected customers that adequately represent the market for this software or whose operational environments appropriately cover possible environments.

These customers then either run test scenarios prescribed by the producer or they run the product on a trial basis under realistic conditions. They give feedback to the producer about the problems they encountered along with general comments and impressions about the new product. The producer can then make the specific adjustments.

Alpha and beta testing

Such testing of preliminary versions by representative customers is also called →alpha testing or →beta testing. Alpha tests are carried out at the producer's location, while beta tests are carried out at the customer's site.

A field test should not replace an internal system test run by the producer (even if some producers do exactly this). Only when the system test has proven that the software is stable enough, the new product should be given to potential customers for a field test.

3.6   Testing New Product Versions

Until now, it was assumed that a software development project is finished upon passing the acceptance test and deployment of the new product. Reality looks very different. The first deployment marks only the beginning of the software life cycle. Once it is installed, it will often be used for years or decades and is changed, updated, and extended many times. Each time that happens, a new →version of the original product is created. This chapter explains what must be considered when testing such new product versions.

3.6.1   Software Maintenance

Software does not wear out. Contrary to "classical" industry products, the purpose of software maintenance is not to maintain the ability to operate or to repair damages caused by heavy use. Defects do not originate from wear and tear. They are design faults that already exist in the original version. We speak of software maintenance when a product is adapted to new operational conditions (adaptive maintenance), or when defects are eliminated (corrective maintenance). Testing whether such changes work can be very difficult as the system's specifications are often out of date or missing, especially in case of legacy systems.

The VSR-System had been distributed and installed after intense testing. In order to find out weaknesses that had not been found previously, a central hotline generates an analysis of all requests that come in from the field. Here are some examples:

Example:
Analysis of VSR hotline requests

1. A few dealers use the system on a platform with an old version of the operating system that is not recommended. In such environments, sometimes the host access causes system crashes.
2. Many customers consider the selection of extra equipment to be awkward, especially when they want to compare prices between different packages of extra equipment. Many users would therefore like to save equipment configurations and to be able to retrieve them after a change.
3. Some of the seldom-occurring insurance prices cannot be calculated at all, because implementing the corresponding calculation was forgotten in the insurance component.
4. Sometimes it takes more than 15 minutes before a car order is confirmed from the server. The system cuts the connection after 15 minutes in order to avoid having unused connections remain open. The customers are angry with this, because they waste a lot of time having to wait in vain for the confirmation of the purchase order. The dealer then has to repeat inputting the order and then must mail the confirmation to the customer.

Problem 1 is the responsibility of the dealer, because they run the system on a platform for which the system was not intended. Still, the software producer might change the program to allow it to be able to also run on this platform, maybe in order to spare the dealer the cost of a hardware upgrade.

Problems like number 2 will always arise, regardless of how well and complete the requirements were originally analyzed. This is due to the fact that the new system will generate many new experiences and therefore new requirements will naturally arise.

Problem 3 could have been detected during the system test. But testing cannot guarantee that a system is completely fault-free. It can only provide a sample

Improve the test plan

with a certain probability to reveal failures. A good test manager will anaylize which kind of testing would have detected this problem and will adequately improve or extend their test plan.

Problem 4 had been detected in the integration test and had been solved. The VSR-System waits for a confirmation from the server for more than 15 minutes without stopping the connection. Sometimes, it happens that there is a long waiting time because batch processes are run in the host computer. The fact that the customer does not want to wait in the shop for such a long time is another subject.

These four examples represent typical problems that will be found in even the most mature software system:

1. The system is run under new operating conditions that were not pre-dictable and were not planned.
2. The customers express new wishes.
3. Functions are necessary for rarely occurring special cases that were not anticipated.
4. Crashes that happen rarely or only after very long uptime are reported. These crashes are often caused by external influences.

Therefore after its deployment, every software system requires certain corrections and improvements. In this context, we speak of software maintenance and software support. But the fact that maintenance is necessary in any case must not be used as pretext for cutting down on component, integration, or system testing. Like "We must continuously publish updates anyway, so we don't need to take testing so seriously, even if we miss defects". Managers behaving in that way have not understood the true costs of failures.

Testing after maintenance   The overall test strategy is easy: anything new or changed should be tested, and, to avoid side effects, the remainder of the system should be regression tested (see section 3.7.4).

Testing after change of environment   Even if the system is unchanged, if only its environment is changed, maintenance testing is necessary.

For example, if the system was migrated from one platform to another testing should repeat the operational tests within the new environment.

Testing for retirement   If a system is scheduled for retirement then some testing is also useful. Such testing for the retirement of a system should include the testing of data archiving or data migration into the future system.

3.6.2   Release Development

Apart from maintenance work necessary because of failures, there are changes and extensions to the product that project management has intended from the beginning.

In the development plan for VSR release 2, the following work is scheduled:

1. New communication software is installed on the host in the car manufacturer's computing center, therefore the VSR communication module must be adapted to it.
2. Certain system extensions that could not be finished in release 1 are now delivered in release 2.
3. The installation base shall be extended to the U.S. dealer network. Therefore specific adaptations necessary for each country must be integrated and all the manuals and the user interface must be translated.

Example:
Planning of the VSR development

These three tasks neither come from defects nor from unforeseen user requests. So, they are not part of ordinary maintenance, but normal further product development.

The first point results from a planned change of a neighbor system. Point 2 is functionality that had been planned from the beginning, but could not be implemented as early as intended. Point 3 represents extensions that become necessary in the course of a planned market expansion.

Therefore, a software product is certainly not finished with the release of the first version. Instead, additional development is continuously occurring. An improved product version will be delivered at certain intervals, e.g., once a year. It is best to synchronize these →releases with the ongoing maintenance work. For example, every half-year a new version is introduced: a maintenance update and a genuine functional update.

After each release, the project effectively starts over, running through all the project phases. This approach is called iterative software development. Nowadays this is the usual way of developing software[19].

How must testing respond to this? Do we have to completely rerun all the test levels for every release of the product? Yes, if possible! Like in maintenance testing, anything new or changed should be tested, and the

Testing new releases

---

19.   This aspect is not shown in the general V-model. Only more modern life cycle models show iterations explicitly (see [Jacobson 99], [Beck 00], [Beedle 01]).

remainder of the system should be regression tested in order to find unexpected side effects (see section 3.7.4).

3.6.3   Testing in Incremental Development

Incremental development means that the project is not done in one (possibly large) piece, but as a series of smaller developments and deliveries. System functionality and reliability requirements will grow over time, from an early version only for the development group or for special users, to versions released to final customers later. Each increment, added to other increments developed previously, forms a growing partial system.

Incremental models try to reduce the risk of developing the wrong system by delivering useful parts of the system early and getting customer feedback.

Examples of incremental models are: Prototyping, Rapid Application Development (RAD) [Martin 91], Rational Unified Process (RUP), Evolutionary Development [Gilb 05], use of the Spiral Model [Boehm 86] and so-called "agile" development methods such as Extreme Programming (XP) [Beck 00], Dynamic Systems Development Method (DSDM) [Stapleton 02], or SCRUM [Beedle 01].

Testing must be adapted to such development models, and continuous integration testing and regression testing are necessary. There should be reusable test cases for every component and increment, and it should be reused and updated for every additional increment. If this is not the case, the product's reliability tends to decrease over time instead of increasing.

The practical way to run such a project is to run several V-models in sequence, where every next "V" reuses existing test material and adds the tests necessary for new development or for higher reliability requirements.

Figure 3–5
Testing in incremental development

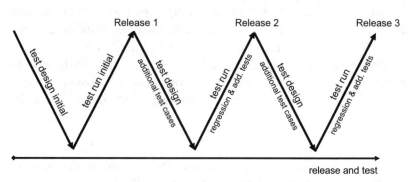

3.7   Generic Types of Testing

The previous chapters gave a detailed view of testing in the software life-cycle, distinguishing several test levels. Focus and objectives change when testing in these different levels. And different types of testing are relevant on each test level.

The following types of testing can be distinguished:

- functional testing
- nonfunctional testing
- testing of software structure
- testing related to changes

3.7.1   Functional Testing

Functional testing includes all kind of tests which verify a system's input-output behavior. To design functional test cases the black box testing methods from section 5.1 are used, and the test bases are the functional requirements.

→Functional requirements specify the behavior of the system; they describe "what" the system must be able to do. Implementation of these requirements is a precondition for the system to be applicable. Characteristics of functionality, according to [ISO 9126], are suitability, accuracy, interoperability, and security.

The (individual) customer's or the market's requirements of a software system are documented in a requirements management system (see section 7.1). Text based requirements specifications are still in use as well. A format for this document is available in [IEEE 830].

The following text shows a part of the requirements paper concerning price calculation for the system VSR (see section 3.2.3 for the specification):

R 100:   The user can choose a vehicle model from the current model list for configuration.

R 101:   For a chosen model, the deliverable extra equipment items are indicated. The user can choose the desired individual equipment from this list.

R 102:   The total price of the chosen configuration is calculated from current price lists and shown continuously.

Example:
Requirements
to the VSR-System

Requirements-based testing

In requirements-based testing, the released requirements are used as the basis for testing. For each requirement, at least one test case is designed and documented in the test specification. The test specification is then also reviewed. The testing of requirement 102 of the example shown above could look like this:

Example:
Requirements-based
testing

T 102.1: A vehicle model is chosen; its base price according to the sales manual is indicated.

T 102.2: A special equipment item is selected; the price of this accessory is added.

T 102.3: A special equipment item is deselected; the price falls accordingly.

T 102.4: Three special equipment items are selected; the discount comes into effect as defined in the specification …

Usually, more than one test case is needed to test a functional requirement. Requirement 102 in the example contains several rules for different price calculations. These must be covered by a set of test cases (102.1 – 102.4 in the example above). Using black box test methods (e.g., →equivalence partitioning) these test cases can be further refined and extended if desired. The decisive fact is: if the defined test cases (or a minimal subset of them) have run without failure, the appropriate functionality is considered validated.

Requirements-based functional testing as shown above is mainly used in system testing and acceptance testing. If a software system's purpose is to automate or support a certain business process of the customer, business-process-based testing or use-case-oriented testing are other similar suitable testing methods (see section 5.1.5).

Example:
Testing based on business
procedure

From the dealer's point of view, VSR supports him in the sales process. This process can, for example, look like this:

- The customer selects a type of vehicle they are interested in from the available models.
- They get the information about the type of extra equipment and prices and select the desired car with extra equipment.
- The dealer suggests alternative ways of financing the car.
- The customer decides and signs the sales contract.

A business process analysis (which is usually elaborated as part of the requirements analysis) shows which business processes are relevant, and how often and in which context they appear. It also shows which persons, enterprises, and external systems are involved. Test scenarios simulating typical business processes are constructed based on this analysis. The test scenarios are prioritized using the frequency and the relevance of the particular business processes.

Requirements-based testing focuses on single system functions (e.g., the transmission of a purchase order). Business-process-based testing, however, focuses on the whole process consisting of many steps (e.g., the sales conversation, consisting of configuring a car, agreeing on the purchase contract, and the transmission of the purchase order). This means a sequence of several tests.

Of course, for the users of the VirtualShowRoom system, it is not enough to see if they can choose and then buy a car. More important for ultimate acceptance is often how easily they can use the system. This depends on how easy it is to work with the system, if it reacts quickly enough, and if it returns easily understood information. Therefore, along with the functional criteria, the nonfunctional criteria must also be checked and tested.

3.7.2 Nonfunctional Testing

→Nonfunctional requirements do not describe the functions, but the attributes of the functional behavior, or the attributes of the system as a whole, i.e., "how well" or with what quality the (partial) system should carry out its function. The implementation of such requirements has a great influence on customer and user satisfaction with the product and how much they enjoy its use. Characteristics of these requirements are, according to [ISO 9126], reliability, usability, and efficiency. In an indirect manner, the ability of the system to be changed and to be installed in new environments also has an influence on customer satisfaction. The faster and the easier a system can be adapted to changed requirements, the more satisfied the customer and the user will be. These two characteristics are also important for the supplier, as maintenance is a major cost driver!

According to [Myers 79], the following nonfunctional system characteristics should be considered in the tests (usually in system testing):

- →**Load test:** Measuring of the system behavior for increasing system loads (e.g., the number of users that work simultaneously, number of transactions)

- →**Performance test:** Measuring of the processing speed and response time for particular use cases, usually dependent on increasing load
- →**Volume test:** Observation of the system behavior dependent on the amount of data (e.g., processing of very large files)
- →**Stress test:** Observation of the system behavior when it is overloaded
- **Testing of security** against unauthorized access, denial of service attacks etc.
- **Stability** or reliability test during permanent operation (e.g., mean time between failures or failure rate with a given user profile)
- →**Robustness test:** Measuring the system's response to operating errors, or wrong programming, or hardware failure, etc., as well as examination of exception handling and recovery
- **Testing of compatibility and data conversion:** Examination of compatibility to given systems, import/export of data etc.
- **Testing of different configurations of the system**, e.g., different versions of the operating system, user interface language, hardware platform, etc. (→back-to-back testing)
- **Usability test:** Examination of the ease of learning the system, ease and efficiency of operation, understandability of the system output, etc., always with respect to the needs of a specific group of users ([ISO 9241], [ISO 9126])
- **Checking of the documentation** for compliance with system behavior (e.g., user manual and GUI)
- **Checking of maintainability:** Assessing the understandability of the system documentation and whether it is up to date; checking if the system has a modular structure, etc.

A major problem in testing nonfunctional requirements is the often imprecise and incomplete character of these requirements. Expressions like "the system should be easy to operate" and "the system should be fast" are not testable in this form. Nonfunctional requirements should be expressed in a testable way.

Hint
- Representatives of the system test personnel should participate in early requirement reviews and make sure that every nonfunctional requirement can be measured and is testable.

Furthermore, there are many nonfunctional requirements that are so fundamental that nobody really thinks about mentioning them in the requirement paper (presumed matters of fact). Even such implicit requirements[20] must be validated because they may be relevant.

The VSR-System is designed for the use on a market-leading operating system. It is obvious that the recommended or usual user interface conventions are followed for the "look and feel" of the VSR-GUI. The DreamCar-GUI (see figure 3-3) violates these conventions in several aspects. Even if no particular requirement is specified, such deviations can and must be seen as faults or defects.

Example:
Presumed requirements

In order to test nonfunctional characteristics, it makes sense to reuse existing functional tests. An elegant general testing approach could look like this:

Testing nonfunctional
requirements

■ Scenarios that represent a cross-section of the functionality of the entire system are selected from the functional tests. The nonfunctional property must be observable in the corresponding test scenario. When executing the test scenario, the nonfunctional characteristic is measured. If the resulting value is inside a given limit, the test is considered "passed". The functional test practically serves as a vehicle for determining the nonfunctional system characteristics.

3.7.3   Testing of Software Structure

Structural techniques (white box testing) use information about the test object's internal code structure or architecture (statements or decisions, a calling hierarchy, menu structures). Also, abstract models of the software may be used (e.g., a process flow model or state transition model).

The objective is to design and run enough test cases to, if possible, completely cover all structural items. Structural techniques approaches are most used in component and integration testing, but can also be applied at system, system integration, or acceptance testing (e.g., to cover menu structures). Structural techniques are covered in section 4.2 and chapter 5 in more detail.

---

20.   This is also true for functionality. The "of course the system has to do X" implicit requirement is a major problem for testing.

3.7.4   Testing Related to Changes and Regression Testing

When existing software is changed, defects are repaired, or new parts are added, the changed parts must be →retested. In addition, there is the risk of side effects. In order to address them, existing test cases are repeated; these tests are called regression tests.

Regression testing

The regression test is a retest of a previously tested program following modification, to ensure that faults have not been introduced or uncovered as a result of the changes made.

Such faults often arise as unplanned side effects of program changes. This means regression testing may be performed at all test levels, and applies to functional, nonfunctional, and →structural testing. Test cases that are used in regression testing run many times and thus have to be well documented and reusable. Therefore, they are strong candidates for →test automation.

It must be determined how extensive a regression test has to be. There are the following possibilities:

Volume of the regression test

1. Rerunning of all the tests that have detected faults which have been fixed in the new software release (defect retest, confirmation testing).
2. Testing of all program parts that were changed or corrected (testing of altered functionality).
3. Testing of all program parts or elements that were newly integrated (testing of new functionality).
4. Testing of the whole system (complete regression test).

A bare retest (1) as well as tests that only execute the area of modifications (2 and 3) are not enough, because in software systems, simple local code changes can create side effects in any other, arbitrarily distant, system parts.

Alterations can have unexpected side effects

If the test covers only altered or new code parts, the test neglects the consequences these alterations can have on unaltered parts. The trouble with software is its complexity. With reasonable cost, it can only be roughly estimated where such unwanted consequences can occur. This is particularly difficult for changes of systems with insufficient documentation or missing requirements, which, unfortunately, is often the case in old systems.

Complete regression test

In addition to the retesting of corrected faults and to the testing of altered functions, all existing test cases should be repeated. Only in this case would the test be as safe as the testing done with the original program version. Such a complete regression test should also be run if the system environment has been changed as this could have effects on every part of the system.

In practice, a complete regression test is usually too time consuming and costly. Therefore, we are looking for criteria that can help to choose which old test cases can be omitted without losing too much information. As always, in testing this means balancing risk and cost. The best way to determine this balance is to make an impact analysis of the changes, trying to determine where side effects may occur. The following strategies are often used to decide on this subject:

- Only the high priority tests according to the test plan are repeated.
- In the functional test, certain variations (special cases) are omitted.
- Restrictions of the tests to certain configurations only (e.g., testing of the English product version only, testing of one operating system version only).
- Restriction of the test to certain subsystems or test levels.

Selection of regression test cases

Generally, the rules listed here refer to the system test. On the lower test levels, regression test criteria can also be based on design or architecture documents (e.g., class hierarchy) or white box information. Further information can be found in [Kung 95], [Rothermel 94], [Winter 98], and [Binder 99]. There, the authors not only describe special problems in regression testing object-oriented programs, but also elaborately describe the general principles of regression testing.

Excursion

3.8 Summary

- The general V-model defines basic test levels: component test, integration test, system test and acceptance test. It distinguishes between verification and validation. These general characteristics of good testing are applicable to any life cycle model:
  - For every development phase there is a corresponding test level
  - The objectives of testing are changing, and specific for each test level
  - The design of tests for a given test level should begin as early as possible, i.e., during the corresponding development activity
  - Testers should be involved in reviewing development information as early as possible
  - The number and intensity of the test levels may be tailored according to the specific needs of the project

■ The V-model uses the fact that it is cheaper to repair defects a short time after they have been introduced than after a long time. If defects remain undetected over several phases of the project, they lead to new defects in documents and products depending on the original defective product. Thus, in general, it is more costly to repair a defect the later it is detected. The defect leads to a so-called "ripple effect".

■ The component test examines single software components. The integration test examines the collaboration of these components. System tests examine the entire system from the perspective of the future users. In the acceptance test, the client checks the product for acceptance respective to the contract and acceptance by operation and the users. If the system is supposed to be installed in many operational environments, then field tests provide an additional opportunity to get experience with the system through running preliminary versions.

■ Defect correction (maintenance) and further development (enhancement) continuously alter and extend the software product throughout its life. All these altered versions must be tested again. Risk analysis must be used to determine the amount of the new tests as well as the regression tests.

■ There are several types of test: Functional testing, nonfunctional testing, testing of software structure, testing related to changes, and regression testing.

4 Static Testing

Static examinations, like reviews, tool supported document and code analyses, can be successfully used for quality improvement. This chapter presents the specific possibilities and techniques for such examinations.

An often underrated test method is the so-called static test, consisting of manual checking and static analysis. Contrary to the dynamic test (see chapter 5), the test object is not executed with test data, but is analyzed instead. This analysis can be done by using one or several people to intensively inspect a document, or by using specific tools. All documents in a software development project can be inspected manually, as well as any document of value outside software projects. Tool-supported static analysis can only be done with documents that follow rules whose checking can be automated.

The main goal of examination is to find defects and deviations from the existing specifications, defined standards, or even the project plan. The results of these examinations are additionally used to optimize the development process. The basic idea is defect prevention: defects and deviations should be recognized as early as possible before they have any effect in the further process of the development where they would result in expensive rework.

4.1 Structured Group Examinations

4.1.1 Foundations

Reviews apply the human analytical capabilities to check and evaluate complex issues. This is done through intensive reading and trying to understand the documents that are examined.

Systematic use of the human capability to think and analyze

There are different techniques for checking documents. They can be distinguished by the intensity, formality, necessary resources (staff and time), as well as by their objectives. Below, the different techniques are explained in more detail. Unfortunately, there is no uniform terminology concerning static analysis techniques. The terms used here are analogous to the terms in the ISTQB syllabus and [IEEE 1028] (see glossary in the appendix). Detailed descriptions can be found in [Freedman 90], [Gilb 96].

4.1.2   Reviews

Review is a common generic term for all the different human static analysis techniques, as well as the term for a specific document examination technique. Another term, often used with the same meaning, is →inspection. However, "inspection" is defined as a special, formal review using data collection and special rules [Fagan 76], [IEEE 1028], [Gilb 96]. All documents can be subjected to a review or an inspection, for example contracts, requirements definitions, design specifications, program code, test plans, and manuals. Often, reviews are the only possibility to check the semantics of a document. Reviews rely on the colleagues of the author to provide feedback. Because of this, they are also called →peer reviews.

Means to assure quality   Reviews are an efficient means to assure the quality of the examined documents. Ideally, they should be performed as soon as possible after a document is completed in order to find mistakes and inconsistencies early. The verifying examinations at the end of a phase in the general V-model normally use reviews (so-called phase exit reviews). Eliminating defects leads to improved quality of the documents and has a positive influence on the whole development process, because development is continued with documents that have less or even no defects.

Positive effects   In addition to defect reduction, reviews have the following positive effects:

- It results in cheaper defect elimination. If defects are recognized and eliminated early, productivity in development is increased because fewer resources are needed for defect recognition and elimination later, when it is substantially more expensive. These resources can instead be used for development (see chapter 3).
- It results in shortened development time.
- If defects are recognized and corrected early, costs and time needed for execution of dynamic tests (see chapter 5) decrease, because there are fewer defects in the test object.

- Because of the smaller number of defects, cost reduction can be expected during the whole lifecycle of a product. For example, a review may detect and clarify inconsistent and imprecise customer wishes in the requirements. Foreseeable change requests after installation of the software system can thus be avoided.
- A reduced failure rate during operation of the system can be expected.
- As the examinations are done using a team of people, reviews lead to mutual learning. People improve their working methods, and reviews will thus lead to enhanced quality of the products that are later produced.
- As several persons are involved in a review, a clear and understandable description of the facts is required. Often the necessity to formulate a clear document lets the author find forgotten issues.
- The whole team feels responsible for the quality of the examined object and the group will gain a common understanding of it.

Potential problems

The following problems can arise: In a badly moderated review session, the author may feel that he himself and not the document is subject to critical scrutiny. Motivation to subject documents to a review will thus be destroyed. One book [Freedman 90] extensively discusses how to solve problems with reviews.

Reviews costs and savings

The costs caused by reviews are estimated to be 10–15 % of the development budget. The costs include the activities of the review process itself, the analysis of the review data, and the effort for their implementation for process improvement. Savings are estimated to be about 14–25 % [Bush 90]. The extra effort for the reviews themselves is included in this calculation.

If reviews are systematically used and efficiently run, more than 70% of the defects in a document can be found and repaired before they are unknowingly inherited by the next work steps [Gilb 96].

- Documents with a formal structure should be analyzed using a (static analysis) tool that checks this structure before the review. The tool can examine many aspects and can detect defects or deviations that do not need to be checked in a review (see section 4.2)

Hint

The following factors are decisive for success when using reviews (as suggested by [IEEE1028]):

- Every review has a clear goal which is formulated beforehand.
- The "right" people are chosen as review participants based on their subject knowledge and skills.

4.1.3   The General Process

The term "review" describes a whole group of static examinations. The different techniques are described in section 4.1.5. The process underlying all examinations is briefly described here in accordance with the IEEE Standard for Software Reviews [IEEE 1028].

A review requires six work steps: planning, overview, preparation, review meeting, rework, and follow-up.

Planning

Reviews must certainly be planned

During overall planning, management must decide which documents in the software development process are subject to which review technique. The estimated effort must be included in the project plans. Several analyses show optimal checking time for reviewing documents and code [Gilb 96]. During planning of the individual review, the review leader selects technically competent staff and assembles a review team. In cooperation with the author of the document to be reviewed, she makes sure that the document is in a →reviewable state, i.e., it is complete enough and the work on it has been finished. In more formal reviews, entry criteria (and the corresponding exit criteria) may be set and checked.

Different viewpoints improve the result

Looking at documents from different perspectives may be more effective than an unfocused review. A review is, in most cases, more successful when the examined document is read from different viewpoints, or if every person only checks particular aspects. The viewpoints or aspects to be used should be determined while planning the review. It may also be decided not to look at the whole document, but to prioritize parts with the highest risk, or to review samples only, in order to check the general quality of the document.

If an overview meeting is considered necessary, time and place must be chosen.

Overview

The overview (or kickoff) serves to provide those involved in the review with all necessary information. This can happen through a written invitation or a first meeting when the review team is organized. The purpose is to share information about the document to be reviewed ("the review object"), and the significance and the objective of the planned review. If the involved people are not familiar with the domain or application area of the review object, then there can be a short introduction to the material, as well a description of how it fits into the application or environment.

In addition to the review object, those involved must have access to other documents. These include the documents that must be used to decide if a particular statement is wrong or correct. The review is done against these documents (e.g., requirements specification, design, guidelines, or standards). Such documents are also called base documents or baseline. Furthermore, review criteria (for example checklists) are very useful in order to support a structured process.

Preparation

The members of the review team must prepare individually for the review meeting. A successful review meeting is only possible with adequate preparation. The reviewers intensively study the review object and check it against the documents given as a basis for it. They note deficiencies, questions, or comments.

Intensively study of the review object

Review meeting[21]

The review meeting is led by a review leader or →moderator. Managing and participating in reviews requires good people skills in order to protect the participating people and motivate them to best contribute to the review.

The review leader must ensure that all experts will be able to express their opinion without fear that the product will be evaluated and not the author, and that conflicts will be prevented or resolved.

Usually, the review meeting has a time limit. The objective is to decide if the review object has met the requirements and complies with the standards, as well as to find defects. The result is a recommendation to accept,

---

21. IEEE Standard 1028 calls this "Examination".

repair, or rewrite the document. All the reviewers should agree upon the findings of this evaluation and the general result.

Following are the general rules for a review meeting[22]:

1. The review meeting is limited to two hours. If necessary, another meeting is called, not before the next day.
2. The moderator has the right to cancel or discontinue a meeting if one or more experts (reviewers) don't appear, or if they are insufficiently prepared.
3. The document subjected to review (the examination object) is subject to discussion, not the author:
    - The reviewers have to watch their expressions and their way of expressing themselves.
    - The author should not defend himself or the document. (That means, the author should not be attacked or forced into a defensive position. Justification or explanation of their decisions is however partially seen as legitimate and helpful.)
4. The moderator should not be a reviewer at the same time.
5. General style questions (outside the guidelines) shall not be discussed.
6. Developing solutions and their discussion is not a task of the review team.
7. Every reviewer must have the opportunity to adequately present their issues.
8. The protocol must describe the consensus of the reviewers.
9. Issues must not be written as commands to the author (additional concrete suggestions for improvement or correction are sometimes considered useful and sensible for quality improvement).
10. The issues must be weighted[23] as:
    - Critical defect (the review object is not suitable for its purpose, the defect must be corrected before the object is approved)
    - Major defect (the usability of the review object is affected, the defect should be corrected before the approval)
    - Minor defect (small deviation, hardly affects the usage)
    - Good (flawless, this area should not be changed during rework)

---

22. Some of these rules do not apply to all kinds of reviews of the IEEE Standard 1028.
23. See section 6.6.3: →Severity class 2 and 3 defects can be seen as major defects and class 4 and 5 as minor defects.

11. The review team shall make a recommendation for the acceptance of the review object (see follow up):

   - Accept (without changes)

   - Accept (with changes, no further review)

   - Do not accept (further review or other checking measures are necessary)

12. At the end of the meetings, all the session participants should sign the protocol

The protocol contains a list of the issues/findings that were discussed in the meeting. An additional review summary report should collect all important data about the review itself, i.e., the review object, the people involved, their roles (see section 4.1.4), a short summary of the most important issues, and the result of the review with the recommendation of the reviewers. When executing a formal review, formal exit criteria may be checked.

Protocol and summary of the results

Rework

The manager decides whether to follow the recommendation or to select a different approach, for which they would have to take the entire responsibility. Usually, the author will eliminate the defects on the basis of the review results.

Follow up

The correction of the defects must be followed up, usually by the manager, moderator, or by someone especially assigned this responsibility. If the result of the first review was not acceptable, another review should be scheduled. The process described here can be rerun, but usually it is done in a shortened way, checking only changed areas.

Second review

A thorough evaluation of the review meetings and their results should then be done to improve the review process, to adapt the used guidelines and checklists to the specific conditions, and to keep them up to date. In order to achieve this it is necessary to collect and evaluate measurement data.

Recurring, or frequently occurring, defect types point to deficiencies in the software development process or in the technical knowledge of the particular people. Necessary improvements of the development process should be planned and implemented. Such defect types should be

Deficiencies in the software development process

included in the checklists. Lack of technical knowledge must be compensated for by training.

4.1.4   Roles and Responsibilities

The description of the general approach already gave some information on the roles and responsibilities, and this section presents the people involved.

Manager   The development manager selects the objects to be reviewed and confirms that the base documents, as well as the necessary resources, are available. They also choose the participating people.

Still, representatives of the management level should not participate in the review meeting in case the author or some reviewers are scared of the possibility that the manager may use the review to evaluate them as a person. Thus, a "free" discussion among the review participants is probably made impossible. Another reason is that the manager often does not have the necessary understanding of technical documents. In a review, the technical content is to be checked, thus the manager is not qualified to participate. Management reviews of project plans and the like are a different thing.

Moderator   The moderator is responsible for: the administrative tasks pertaining to the review, planning and preparation, ensuring that the review is conducted in an orderly manner and meets its objectives, collecting review data, and issuing the review report.

The moderator is crucial for the success of the review. First and foremost, they must be a good meeting leader, leading the meeting efficiently and in a diplomatic way. They must be able to stop unnecessary discussions without offending the participants, to mediate when there are conflicting points of view, and to understand discussions "between the lines". They must be neutral and must not state their own opinion about the review object.

Author   The author is the creator of the document that is the subject of a review. If several people have been involved in the creation, one person with lead responsibility should be appointed; this person takes over the role of the author.

The author is responsible for the review object meeting its review entry criteria (generally that the document is in a reasonably complete state), for contributing to the review based on their special knowledge and understanding of the document, and for performing any rework required to make the review object meet its review exit criteria.

It is important that the author does not interpret the issues raised on the document as personal criticism. The author must understand that a review is only done to help improve the product.

The reviewers, sometimes also called inspectors, are several (usually a maximum of five) technical experts that shall check the review object after individual preparation.

Reviewer

They shall identify and describe problems in the review object. They shall represent different viewpoints (for example sponsor, requirements, design, code, safety, test, etc.). Only those viewpoints pertinent to the review of the product should be presented.

Some reviewers should be assigned specific review topics to ensure effective coverage. For example, one reviewer may focus on conformance with a specific standard, another on syntax, and another on overall coherence. The moderator should assign these roles when planning the review.

The reviewers shall adequately prepare for the meeting. Insufficient or deficient parts of the review object must be labeled accordingly and the deficiencies must be documented for the author in such a way that they can be corrected. The reviewers should also label the good parts in the document.

The recorder (or scribe) shall document the findings (problems, action items, decisions, and recommendations) made by the review team. The recorder must be able to record in a short and precise way, capturing the essence of the discussion. This may not be easy as contributions are often not clear or well expressed. It can make sense to have the author assume the role of recorder. The author knows exactly how precisely and how detailed the contributions of the reviewers need to be recorded in order to have enough information for follow up.

Recorder

Possible difficulties

Reviews may fail due to several causes:

Reasons for reviews to fail

- The required persons are not available or do not have the required qualification or technical aptitude. This is especially true for the moderator, because they must have more psychological than technical skills. This may be solved by training or by using qualified staff from consulting companies.
- Inaccurate estimates during resource planning by management may result in time pressure, which then causes unsatisfactory review results. Sometimes, a less costly review type can bring relief.

■ If reviews fail due to lack of preparation, this is mostly because the wrong reviewers were chosen. If the reviewer does not realize the importance of the review and its great effect on quality improvement, and the review fails because of this, then figures must be shown that prove the productive benefit of the review.

■ A review can also fail because of missing or insufficient documentation. Prior to the review, a check must be done to verify that all the needed documents exist and that they are sufficiently descriptive. Only when this is the case can a review be carried out.

■ The review process cannot be successful if management support is lacking, because the necessary resources will not be provided and the results will not be used for process improvement. Unfortunately, this is often the case.

Detailed hints for solving these problems are described in [Freedman 90].

4.1.5   Types of Reviews

Two main groups of reviews can be distinguished depending on the examined review object:

■ Reviews pertaining to technical products or partial products that have been created during the development process
■ Reviews that analyze project plans and the development process

Excursion   The purpose of a →management review [IEEE 1028][24] (or project review) is to monitor progress, determine the status of plans and schedules, confirm requirements and their system allocation, or evaluate the effectiveness of management approaches used to achieve fitness for purpose.

The project as a whole, as well as the determination of its current state, is the review object. The state of the project is evaluated with respect to technical, economic, time, and management aspects.

Management reviews are often performed when reaching a milestone in the project, when completing a main phase in the software development process, or as a "post-mortem"-analysis, in order to learn from the finished project.

In the following sections, the first group of reviews is described in more detail. We can distinguish between the following review types: →walk-

---

24. In [ISO 8402] the management review is defined in a more narrow way as "a formal evaluation by top management of the status and adequacy of the quality system in relation to quality policy and objectives".

through, inspection, →technical review, and →informal review. In the particular descriptions, the focus is laid on the main differences between the particular review type and the basic review process (see section 4.1.3).

Walkthrough

A walkthrough[25] is an informal review method with the purpose of finding defects, ambiguities, and problems in the written documentation. The author presents the document to the reviewers in the review meeting.

The purpose of educating an audience regarding a software product is mentioned in [IEEE 1028]. Main objectives are to find anomalies, to improve the product, to consider alternative implementations, and to evaluate conformance to standards and specifications.

The focus of the meeting is the walkthrough (without time limit). The preparation is the least compared to the other types of reviews; it can even be omitted sometimes[26].

In the meeting, the author presents the product. Usually, typical use cases, also called scenarios, are walked through according to the course of events. Also, single use cases can be simulated. The reviewers try to reveal possible defects and problems by spontaneously asking questions.

Discussion of typical usage situations

This process is suitable for small development teams of 5 to 10 persons and causes little effort, because preparation and follow up do not take many resources and are not mandatory. A walkthrough can be used for checking "noncritical" documents.

Suitable for small development teams

Due to the fact that the author chairs the meeting, the author has a great influence. This can have a detrimental effect on the result if the author does not want a discussion of the critical parts of the review object. The author is responsible for follow up; there is no more checking involved.

The following approaches are also possible for a walkthrough: Before the meeting the reviewers prepare, the results are written in a protocol, and the findings are listed instead of letting the author note them. In practice there is a wide variation from informal to formal walkthroughs.

---

25. Also called "structured walkthrough".
26. According to [IEEE 1028], the participants should receive the documents in advance and should have prepared for the meeting.

Inspection

Formal process

The inspection is the most formal review. It follows a formal, prescribed process. Every person usually chosen from the direct colleagues of the author, has a defined role. The course of events is defined by rules. Check-lists containing inspection criteria (formal entry and exit criteria) for the individual aspects are used.

The focus is finding unclear points and possible defects, measuring document quality, and improving the quality of the product and the development process. The objectives of the inspection are determined during planning, and only a specific number of aspects will be examined. The inspection object is checked with respect to formal entry criteria prior to starting. The inspectors prepare themselves using procedures, standards, and checklists.

Traditionally, this method of reviewing has been called design inspection or code inspection. The name points to the documents that are subject to an inspection (see [Fagan 76]). However, inspections can be used for any document where formal evaluation criteria exist.

Inspection meeting

The inspection meeting follows this agenda: A moderator leads the meeting. The moderator first presents the participants and their roles, as well with a short introduction to the topics to be checked. The moderator asks every participant if he or she is adequately prepared. It may be asked how much time the reviewer has used and how many issues were found. The group may review the checklists chosen for the inspection in order to determine that everyone is well prepared for the meeting.

Issues of a general nature are then discussed and written to the protocol.

A reviewer[27] presents the contents of the inspection object in a short and logical way. If it is considered useful, passages can also be read aloud. The reviewers ask questions during this procedure, and the selected aspects of the inspection are intensely checked. The author answers questions, but remains passive in general. If author and reviewer disagree about an issue, this may be discussed at the end of the meeting.

The moderator must intervene if the discussion is getting out of control. The moderator also makes sure that the meeting covers all aspects to be evaluated as well as the whole document. The moderator makes sure that the recorder keeps track of all the issues and ambiguities that are detected.

---

27.   IEEE 1028 says "reader".

At the end of the meeting all recorded items are reviewed for completeness. Issues where there was disagreement are discussed in order to resolve whether or not they are defects. If no resolution is reached, this is written in the protocol.

Finally, a judgment is reached about the inspection object as a whole. It is decided if the inspection object must be reworked or not. In inspections, follow-up and re-inspection are formally regulated.

In an inspection, data are also collected for general quality assessment of the development process and the inspection process. Therefore, the inspection also serves to improve the development process, in addition to assessing the inspected documents. The data are analyzed in order to find weaknesses in the development process. After improvement of the process, the effect of the alteration is checked by comparing the collected data before the change to the current data.

Additional assessment of the development and inspection process

Technical review

In a technical review, the focus of attention is compliance of the document with the specification, fitness for its intended purpose, and compliance to standards. During preparation, the reviewers inspect the review object according to the specified review criteria.

Does the review object fulfill its purpose?

The reviewers must be technically qualified experts. Some of them should not be project participants, in order to avoid "project blindness". Management does not participate. Background for the review is only the "official" specification and the specified tasks for the review. The reviewers write down their comments and pass them to the moderator before the review meeting[28]. The moderator (who in the ideal case is properly trained) sets the priority for these findings according to their presumable importance. During the review meeting, only selected important remarks are discussed.

Technical experts as reviewers

Most of the effort lies in the preparation work. During the meeting, normally not attended by the author, the recorder notes all the issues and prepares the final documentation of the results.

High preparation effort

The review result must be approved unanimously by all involved, and signed by everyone. Disagreement should be noted in the protocol. It is not the job of the review participants to decide on the consequences of the

---

28.   In [IEEE 1028] this also applies to inspection.

result, as that is a management responsibility. If the review is highly formalized, entry and exit criteria of the review may also be defined.

In practice very different versions of the technical review are found, from a very informal to a strictly defined, formal process.

Informal review

The informal review is a light version of a review. However, it more or less follows the general procedure for reviews (see section 4.1.3) in a simplified way. In most cases, the author initiates an informal review. Planning is restricted to choosing reviewers and asking them to deliver their remarks at a certain point in time. Often, there is no meeting or exchange of the findings. In such cases, the review is just an author reader cycle. The informal review is a kind of cross-read by one or more colleagues. The results need not be explicitly documented; a list of remarks or the revised document is enough.

Pair programming, buddy testing, code swapping, and the like are each a type of informal review. The informal review is very common and has a high acceptance due to the minimal effort required.

Selection criteria

Selection of type of review   The type of review that should be used depends very much on the requested quality and the effort that has to be spent. It depends on the project environment, and specific recommendations cannot be given. It must be decided in each particular case which type of review is appropriate. Below, some questions and criteria are given that should help to make the selection of specific review types easier:

- The form in which the result of the review should be presented can help select the review type. Is detailed documentation necessary, or is it enough to implement the checking results informally?
- Will it be difficult or easy to find a date and time for the review? It can be very difficult to bring together 5 or 7 technical experts for one or more meetings.
- Is it necessary to have technical knowledge from different disciplines?
- How many qualified review participants are necessary? Will the reviewers be motivated?
- Is the preparation effort appropriate with respect to the benefit of the review (the expected result)?

- How formally written is the review object? Is it possible to perform tool-supported analyses?
- How much management support is available? Will management curtail reviews when the work is done under time pressure?

Notes

As we already said in the beginning of the chapter, there are no uniform descriptions of the individual types of review. There is no clear boundary between the different review types, and the same terms are used with different meanings.

Generally, it can be said that the type of a review is very much determined by the organization that uses it. The reviews are tailored for the specific needs and requirements of a project. This has a positive influence on their effectiveness.

Types of reviews depend on the organization where they are used

A cooperative collaboration between the people involved in software development can be considered beneficial to quality. If people examine each other's work results, defects and ambiguities can be revealed. From this point of view, pair programming, as it is suggested in →Extreme Programming, can be regarded as a permanent "two-person-review" [Beck 00].

In distributed project teams, there may be difficulties organizing review meetings. Modern ways of organizing reviews include structured discussion by Internet, video, telephone conferences, etc.

Success Factors

When using reviews the following factors are crucial for success and must be taken into consideration:

- Reviews serve the purpose of improving the examined documents. Detecting findings, such as unclear points and deviations, is a wanted and required effect. The findings must be formulated in a neutral and objective way.
- Human and psychological factors have a strong influence in a review. The author of the examined document should feel that the review is a positive experience.
- Depending on the type and level of the examined document, and the state of knowledge of the participating people, a different but appropriate kind of review should be chosen.

- Checklists and guidelines are used in order to increase the effectiveness of detecting findings during reviews.
- Training is necessary, especially for more formal kinds of reviews, such as inspections.
- Management can support a good review process by planning sufficient resources (time and personnel) for document reviews in the software development process.
- A very important aspect of the successful use of reviews is continuous learning from the reviews themselves, i.e., review process improvement.

4.2   Static Analysis

Analysis without execution of program

The objective of static analysis is, as with reviews, to reveal defects or parts that are defect-prone in a document. However, in static analysis, tools do the analysis.

For example, even spell checkers can be regarded as a form of →static analyzers that find mistakes in texts and therefore contribute to quality improvement. The term "static analysis" points to the fact that this form of checking does not contain an execution of the checked objects (of a program). An additional objective is to derive measurements, or metrics, in order to measure and prove the quality of the object.

Formal documents

The document to be analyzed must follow a certain formal structure in order to be checked by a tool. Static analysis only makes sense with the support of tools. Formal documents can be, for example, the technical requirements, the software architecture, or the software design. An example is the modeling of class diagrams in UML[29]. Generated outputs in HTML[30] or XML[31] can also be subjected to tool supported static analysis. Formal models developed during the design phases can also be analyzed and inconsistencies can be detected. Unfortunately, in practice, the program code is often the one and only formal document of the software development that can be subjected to static analysis.

Static analysis tools are typically used by developers, before or during component or integration testing, in order to check if guidelines or pro-

---

29.   UML – Unified Modeling Language [URL: UML]
30.   HTML – HyperText Markup Language [URL: HTML]
31.   XML – Extensible Markup Language [URL: XML]

gramming conventions are adhered to. During integration testing, adherence to interface guidelines is analyzed.

Analysis tools often produce a long list of warnings and comments. In order to effectively use the tools, the mass of generated information must be handled intelligently; for example, by configuring the tool. Otherwise the tools might be avoided.

Static analysis and reviews are closely related. If a static analysis is performed before the review, a number of defects can be found and the number of the aspects to be checked in the review clearly decreases. Due to the fact that static analysis is tool-supported, the effort is much less than in a review.

Static analysis and reviews

- If documents are formal enough to allow tool-supported static analysis, then this should definitely be performed before the document reviews because faults and inconsistencies can be detected conveniently and cheaply and the reviews can be shortened.
- Generally, static analysis should be used even if no review is planned. Each located and removed discrepancy increases the quality of the document.

Hint

Not all defects can be found using static testing, though. Some defects become apparent only when the program is executed (that means at run time), and cannot be recognized before. For example, if the value of the denominator in a division is stored in a variable, that variable can be assigned the value zero. This leads to a failure at run time. In static analysis, this defect cannot easily be found, except for when this variable is assigned the value zero by a constant having zero as its value. Alternatively, all possible paths through the operations are analyzed and the operation can be flagged as potentially dangerous.

On the other hand, some inconsistencies and defect-prone areas in a program are difficult to find by dynamic testing. Detecting violation of programming standards or use of forbidden error-prone program constructs is only possible with static analysis (or reviews).

All compilers carry out a static analysis of the program test by making sure that the correct syntax of the programming language is used. Most compilers provide additional information, which can be derived by static analysis (see section 4.2.1). In addition to compilers, other tools are so-called analyzers. These are used for performing individual or group analyses.

The compiler is an analysis tool

The following defects and constructions that bear the danger of producing problems can be detected by static analysis:

- Syntax violation
- Deviation from conventions and standards
- →Control flow anomalies
- →Data flow anomalies.

Finding security problems Static analysis can be used in order to detect security problems. Many security holes occur because certain error-prone program constructs are used and necessary checks are not done. Examples are lack of buffer overflow protection, or failing to check that input data may be out of bounds. Tools can find such deficiencies because they often have a certain "pattern", which can be searched for and found.

4.2.1   The Compiler as Static Analysis Tool

Violation of the programming language syntax is detected by static analysis and reported as a fault or warning. Many compilers also generate further information and perform other checks. Examples are:

- Generating a cross reference list of the different program elements (e.g., variables, functions)
- Checking for correct data type usage by data and variables in programming languages with strict typing
- Detecting undeclared variables
- Detecting code that is not reachable
- Detecting overflow or underflow of field boundaries (static addressing)
- Checking of interface consistency
- Detecting the use of all labels as jump start or jump target

The information is usually provided in the form of lists. A result reported as "suspicious" by the tool is not always a fault. Therefore, further investigation is necessary.

4.2.2   Examination of Compliance to Conventions and Standards

Compliance to conventions and standards can also be checked with tools; for example, if most programming regulations and standards have been respected. This way of inspecting takes little time and almost no personnel resources. In any case, only guidelines that can be verified by tools should be accepted in a project. Every other regulation usually proves to be bureaucratic waste anyway. Furthermore, there often is an additional advantage: if the programmers know that the program code is checked for compliance to the programming guidelines, their willingness to work according to the guidelines is much higher than without an automatic test.

4.2.3   Data Flow Analysis

→Data flow analysis is another means to reveal defects. Here, the usage of data on →paths through the program code is checked. It is not always possible to detect defects. Instead, we speak of →anomalies, or data flow anomalies. Anomaly means an inconsistency that can lead to failure, but does not necessarily do so. An anomaly may be flagged as a risk.

Data use analysis

For example, data flow anomalies are reading variables without previous initialization, or not using the value of a variable at all. The usage of every single variable is inspected during the analysis. The following three types of usage or states of variables are distinguished:

- **Defined (d)**: the variable is assigned a value
- **Referenced (r)**: the value of the variable is read and/or used
- **Undefined (u)**: the variable has no defined value

We can distinguish three types of data flow anomalies:

Data flow anomalies

- **ur-anomaly**: An undefined value (u) of a variable is read on a program path (r)
- **du-anomaly**: The variable is assigned a value (d) that becomes invalid/undefined (u) without having been used in the meantime
- **dd-anomaly**: The variable receives a value for the second time (d) and the first value had not been used (d)

The different anomalies are explained referring to the following example (in C++). The following function is supposed to exchange the integer values of the parameters Max and Min with the help of the variable Help, if the value of the variable Min is greater that the value of the variable Max:

Example for anomalies

```
void exchange (int& Min, int& Max) {
    int Help;
        if (Min > Max) {
        Max = Help;
        Max = Min;
        Help = Min;
        }
}
```

After the analysis of the usage of the single variables, the following anomalies can be detected:

- **ur-anomaly** of the variable Help: The domain of the variable is limited to the function. The first usage of the variable is on the right side of an assignment. At this time, the variable still has an undefined value, which is referenced there. There was no initialization of the variable when it was declared (this anomaly is also recognized by usual compilers, if a high warning level is activated).
- **dd-anomaly** of the variable Max: The variable is used twice consecutively on the left side of an assignment and therefore is assigned a value twice. Either the first assignment can be omitted or the use of the first value (before the second assignment) has been forgotten.
- **du-anomaly** of the variable Help: In the last assignment of the function the variable Help is assigned another value that cannot be used anywhere, because the variable is only valid inside the function.

Data flow anomalies are usually not that obvious

In this example, the anomalies are obvious. But it must be considered that between the particular statements that cause these anomalies there could be an arbitrary number of other statements. The anomalies would not be as obvious anymore and could easily be missed by a manual check, e.g., a review. A tool for analyzing data flow can, however, detect the anomalies.

Not every anomaly leads directly to an incorrect behavior. For example, a "du"-anomaly does not always have direct effects; the program could still run properly. The question arises why this particular assignment is at this position in the program, just before the end of the block where the variable is valid. Usually, an exact examination of the program parts where trouble is indicated is worthwhile and further inconsistencies can be discovered.

4.2.4   Control Flow Analysis

Control flow graph

In figure 4-1, a program structure is represented as a control flow graph. In this directed graph, the statements of the program are represented with nodes. Sequences of statements are also represented with a single node, because inside the sequence there can be no change in the course of program execution. If the first statement of the sequence is executed, the others are also executed.

Changes in the course of program execution are represented by decisions, e.g., in "IF"-statements. If the calculated value of the condition is "true", then the program continues in the part that begins with "THEN". If the condition is "false", then the "ELSE"- part is executed. Loops lead to previous statements, resulting in repeated execution of a part of the graph.

Due to the clarity of the control flow graph, the sequence in the program structure can easily be understood and possible anomalies can be detected. These anomalies could be jumps out of a loop body, or a program structure that has several exits. These anomalies may not necessarily lead to failure, but they are not in accordance with the principles of structured programming. It is assumed that the graph is not generated manually, but that it is generated by a tool that guarantees an exact mapping of the program text in the graph.

Control flow anomalies

If parts of the graph or the whole graph are very complex, and the relations, as well as the course of events, are not understandable, then a revision of the program text should be done, because complex sequence structures often bear a great risk of errors.

In addition to graphs, a tool can generate predecessor-successor tables that show how every statement is related to the other statements. If there is a statement that does not have a predecessor, then this statement is unreachable (so-called dead code). Thus a defect or at least an anomaly is detected. Only the first and last statements of a program are allowed to not have a predecessor or successor. For programs with several entrance and/or exit points, the same applies.

Excursion:
Predecessor-successor
table

4.2.5   Determining Metrics

In addition to the mentioned analyses, static analysis tools also provide measurement values. Quality characteristics can be measured with measurement values, or metrics. The measured values must be checked, though, to see if they meet the specified requirements [ISO 9126]. An overview of currently used metrics can be found in [Fenton 91].

Measuring of quality
characteristics

The definition of metrics for certain characteristics of software is based on the intent to gain a quantitative measure of software whose nature is abstract. Therefore, a metric can only provide statements concerning the one aspect that is examined, and the measurement values that are calculated are only interesting in comparison to numbers from other programs or program parts that are examined.

In the following, a closer look at a certain metric will be taken: the →cyclomatic number (McCabe number [McCabe 76]). The cyclomatic number measures the structural complexity of program code. The basis of this calculation is the control flow graph.

Cyclomatic number

*The original formula is
v(G) = e - n + 2p, where p is
the number of connected
program parts. We use p=1,
because there is only one
part which is analyzed.

For a control flow graph G of a program or a program part the cyclomatic number can be computed like this:*

$$v(G) = e - n + 2$$

v(G) = cyclomatic number of the graph G
e   = number of edges in the control flow graph
n   = number of nodes in the control flow graph

Example of the calculation of the cyclomatic number

A program part is represented by the graph of figure 4-1. It is a function that can be called. Thus, the cyclomatic number can be calculated like this:

$$v\,(G) = e\text{-}n + 2 = 17\text{-}13 + 2 = 6$$

with
e = number of edges in the graph = 17
n = number of nodes in the graph = 13

Figure 4–1
Control flow graph for the calculation of the cyclomatic number (identical to figure 2-2)

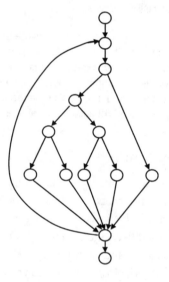

The value of 6 is, according to McCabe, acceptable and in the middle of the range. We assume that a value higher than 10 can not be tolerated and rework of the program code has to take place.

The cyclomatic number gives information about the testing effort

The cyclomatic number can be used to estimate the testability and the maintainability of the particular program part. The cyclomatic number specifies the number of independent paths in the program part[32]. If 100%

32. All linearly independent paths are meant.

branch coverage (see section 5.2.2) is intended, then all these independent paths of the control flow graph have to be executed at least once. Therefore, the cyclomatic number provides important information concerning the volume of the test. Understanding a program is essential for its maintenance. The higher the value of the cyclomatic number, the more difficult it is to understand a certain program part.

The cyclomatic number has been very much discussed since its publication. One of its drawbacks is that the complexity of the conditions, which lead to the selection of the control flow, is not taken into account. Whether a condition consists of several partial atomic conditions with logical operators, or is a single condition, does not influence the calculation of the cyclomatic number. Many extensions and adaptations have been published concerning this matter.

Excursion

4.3 Summary

Several pairs of eyes see more than a single pair of eyes. This is also true in software development. This is the main principle for the reviews that are performed for checking and for improving quality. Several people inspect the documents and discuss them in a meeting and the results are recorded.

- A fundamental review process consists of the following activities: planning, overview, preparation, review meeting, rework and follow-up. The roles of the participants are manager, moderator, author, reviewer and recorder.
- There are several types of reviews. Unfortunately, the terminology is defined differently in all literature and standards.
- The walkthrough is an informal procedure where the author presents their document to the reviewers in the meeting. There is little preparation for the meeting. The walkthrough is especially suitable for small development teams, for discussing alternatives, and for educating people.
- The inspection is the most formal review process. Preparation is done using checklists, there are defined entry and exit criteria, the meeting is chaired by a trained moderator, and data are collected and used for quality improvement of both development and the inspection process itself.
- In the technical review, the individual reviewers' results are presented to the review leader prior to the meeting. The meeting is then priori-

tized by assumed importance of the individual issues. The author does not participate. Checking is done using documents only.

- The informal review is not based on a formal procedure. It is not prescribed in which form the results have to be presented. Because this type of review can be performed with minimal effort, its acceptance is very high, and in practice it is very commonly used.

- Generally, the type of review used is very much determined by the specific environment, i.e., the specific organization and project for which the review is used. The reviews are tailored to meet the specific needs and requirements which increases their efficiency. It is important to establish a cooperative and collaborative atmosphere amongst the people involved in the software development.

- In addition to the reviews, a whole series of checks can be done for documents that have a formalized structure. These checks are called static analyses. The test object is not executed during a static analysis.

- The compiler is the most common analysis tool and reveals syntax errors in the program code. Usually, compilers provide even more checking and information.

- Analysis tools can also show violation of standards and other conventions.

- Tools are available for detecting anomalies in the data and control flows of the program. Useful information about control and data flows is generated, which often points to parts that could contain defects.

- Metrics are used to measure quality. One such metric is the cyclomatic number, which calculates the number of independent paths in the checked program. It is possible to gain information on the structure and the testing effort.

- Generally, static analyses should be performed first, before a document is subjected to reviewing. Static analyses provide a cheap means to detect defects and thus make the reviews cheaper.

5 Dynamic Analysis – Test Design Techniques

This chapter describes techniques for testing of software by executing the test-objects on a computer. It presents the different techniques for specifying test cases and for defining test exit criteria, and then explains them by examples. These techniques are divided into black box testing and white box testing. Additional test design methods conclude this chapter.

In most cases, testing of software is seen as the execution of the test object on a computer. For further clarification, the phrase →*dynamic* analysis is used. The test object (program) must be executable. It is provided with input data before it is executed. In the lower test stages (component and integration testing) the test object cannot be run alone, but must be embedded into a test bed to obtain an executable program (see figure 5-1).

Execution of the test object on a computer

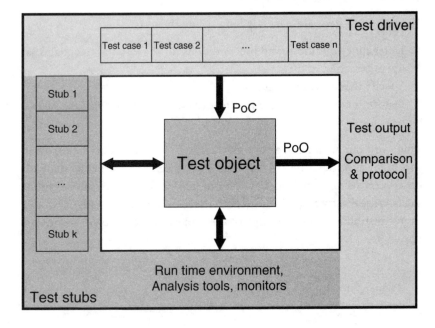

Figure 5–1
Test bed

Test bed necessary

The test object will usually call different parts of the program through predefined interfaces. These parts of the program are substituted by place-holders called stubs whenever these parts are not yet implemented, and therefore not ready to be used if they are supposed to be simulated for this particular test of the test object. Stubs simulate the input/output behavior of that part of the program that usually would be called by the test object[33].

Furthermore, the test bed must supply the test object with input data. In most cases, it is necessary to simulate a part of the program that is supposed to call the test object. The test driver does this. Driver and stub combined establish the test bed, which constitutes the executable program together with the test object.

The tester must often create the test bed, or the tester must expand or modify standard (generic) test beds, adjusting them to the interfaces of the test object. Test bed generators can be used as well (section 7.1.4). Having such an executable test object empowers the tester to start the dynamic analysis.

Systematic approach at determination of the test cases

When executing a program, testing must expose failures and verify as many requirements as possible with as little expense as possible. To reach this goal, a systematic approach is necessary. Unstructured testing, usually "by gut feeling", does not offer any guarantee. The tester should test as many situations as possible, but it is best to test all possible situations that are processed by the test object.

Incremental approach

The following steps are necessary to execute the tests:

- Determine conditions and preconditions for the test and the goals that are to be achieved
- Specify the individual test cases
- Determine how to execute the tests (usually chaining together several test cases)

This work can be done in a very informal way (i.e., undocumented), or in a formal way as described in this chapter. The degree of formality depends on several factors, such as application area of the system (for example safety critical software), maturity of the development and test process, and time constraints and knowledge of the project participants, to mention a few.

---

33. Contrary to stubs, with its rudimental functionality, the →dummy or →mock-up offers additional functionality for testing purposes.

At the beginning of this activity, the test basis is analyzed to determine what must be tested. For example, a test should show that time constraints are met or a particular transaction is correctly executed. We determine the test objectives for demonstrating that requirements are met. The failure risk should especially be taken into account. Necessary preconditions and conditions for the test are determined, an example being the necessary data in a database.

Conditions, preconditions, and goals

It must be determined how the individual requirements and the test cases relate to each other. Thus, it is possible to determine the coverage of the requirements by the tests. It will also be easier to estimate the effect of requirement changes on the test (implementing new test cases or changing existing ones).

Part of the specification of the individual test cases is determining test input data for the test object. They are determined by the methods described in this chapter.

Test case specification

However, the preconditions for executing the test case, as well as the expected results and expected postconditions are important, in determining if there is a failure (detailed descriptions can be found in [IEEE 829]).

The expected results (output, change of internal states, etc.) should be determined before executing the test cases. Otherwise, it often happens that an incorrect result is interpreted as correct, thus missing detection of a failure.

Determine expected result and behavior

It does not make much sense to execute an individual test case. Test cases should be grouped in such a way that a whole sequence of test cases is executed (test sequence or test scenario). Such a test sequence is documented in the →test procedure specifications or test instructions. The document commonly groups the test cases by topic or by test objectives. It should also be possible to find information about test priorities, and technical and logical dependencies between the tests and regression test cases. Finally, the timing of the test execution (assigning tests to testers and determining the point of time for execution) is described in the →test schedule.

Test case execution

In order to be able to execute a test sequence a →test script is required. The test script contains, most often in a programming language or a similar notation, instructions for automatically executing the test sequence. The corresponding preconditions can be set and the actual and expected results can be compared in the test script. JUnit is an example of a framework, which allows for easy programming of test scripts in Java [URL: xunit].

Black box and white box
techniques

Several different approaches are available for testing the test object. They can be categorized into two groups: black box and white box[34] testing. To be more precise: test case design techniques, because these techniques support the identification of the respective test cases.

Using black box testing, the test object is seen as a black box. Test cases are derived from the specification of the test object. The behavior of the test object is watched from the outside (PoO – →Point of Observation is outside the test object). It is not possible to control the operating sequence of the test object other than choosing the adequate input test data (the PoC – →Point of Control is situated outside of test object, too). Test cases are designed by using the specification or the requirements of the test object.

In white box testing, the source code is known and used for test design. While executing the test cases, the internal processing of the test object, as well as the output, is analyzed (the Point of Observation is inside of the test object). Direct intervention in the process of the test object is possible, but should be used only in special situations, e.g. to execute negative testing when the component's interface is not capable of initiating the provoked failure (the Point of Control can be located inside the test object). Test cases are designed to cover the program structure of the test object (figure 5-2).

Figure 5–2
PoC and PoO at black box
and white box techniques

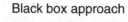

| Black box approach | White box approach |

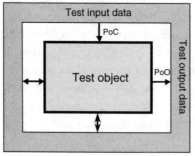
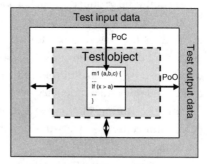

PoC and PoO "outside"   PoC and/or PoO "inside"
the test object   the test object

---

34. Sometimes called "glass box testing" or "open box testing", because of the lack of transparency in a white box. Nevertheless, these terms are not in widespread use.

White box testing is also called structural testing, because the test designer considers the structure (component hierarchy, flow control, data flow) of the test object. The black box testing techniques are known as functional or behavioral testing techniques, because of the observation of the input/output behavior [Beizer 95]. The functionality of the test object is the center of attention. White box testing can be applied at the lower levels of the testing, i.e., component and integration test.

Black box testing is predominantly used for higher levels of testing even though it is reasonable in component tests. Any test design before the code is written (test-first programming, test-driven development) is essentially black box driven.

Most test methods can clearly be assigned to one of the two categories. Some have elements of both, and are sometimes called "grey box techniques". In the following two chapters, black box and white box techniques are described in detail. Intuitive or experience-based testing can be said to be a black box technique. However, it is described in a different chapter as it is not a systematic technique.

5.1   Black Box Testing Techniques

Using black box testing, the inner structure and design of the test object is unknown, or not considered. The test cases are derived from the specification, or they are already available as part of the specification. A test with all possible input data combinations would be a complete test, but this is unrealistic considering the enormous number of combinations (section 2.1.4). Test design must make a reasonable selection of all possible test cases. There are a couple of methods to do exactly that, which will be introduced below.

5.1.1   Equivalence Class Partitioning

The domain of possible input data for each input data element is divided into →equivalence classes (equivalence class partitioning). An equivalence class is a group of data values where the tester assumes that the test object processes them in the same way. The test of one representative of the equivalence class is seen as sufficient because it is assumed that for any other input value of the same equivalence class the test object will not show a different reaction or behavior. Besides equivalence classes for correct input, those for incorrect input values must be tested as well.

Input domains are divided into equivalence classes

The example for the calculation of the Christmas bonus from section 2.2.2 is revisited here to clarify the facts. As a reminder: The program shall calculate the Christmas bonus of the employees depending on the affiliation to the company. The following text is part of the description of the requirements: "Employees receive a Christmas bonus equal to 50% of their monthly income if they have been working for the company for more than three years, employees who have been employed for more than five years receive a 75% bonus, and those with more than eight years of employment are awarded a 100% bonus."

Four different equivalence classes with correct input values (correct, or "valid" equivalence classes, vEC) can be derived very easily from the calculation of the bonus by considering the length of employment.

Table 5–1
*Correct equivalence classes
and representatives*

Parameter	Equivalence classes	Representative values
Bonus calculation program, duration of employment in years	vEC_1: $0 <= x <= 3$	2
	vEC_2: $3 < x <= 5$	4
	vEC_3: $5 < x <= 8$	7
	vEC_4: $x > 8$	12

In section 2.2.2, the input values 2, 4, 7, 12 (compare table 2-2) were chosen. Every value is a representative for one of the four equivalence classes. It is assumed that test execution with input values like 1, 6, 9, and 17 does not lead to further insights and therefore not exposes further failures. With this assumption, it is not necessary to execute those extra test cases.

Besides the correct input values, incorrect values must be tested. Equivalence classes for incorrect input values must be derived as well, and test cases with representatives of these classes must be executed. In the example we used earlier, there are the following two invalid equivalence classes (iEC)[35]:

Table 5–2
*Invalid equivalence classes
and representatives*

Parameter	Equivalence classes	Representative values
Bonus calculation program, duration of employment in years	iEC_1: $x < 0$ ("Negative" – thus incorrect – staff membership in a company)	-3
	iEC_2: $x > 70$ (Unrealistically long and incorrect staff membership in a company[a])	80

a. The value 70 is chosen rather randomly by judging nobody would be employed for such a long time. The maximum value for company affiliation has to be aligned with the customer's opinion.

35. A correct term would be "equivalence classes for invalid values" instead of "invalid equivalence class", because the equivalence class in itself is not invalid, only the values of this class, for the specified input.

The following describes how to systematically derive the test cases. For every input data element that should be tested (e.g., function/method parameter at component tests or input screen field at system tests) the domain of all possible inputs should be determined. This domain is then partitioned into equivalence classes. First, the subdomain of correct inputs is found. This is the equivalence class of all correct input values. The test object should process these values according to the specification. The values outside of this domain are seen as equivalence classes with incorrect input values. For these values as well, it must be tested how the test object behaves.

Systematic derivation of the test cases

The next step is to refine the equivalence classes. If the test object's specification tells that some elements of equivalence classes are processed differently, they should be assigned to a new (sub)equivalence class. The equivalence classes should be divided until each different requirement corresponds to an equivalence class. For every single equivalence class, a representative value should be chosen for testing.

Further partitioning of the equivalence classes

To complete the test cases, the tester must define the preconditions and the expected result for every test case.

The same principle of dividing into equivalence classes can also be used for the output data. Admittedly, identification of the individual test cases is more expensive, because for every output-representative (output value) the corresponding input value combination causing this output must be determined. For the output values as well, the equivalence classes with incorrect values must not be disregarded.

Equivalence classes for output values

Partitioning into equivalence classes and selecting the representatives should be carefully done. The probability of failure detection is highly dependent upon the quality of the partitioning, as well as which test cases are executed. Usually, it is not trivial to identify the equivalence classes from the specification or from other documents.

The best test values are certainly those verifying the boundaries of the equivalence classes. There are often misunderstandings or inaccuracies in the requirements at these spots, because our natural language is not precise enough to accurately define the limits of the equivalence classes. The colloquial phrase "... more than 3 years..." within the requirements might mean the value 3 being inside (EC: $x \geq 3$) or outside of the equivalence class (EC: $x > 3$). An additional test case with $x = 3$ might detect a misinterpretation and therefore failure. Section 5.1.2 discusses in detail the analysis of the boundary values for equivalence classes.

Boundaries of the equivalence classes

*Example: Equivalence
class construction
for integer values*

To clarify the procedure for building equivalence classes, all possible equivalence classes for an integer input value are to be identified. The following equivalence classes result for the integer parameter extras of the function `calculate_price()`:

Table 5–3
*Equivalence classes
for integer input values*

Parameter	Equivalence classes
extras	vEC_1: [MIN_INT,…, MAX_INT] [a]
	iEC_1: NaN (Not a Number)

a. MIN_INT and MAX_INT each describe the minimum and maximum whole number that the computer is able to use. These can vary depending on the used hardware.

Notice that the domain contrary to plain mathematics is limited on a computer by its maximum and minimum. Using values outside the computer domain often leads to failures, because this situation is not handled correctly.

The equivalence class for incorrect values is derived from the following consideration: Incorrect values are numbers that are greater or smaller than the range of the applicable interval or every nonnumeric value[36]. If it is assumed that the program's reaction on an incorrect value is always the same (e.g., an exception handling that delivers the error code NOT_VALID), then it is sufficient to map all possible incorrect values on one common equivalence class (named NaN for "Not a Number" here). Part of this equivalence class is the floating point numbers because it is expected that the program reacts with an error message to inputs such as "3.5". In this case, the equivalence class partitioning method does not require any further subdivision, as the same reaction is expected in every case of wrong input. However, an experienced tester will always include a test case with a floating-point number in order to determine if the program rounds the number and continues with the rounded integer number. The basis of such an additional test case is intuition or experience based testing (see section 5.3).

It is reasonable to further divide the equivalence classes with correct values because negative and positive values often must be treated differently. Zero is a further input value that often leads to failures, therefore, it is often interesting to test.

Table 5–4
*Equivalence classes and
representatives for integer
values*

Parameter	Equivalence classes	Representatives
extras	vEC_1: [MIN_INT, …, 0[[a]	-123
	vEC_2: [0, …, MAX_INT]	654
	iEC_1: NaN (Not a Number)	"f"

a. '[' Specifies an open interval until just below the given value, but not including it. The definition [MIN_INT, … , -1] is equivalent because we deal with integer numbers in this case.

36. It depends on the given programming language and the used compiler which incorrect values the compiler or run time system is able to identify, e.g., while attempting to call the function from the test driver. In the example, it is assumed that the compiler or run time system cannot recognize incorrect values and that the processing of those values must be examined in the dynamic test.

The representative values for the three equivalence classes have been randomly chosen. The boundary values (see section 5.1.2) of the respective equivalence classes should be added: MIN_INT, -1, 0, MAX_INT. The equivalence class for incorrect values has no boundary values.

Result: For the test of the integer parameter extras, the equivalence class method, taking into account boundary values, generates the following seven test values:

{"f", MIN_INT, -123, -1, 0, 654, MAX_INT}.

For every input value the expected outputs or reactions of the test object should be defined in order to decide after test execution whether a failure occurred or not.

For the integer input data of the example, it is very easy to determine equivalence classes and the corresponding representative test values. Besides the basic data types, data structures and sets of objects can occur. It must then be decided in each case with which representative values to execute the test case.

Equivalence classes of input values, which are not basic data types

---

The following example should clarify this: A traveler can be a child, a teenager, an adult, a student, a person on welfare, or a retired person. If the test object needs to react differently to each kind of traveler, then every possibility must be verified with an additional test case. If there is no requirement for different reactions for each person type, then one test case might be sufficient. In this case, any randomly chosen but correct value can be chosen for the traveler.

Example for input values to be selected from a set

If the test object is the component that calculates the fare, and the fare depends on the type of person, then certainly six different test cases for the traveler must be provided. It is probable that the fare is calculated differently for each traveler. Details must be looked up in the requirements. Each calculation must be verified by a test to prove the correctness of the calculations and to find failures.

For the test of the component that handles the seat reservation, it might be sufficient to choose only one representative, e.g., an adult, for the traveler. Presumably, it is not relevant if a teenager or a retired person takes the seat. Here, as well, the requirements may tell otherwise and should be analyzed. The tester should be aware, though, that in case she executes the test with the input "adult" only, she will not be able to verify anything about the correctness of the seat reservation for any of the five other traveler types.

Hint for determining equivalence classes

The following hints can help determine equivalence classes:

- For the inputs as well as for the outputs, identify the restrictions and conditions in the specification.
- For every restriction or condition, partition into equivalence classes:
  - If a continuous numerical domain is specified, then create one valid and two invalid equivalence classes.
  - If a number of values should be entered, then create one valid (with all possible correct values) and two invalid equivalence classes (less and more than the correct number).
  - If a set of values is specified where each value may possibly be treated differently, then create one valid equivalence class for each value of the set (containing exactly this one value) and one additional invalid equivalence class (containing all possible other values).
  - If there is a condition that must be fulfilled, then create one valid and one invalid equivalence class to test the condition fulfilled and not fulfilled.
- If there is any doubt that the values of one equivalence class are treated equally, the equivalence class should be further divided into subclasses.

Test Cases

Combination of the representatives

Usually, the test object has more than one input parameter. The equivalence class technique results in at least two equivalence classes (one valid and one invalid) for each of these parameters of the test object. Therefore, there are at least two representative values that must be used as test input for each parameter.

In order to specify a test case, each parameter must be assigned an input value. For this purpose, a decision must be made about which of the available values should be combined together to form test cases. In order to guarantee triggering all test object reactions (modeled by the equivalence class division), the input values, i.e., the representatives of the according equivalence classes, must be combined using the following rules:

Rules for test case determination

- The representative values of all valid equivalence classes should be combined to test cases, meaning that all possible combinations of valid equivalence classes will be covered. Any of those combinations builds a "valid test case" or a "positive test case".

Separate test of the invalid value

- The representative value of an invalid equivalence class can only be combined with (arbitrary) representatives of other *valid* equivalence classes. Thus, every invalid equivalence class leads to an additional "invalid test case" or "negative test case".

The number of "valid" test cases is the product of the number of valid equivalence classes per parameter. Because of this multiplicative combination, even a few parameters can generate hundreds of "valid test cases". Since it is seldom possible to use that many test cases, more rules are necessary to reduce the number of "valid" test cases:

Restriction of the number of test cases

▪ Combine the test cases and sort them by frequency of occurrence (typical usage profile). Prioritize the test cases in this order. That way only the "relevant" test cases (often appearing combinations) are tested.

Rules for test case restriction

▪ Test cases including boundary values or boundary value combinations are preferred.

▪ Combine every representative of one equivalence class with every representative of other equivalence classes (i.e., dual combinations instead of complete combinations).

▪ Ensure as minimum criteria that every representative of an equivalence class appears in at least one test case.

▪ Representatives of invalid equivalence classes should not be combined with representatives of other invalid equivalence classes.

Invalid equivalence classes are not combined in a "multiplicative way". An incorrect value should only be combined with "correct" ones because an incorrect parameter value normally triggers an exception handling. This is usually independent of values of other parameters. If a test case combines more than one incorrect value, defect masking may result and only one of the possible exceptions is actually triggered and tested. On appearance of a failure it is not obvious which of the incorrect values has triggered the effect. This leads to extra time and expense for analysis.

Test invalid values separately

In the following example, the function `calculate_price()` from the VSR-Subsystem *DreamCar* serves as test object (specified in section 3.2.3). We must test if the function calculates the correct total price from its input values. We assume that the inner structure of the function is unknown. Only the functional specification of the function and the external interface are known.

Example: Test of the DreamCar price calculation

```
double calculate_price (
double baseprice,    // base price of the vehicle
double specialprice, // special model addition
double extraprice,   // price of the extras
int extras,          // number of extras
double discount      // dealer's discount
)
```

Step 1:
Identifying the domain
The equivalence class technique is used to derive the required test cases from the input parameters. First, we identify the domain for every input parameter. This results in equivalence classes for valid and invalid values for each parameter (see table 5-5).

Table 5–5
Equivalence classes
for integer input values

Parameter	Equivalence classes
`baseprice`	vEC_{11}: `[MIN_DOUBLE, … , MAX_DOUBLE]` iEC_{11}: `NaN`
`specialprice`	vEC_{21}: `[MIN_DOUBLE, … , MAX_DOUBLE]` iEC_{21}: `NaN`
`extraprice`	vEC_{31}: `[MIN_DOUBLE, … , MAX_DOUBLE]` iEC_{31}: `NaN`
`extras`	vEC_{41}: `[MIN_INT, … , MAX_INT]` iEC_{41}: `NaN`
`discount`	vEC_{51}: `[MIN_DOUBLE, … , MAX_DOUBLE]` iEC_{51}: `NaN`

With this technique, at least one valid and one invalid equivalence class per parameter has been derived exclusively from the interface specifications (test data generators work in a similar way; section 7.1.2).

Step 2:
Refine the equivalence
classes based on the
specification
In order to further subdivide these equivalence classes, information about the functionality is needed. The functional specification delivers this information (section 3.2.3). From this specification the following conclusions relevant for testing can be drawn:

- Parameters 1 to 3 are (vehicle) prices. Prices are not negative. The specification does not define any price limits.
- The value `extras` controls the discount for the supplementary equipment (10 % if `extras` >=3 and 15 % if `extras` >=5). The parameter `extras` defines the number of chosen parts of supplementary equipment and therefore it cannot be negative[37]. The specification does not define an upper limit for this data element.
- The parameter `discount` denotes a general discount and is given as a percentage between 0 and 100. Because the specification text defines the limits for the discount for supplementary equipment as a percentage, the tester can assume that this parameter is entered as a percentage as well. Consultation with the client will otherwise clarify this matter.

These considerations are based not only on the functional specification. Rather the analysis uncovers some "holes" in the specification. The tester "fills" these

---

37. Floating point numbers belong to the equivalence class NaN, see the example for equivalence partition for integer numbers.

holes by making plausible assumptions based on application domain or general knowledge and her testing experience or by asking colleagues (testers or developers). If there is any doubt, consultation with the client is useful. The equivalence classes already defined before can be refined during this analysis, partitioning them into subclasses. The more detailed the equivalence classes are, the more comprehensive the test becomes. The class partition is complete when all conditions in the specification, as well as conditions from the tester's knowledge are incorporated.

Parameter	Equivalence classes	Representatives
baseprice	vEC_{11}: [0, … , MAX_DOUBLE]	20000.00
	iEC_{11}: [MIN_DOUBLE, … , 0[	-1.00
	iEC_{12}: NaN	"abc"
specialprice	vEC_{21}: [0, … , MAX_DOUBLE]	3450.00
	iEC_{21}: [MIN_DOUBLE, … , 0[	-1.00
	iEC_{22}: NaN	"abc"
extraprice	vEC_{31}: [0, … , MAX_DOUBLE]	6000.00
	iEC_{31}: [MIN_DOUBLE, … , 0[	-1.00
	iEC_{32}: NaN	"abc"
extras	vEC_{41}: [0, … , 2]	1
	vEC_{42}: [3, 4]	3
	vEC_{43}: [5, … , MAX_INT]	20
	iEC_{41}: [MIN_INT, … , 0[	-1.00
	iEC_{42}: NaN	"abc"
discount	vEC_{51}: [0, … , 100]	10.00
	iEC_{51}: [MIN_DOUBLE, … , 0[	-1.00
	iEC_{52}:]100, … , MAX_DOUBLE]	101.00
	iEC_{53}: NaN	"abc"

Table 5–6
Further partitioning of the equivalence classes of the parameter of the function Calculate_price() *with representatives*

The result: Altogether 18 equivalence classes are produced, 7 for correct / valid parameter values and 11 for incorrect / invalid ones.

To get input data one representative value must be chosen for every equivalence class. Any value of an equivalence class can be used, according to equivalence class theory. In practice, perfect decomposition is seldom done. Due to an absence of detailed information, lack of time, or just lack of motivation the decomposition is aborted at a certain level. Several equivalence classes might even (incorrectly) overlap[38]. Therefore, the choice of representative values for the test must be made with care. One must remember there could be values inside an equivalence class where the test object could react differently. Usage frequencies of different values of the VSR-System should also be considered.

Step 3:
Select representatives

Hence, in the example, the values for the valid equivalence classes are selected to represent plausible values and values that will probably often appear in practice. For invalid equivalence classes, possible values with low complexity are chosen. The selected values are shown in the table above.

The next step is to combine the values to test cases. Using the above given rules we get 1*1*1*3*1 = 3 "valid" test cases (by combining the representatives of the valid equivalence classes) and 2+2+2+2+3 = 11 negative tests (by separately testing representatives of every invalid class). In total, 14 test cases result from the 18 equivalence classes (table 5-7).

Table 5–7

Further partitioning of the equivalence classes of the parameter Test cases of the function
`Calculate_price()`

| Test case | parameter | | | | | |
	baseprice	special-price	extraprice	extras	discount	result
1	20000.00	3450.00	6000.00	1	10.00	27450.00
2	20000.00	3450.00	6000.00	3	10.00	26850.00
3	20000.00	3450.00	6000.00	20	10.00	26550.00
4	-1.00	3450.00	6000.00	1	10.00	NOT_VALID
5	"abc"	3450.00	6000.00	1	10.00	NOT_VALID
6	20000.00	-1.00	6000.00	1	10.00	NOT_VALID
7	20000.00	"abc"	6000.00	1	10.00	NOT_VALID
8	20000.00	3450.00	-1.00	1	10.00	NOT_VALID
9	20000.00	3450.00	"abc"	1	10.00	NOT_VALID
10	20000.00	3450.00	6000.00	-1.00	10.00	NOT_VALID
11	20000.00	3450.00	6000.00	"abc"	10.00	NOT_VALID
12	20000.00	3450.00	6000.00	1	-1.00	NOT_VALID
13	20000.00	3450.00	6000.00	1	101.00	NOT_VALID
14	20000.00	3450.00	6000.00	1	"abc"	NOT_VALID

For the valid equivalence classes the same representative values were used to ensure that only the variance of one parameter triggers the reaction of the test object.

Because four out of five parameters feature only one valid equivalence class, only a few "valid" test cases result. There is no reason to reduce the number of test cases any further.

After the test inputs have been chosen, the expected outcome should be identified for every test case. For the negative tests this is easy: The expected result is the error code or message generated by the test object. For the "valid" tests, the expected outcome must be calculated (for example by using a spreadsheet).

---

38.   The ideal case is that the identified classes (like equivalence classes in mathematics) are not overlapping (disjoint). This should be strived for, but is not guaranteed by the partitioning technique.

Definition of the Test Completion Criteria

A test completion criterion for the test by equivalence class partitioning can be defined as the percentage of executed equivalence classes in comparison to the total number of specified equivalence classes (→equivalence (class) partition coverage):

EC-coverage = (number of tested EC / total number of EC) * 100 %

Let us assume that 18 equivalence classes have been defined, as in our example, but only 15 have been executed in the chosen test cases. Then the equivalence class coverage is 83%.

EC-coverage = (15/18) * 100% = 83.33%

In the total of 14 test cases (table 5-7), all 18 equivalence classes are contained with at least one representative each. Thus, executing all 14 test cases gives a 100% equivalence class coverage. If the last three test cases are left out due to time limitations, i.e., only 11 instead of 14 test cases are executed, all thee invalid equivalence classes for the parameter discount are not tested and the coverage will be 15/18, for example 83.33%.

Example: Equivalence class coverage

The more thoroughly a test object is planned to be tested, the higher the intended coverage. Before test execution, the predefined coverage serves as a criterion for deciding when the testing is sufficient, and after test execution, it serves as verification if the required test intensity has been reached.

Degree of coverage defines test comprehensiveness

If, in the example above, the intended coverage for equivalence classes is defined as 80% then this can be achieved with only 14 of the 18 tests. The test using equivalence class partitioning can be finished after 14 test cases. Test coverage is a measurable criterion for finishing testing.

The previous example also shows the criticality of the identification of the equivalence classes. If not all the equivalence classes have been identified, then fewer values will be chosen for designing test cases, and fewer test cases will result. A high coverage is achieved, but it has been calculated based on an incorrect total number of equivalence classes. The alleged good result does not reflect the actual intensity of the testing. Test case identification using equivalence class partitioning is only as good as the analysis of the requirements and the following building of the equivalence classes.

The value of the technique

Equivalence class partitioning contributes to a complete test where specified conditions and restrictions are not overlooked. The method also minimizes the generation of unnecessary test cases. Such test cases are the ones having data from the same equivalence classes, and therefore resulting in equal behavior of the test object.

Equivalence classes not only can be determined for inputs and outputs of methods and functions. They can also be prepared for internal values and states, time dependent values (for example before or after an event), and interface parameters. The method can thus be used in system testing, integration testing, and component testing.

However, only single input or output conditions are considered, while possible dependencies or interactions between conditions are ignored. If they are considered, this is very expensive, but can be done through further partitioning of the equivalence classes and by specifying according combinations. This is also called "domain analysis." In combination with fault-oriented techniques, like boundary value analysis, equivalence class partitioning is a very powerful technique.

5.1.2   Boundary Value Analysis

Reasonable addition   Boundary value analysis delivers a very reasonable addition to the test cases that have been identified by the equivalence classes. Faults often appear at the boundaries of equivalence classes. This happens because boundaries are often not defined clearly or programmers misunderstand them. A test with boundary values usually discovers failures. The technique can only be applied if the set of data, which is in one equivalence class, has identifiable boundaries.

Boundary value analysis checks the "border" of the equivalence classes. On every border, the exact boundary value and both nearest adjacent values (inside and outside the equivalence class) are tested. Thereby the minimal possible increment in both directions should be used. For floating point data this can be the defined tolerance. Therefore, three test cases result from every boundary. If the upper boundary of one equivalence class equals the lower boundary of the adjacent equivalence class, then the respective test cases coincide as well.

In many cases there does not exist a real boundary value because the boundary value belongs to another equivalence class. In such cases it can be sufficient to test the boundary with two values: one value, which is just inside of an equivalence class, and another value, that is just outside an equivalence class.

For paying the bonus (table 5-1), four valid equivalence classes were determined and corresponding values chosen for testing the classes. Equivalence classes 3 and 4 are specified with: vEC3: 5 < x <= 8 and vEC4: x > 8. For testing the common boundary of the two equivalence classes, the values 8 and 9 can be chosen. The value 8 lies in vEC3 and is the largest possible value in that equivalence class. The value 9 is the least possible value in vEC4 .The values 7 and 10 do not give any more information because they are further inside their corresponding equivalence classes. Thus, when are the values 8 and 9 sufficient and when should we additionally use the value 7?

Example:
Boundary values for bonus

It can help to look at the implementation. The program will probably contain the instruction if (x>8). Which wrong implementation of this condition can be found by which test cases? The test values 7, 8 and 9 generate the truth values false, false and true in the if-statement and the corresponding program parts are executed. Test value 7 does not seem to add any value because test value 8 already generates the truth value false. Wrong implementation of the statement if (x>=8) leads to the truth values false, true and true. Even here, a test with the value 7 does not lead to any new results and can thus be omitted. Only a wrong implementation of if (x<>8) and the truth values true, false and true can only be found with test case value 7. The values 8 and 9 deliver the expected results or the same ones as with the correct implementation.

Hint: Wrong implementation of the instruction in if (x<8) with true, false and false and in if (x<=8) with true, true and false always result in two differences between actual and expected result and can be found by test cases with the values 8 and 9.

As the equivalence classes vEC3 and vEC4 are neighbor classes, a test with the input data 7 and 8 must lead to the specified output of vEC3 (75% bonus). A wrong implementation of a logic query thus leads to wrong results and will be found.

It should be decided when a test with only two values is considered enough or when it is beneficial to test the boundary with three values. The wrong query in the example program, implemented as (if (x<>8)) can be found in a code review as it does not check the boundary of a value area (if (x>8)), but instead checks if two values are unequal. However, this defect can easily be overlooked. Only with a boundary value test with three values can all possible wrong implementations of boundary conditions be found.

For the above example of the test of an integer input value, five new test cases result, thus there will be a total of twelve test cases with the following test input values:

```
{"f",
MIN_INT-1, MIN_INT, MIN_INT+1,
-123,
-1, 0, 1,
654,
MAX_INT-1, MAX_INT, MAX_INT+1}
```

The test case with the input value -1 tests the maximum value of the equivalence class EC1: [MIN_INT, … 0[. This test case also verifies the smallest deviation from the lower boundary (0) of the equivalence class EC2: [0, …, MAX_INT]. The value lies outside this equivalence class. Just notice that values above the uppermost boundary as well as beneath the lowermost boundary cannot always be entered due to technical reasons.

Only test values for the input variable are given in this example. To complete the test cases for each of the twelve values the expected behavior of the test object and the expected outcome must be specified using the test oracle. Additionally, the applicable pre- and post-conditions are necessary.

Here too, we have to decide if the test cost is justified and every boundary with the adjacent values each must be tested with extra test cases. Test cases with values of equivalence classes that do not verify any boundary can be dropped. In the example, these are the test cases with the input values -123 and 654. It is assumed that test cases with values in the middle of an equivalence class do not deliver any new insight. This is because test cases with the maximum and the minimum value inside the equivalence class are already chosen in some test case. In the example these values are MIN_INT +1 and 1, MAX_INT-1.

For the example with the input data element "traveler" given above, no boundaries for the input domain can be found. The input data type is discrete, i.e., a set of the six elements (child, teenager, adult, student, person on welfare, and retired person). Boundaries cannot be identified here. A possible order by age cannot be defined clearly because the person on welfare, for instance, might have any age.

Of course, boundary value analysis can also be applied for output equivalence classes.

Test Cases

Analogous to the test case determination in equivalence class partition, the valid boundaries inside an equivalence class may be combined as test cases. The invalid boundaries must be verified separately and cannot be combined with other invalid boundaries.

Values from the middle of an equivalence class are, in principle, not necessary if the two boundary values in an equivalence class are used for test cases.

The following table lists the boundary values for the valid equivalence classes for verification of the function `calculate_price()`:

Example: Boundary value test for `calculate_price()`

Table 5–8
Boundaries of the parameters of the function `calculate_price()`

Parameter	Lower boundary value [Equivalence class] Upper boundary value
`baseprice`	$0-\delta^a$, `[0,` `0+`δ`, ...,` `MAX_DOUBLE-`δ`,` `MAX_DOUBLE]`, `MAX_DOUBLE+`δ
`specialprice`	Same values as baseprice
`extraprice`	Same values as baseprice

	`-1, [0, 1, 2], 3`
	`2, [3, 4], 5`
	`4, [5, 6, ..., MAX_INT-1, MAX_INT], MAX_INT+1`

`discount`	$0-\delta$,`[0,` `0+`δ`, ...,` `100-`δ`,` `100]`, `100+`δ

a. The accuracy considered here depends on the problem (for example, a given tolerance) and the number representation of the computer.

Considering only those boundaries that can be found inside equivalence classes, we get 4+4+4+9+4 = 25 boundary based values. Of these, two (extras: 1, 3) are already tested in the original equivalence class partitioning in the example before (test cases 1 and 2 in table 5-7). Thus, the following 23 representatives must be used for new test cases.

```
baseprice:      0.00, 0.01³⁹, MAX_DOUBLE-0.01, MAX_DOUBLE
specialprice:   0.00, 0.01, MAX_DOUBLE-0.01, MAX_DOUBLE
extraprice:     0.00, 0.01, MAX_DOUBLE-0.01, MAX_DOUBLE
extras:         0, 2, 4, 5, 6, MAX_INT-1, MAX_INT
discount:       0.00, 0.01, 99.99, 100.00
```

As all values are valid boundaries, they can be combined into test cases (table 5-9).

---

39. For the test cases, `0.01` was assumed to be precise enough.

The expected results of a boundary value test are not always easy to derive from the specification. The experienced tester must thus define reasonable expected results:

	Parameter					
Testcase	**baseprice**	**specialprice**	**extraprice**	**extras**	**discount**	**result**
15	0.00	0.00	0.00	0	0.00	0.00
16	0.01	0.01	0.01	2	0.01	0.03
17	MAX_DOUBLE-0.01	MAX_DOUBLE-0.01	MAX_DOUBLE-0.01	4	99.99	>MAX_DOUBLE
18	MAX_DOUBLE-0.01	3450.00	6000.00	1	10.00	>MAX_DOUBLE
19	20000.00	MAX_DOUBLE-0.01	6000.00	1	10.00	>MAX_DOUBLE
20	20000.00	3450.00	MAX_DOUBLE-0.01	1	10.00	>MAX_DOUBLE
...						

- Test case 15 verifies all valid lower boundaries of equivalence classes of the parameters of calculate_price(). The test case seems not to be very realistic[40]. This is because of the imprecise specification of the functionality, where no lower and upper boundaries are specified (see below).[41]
- Test case 16 is analogous to test case 15, but here we test the precision of the calculation[42].
- Test case 17 combines the next boundaries from the table above. The expected result is rather speculative with a discount of 99.99%. A look into the specification of the method calculate_price() shows that the prices are added. Thus, it makes sense to check the maximal values individually. Test cases 18 to 20 do this. For the other parameters we use the values from test case 1 (table 5-7). Further sensible test cases results when the values of the other parameters are set to 0.00, in order to check if maximal value without further addition are handled correctly and without overflow.
- Analogous to test cases 17 to 20, test cases for MAX_DOUBLE should be run.
- For the still not tested boundary values (extras = 5, 6, MAX_INT-1, MAX_INT and discount = 100.00), more test cases are needed.

Boundary values outside the valid equivalence classes are not used here.

---

40. Remark: A test with 0.00 for the base price is reasonable, but it should be done in system testing, because for this input value, calculate_price() is not necessarily responsible.
41. The dependence between the number of extras and extra price (if no extras are given, there should not be a price given) cannot be checked through equivalence partitioning or boundary value analysis. In order to do this cause-effect analysis [Myers 79] must be used.
42. In order to exactly check the rounding precision, values like for example 0.005 are needed.

The example shows the detrimental effect of imprecise specifications. If the tester communicates with the customer before determining the test cases, and the value ranges of the parameters can be specified more precisely, then the test may be less expensive. This is shown here, as a short example.

Early thinking of testing pays off

The customer has given the following information:

▓ The base price is between $10,000 and $150,000.

▓ The extra prices for the extra items are between $800 and $3,500.

▓ There are a maximum of 25 possible extras, whose prices are between $50 and $750.

▓ The dealer discount is a maximum of 25%.

After specifying the equivalence classes, the following valid boundaries result:

```
baseprice:     10000.00, 10000.01, 149999.99, 150000.00
specialprice:  800.00, 800.01, 3499.99, 3500.00
extraprice:    50.00, 50.01, 18749.99, 18750.00⁴³
extras:        0, 1, 2, 3, 4, 5, 6, 24, 25
discount:      0.00, 0.01, 24.99, 25.00
```

All these values may be freely combined to test cases. For values outside the valid equivalence classes one test case is needed for each. The following values must be used for these:

```
baseprice:     9999.99, 150000.01
specialprice:  799.99, 3500.01
extraprice:    49.99, 18750.01
extras:        -1, 26
discount:      -0.01, 25.01
```

Thus, we see that a more specific specification results in fewer test cases and an easier prediction of the results.

Adding the "boundary values for the machine" (MAX_DOUBLE, MIN_DOUBLE, etc.) is a good idea. This will detect problems with hardware restrictions.

---

43. The maximum price for extra items cannot be specified exactly, because the dependence between number of extras and total price cannot be used. We used the value 25 * 750 = 18750. An extra price of 0 was not included as a further boundary value, because the dependency of the number of extras and the total value of the extras cannot be checked with equivalence class partitioning or boundary value analysis.

As discussed above, it must be decided if it is sufficient to test a boundary with two, instead of three test data. In the following hints we assume that two test vales are sufficient, because a code review has been done and possible totally wrong checks have been found.

Hint on test case design
by boundary analysis

- For an input domain, the boundaries and the adjacent values outside the domain must be considered. Domain: [-1.0; +1.0], test data: -1.0, +1.0 and -1.001, +1.001[44].
- An input file has a restricted number of data records, between 1 and 100. The test values should be 1, 100 and 0, 101.
- If the *output* domains serve as the basis, then the analysis can be done as follows: The output of the test object is an integer value between 500 and 1000. Test outputs that should be achieved: 500, 1000, 499, 1001. Indeed, it can take a certain effort to identify the respective input test data to achieve exactly the required outputs. Generating the invalid outputs can even be impossible, but attempting to do it may find defects.
- If the permitted number of output values is to be tested, proceed just as with the number of input values: If outputs of 1 to 4 data values are allowed, the test outputs to produce are: 1, 4 as well as 0 and 5 data values.
- For ordered sets the first and last element is of special interest for the test.
- If complex data structures are given as input or output, for instance, an empty list or zero matrixes can be considered a boundary value.
- For numeric calculations, values that are close together, as well as values that are far apart, should be taken into consideration as boundary values.
- For invalid equivalence classes, boundary value analysis is only useful when different exception handling for the test object is expected depending on an equivalence class boundary.
- In addition, extremely large data structures, lists, tables, etc. should be chosen. For example, those that exceed buffer, file, or data storage boundaries, in order to check the behavior of the test object in extreme cases.
- For lists and tables, empty and full lists and the first and last elements are of interest, as they often show failures due to incorrect programming (*Off-by-one problem*).

Definition of the Test Completion Criteria

Analogous to the test completion criterion for equivalence class partition, an intended coverage of the boundary values (BV) can also be predefined and calculated after execution of the tests.

BV-Coverage = (number of tested BV/total number of BV) * 100%

---

44. The accuracy to be chosen depends on the specified problem.

Notice that the boundary values, as well as the according adjacent values above and below the boundary, must be counted. However, only unequal values are used for the calculation. Overlapping values of adjacent equivalence classes are counted as one boundary value, because only one test case with the respective input test value is possible.

The value of the technique

Boundary value analysis should be done together with equivalence class partitioning, because faults are discovered more often at the boundaries of the equivalence classes than far inside the classes. Both techniques can be combined easily, but still allow enough freedom in selecting the concrete test data.

In combination with equivalence class partitioning

The technique requires a lot of creativity in order to define the according test data at the boundaries. This aspect is often ignored because the technique appears to be very easy, even though the determination of the relevant boundaries is not at all trivial.

5.1.3   State Transition Testing

In many cases, not only the current input, but also the history of execution or events or inputs, influences the outputs and how the test object will behave. To illustrate the dependence on history →state diagrams are used. They are the basis for designing the test (→state transition testing).

Consider history

The system or test object starts from an initial state and can then come into different states. Events trigger state transitions where an event normally is a function invocation. State transitions can involve actions. Besides the initial state, the other special state is the end-state. →Finite state machines, state diagrams, or state transition tables model this behavior.

[Beizer 95] defines a finite state machine as follows: "An abstract machine (e.g., program, logic circuit, car's transmission) for which the number of states and input symbols are both finite and fixed. A finite state machine consists of states (nodes), transitions (links), inputs (link weights), and outputs (link weights)." The comments given in parenthesis define the notation in a state graph or state transition diagram. A state diagram is a diagram which depicts the states that a system or component can assume, and shows the events or circumstances that cause or result from a change from one state to another [IEEE 610.12].

Definition finite state machine

Example: Stack   The popular example of a stack (figure 5-3) is supposed to clarify the circumstances. The stack, for example a dish stack in a heating device, can adopt three different states: an empty stack, a filled stack, and a full stack.

Figure 5–3

State diagram of a stack

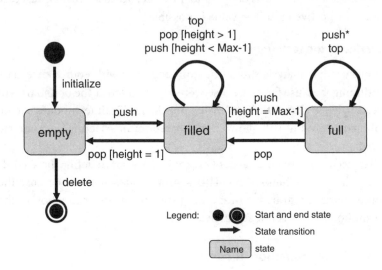

The stack is "empty" after initializing where the maximum height (Max) is defined (current height = 0). By adding an element to the stack (call of the function push), the state changes to "filled" and the current height is incremented. In this state further elements can be added (push, increment height), as well as withdrawn (call of the function pop, decrement height). The uppermost element can also be displayed (call of the function top, height unchanged). Displaying does not alter the stack itself and therefore does not remove any element. If the current height is one less than the maximum (height = Max – 1) and one element is added to the stack (push), then the state of the stack changes from "filled" to "full". No further element can be added. If one element is removed (pop) while the stack is in the state "full", the state is changed back from "full" to "filled". A state transition from filled to empty happens only if the stack consists of just one element which is removed (pop). The stack can only be deleted in the state "empty".

Depending upon the specification, it can be defined which functions (push, pop, top, …) can be called at which state of the stack. It must still be clarified what shall happen when an element is added to a full stack (push*). The function must perform differently than in the case of a just filled stack. The functions must behave differently depending on the state of the stack. Thus, the state of the test object is a decisive element and must be considered when testing.

A possible test case   Example: A stack accepting strings (type: string) shall be tested. A possible test case with pre- and post-condition is the following:

- ▥ Precondition: stack is initialized; state is "empty"
- ▥ Input: push ("hello")
- ▥ Expected result: stack contains "hello"
- ▥ Post-condition: state of the stack is "filled"

Further functions of the stack (display of the current height, display of the maximum height, query if the stack is "empty", ...) are not included in this example because they do not cause any change of the state.

In state transition testing the test object can be a complete system with different system states, as well as a class in an object-oriented system with different states. Whenever the history leads to differing behavior, a state transition test must be applied.

Test object for state transition testing

For the state transition test, different levels of test intensity can be defined. A minimum requirement is to reach all possible states. In the given stack example these states are empty, filled, and full[45]. With an assumed maximum height of 4, all three states are reached after calling the following functions:

Further test cases for the stack example

Test case 1[46]: initialize [empty], push [filled], push, push, push [full].

Yet, not all of the functions of the stack have been called in this test!

Another requirement for the test is to invoke all functions. With the same stack as before, the following sequence of function calls is sufficient for compliance with this requirement:

Test case 2: initialize [empty], push [filled], top, pop [empty], delete.

However, in this sequence as well, still not all the states have been reached.

A state transition test should execute all specified functions of a certain state at least once. The compliance between the specified and the actual behavior of the test object can thus be checked.

Test criteria

In order to identify the necessary test cases, the finite state machine is transformed into a transition tree, which includes certain sequences of transitions ([Chow 78]). The cyclic state transition diagram with potentially infinite sequences of states changes to a transition tree, which corresponds to a representative number of states without cycles. In doing this

---

45. To keep the test effort small the maximum height of the stack should be chosen not too high because the function push must be called a corresponding number of times to reach the state "full".

46. The following test cases are simplified (no precondition and postcondition ...) to keep them properly arranged.

translation, all states must be reached and all transitions of the transition diagram must appear.

The transition tree is built from a transition diagram in the following way:

1. The initial or start state is the root of the tree.
2. For every possible transition from the initial state to a following state in the state transition diagram, the transition tree receives a branch from its root to a node, representing this next state.
3. The process for step 2 is repeated for every leaf in the tree (every newly added node) until one of the following two end-conditions is fulfilled:
    *   The corresponding state is already included in the tree on the way from the root to the node. This end condition corresponds to one pass of a cycle in the transition diagram.
    *   The corresponding state is a final state, and therefore has no further transitions to be considered.

For the stack, the resulting transition tree is shown in figure 5-4.

Figure 5–4
Transition tree
for the stack example

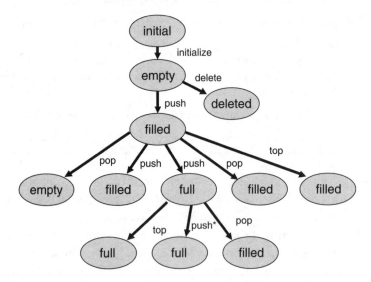

Eight different paths can be produced from the root to each of the end nodes. Each of the paths represents a test case, i.e., a sequence of function calls. Thereby, every state is reached at least once, and every possible function is called in each state according to the specification of the state transition diagram.

In addition to this, the reaction of the state machine for wrong usage must be checked, which means that functions are called in states in which they are not supposed to be called (e.g., to delete the stack while in "full" state). This is a test of robustness to verify how the test object reacts upon incorrect use. Thus, it is tested whether unexpected transitions may appear. The test can be seen as an analogy to the test of unexpected input values.

Wrong usage of the functions

The transition tree should be extended by including a branch for every function from every node. This means that from every state, all the functions should be executed or at least attempted to be executed (figure 5-5).

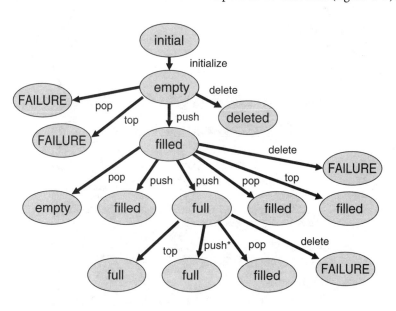

Figure 5–5
Transition tree for the test for robustness

State transition testing is also a good technique for system testing. For example, the test of a Graphical User Interface (GUI) can be designed this way: the Graphical User Interface usually consists of a set of screens and user controls, such as menus and dialog boxes; between those, the user can switch back and forth (menu choices, "OK" button, etc.); if screens and user controls are seen as states and input reactions as state transitions then the Graphical User Interface can be modeled as a finite state machine. Appropriate test cases and the test coverage can be identified by the technique of state transition testing given above.

Example:

Test of the DreamCar-GUI

Figure 5–6

GUI navigation as state graph

For the test of the *DreamCar*-GUI this can look like the following figure:

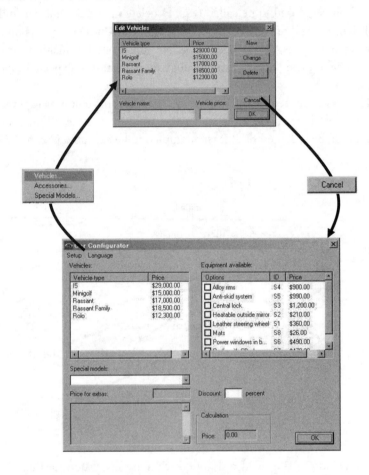

The test starts at the *DreamCar* main screen (state 1). The action[47] "Setup vehicles" triggers the transition into the dialog "Edit vehicle" (state 2). The action "Cancel" ends this dialog and the return to state 1 occurs. Inside a state we can then use tests, which do not change the state. These local tests then verify the actual functionality of the accessed screen. Like this, navigation through arbitrarily complex chains of dialogs can be modeled. The state diagram of the GUI ensures that all dialogs are included and verified in the test.

---

47.   The two-staged menu choice is seen here as an action.

Test Cases

For a complete definition of a state-based test case the following information is necessary:

- The initial state of the test object (component or system)
- The inputs to the test object
- The expected outcome or expected behavior
- The expected final state

Further, for each expected transition of the test case the following aspects must be defined:

- The state before the transition
- The initiating event that triggers the transition
- The expected reaction triggered by the transition
- The next expected state

It is not always easy to identify the states of a test object. Often, the state is not defined by a single variable, but is rather the result from a constellation of values of several variables. These variables may be deeply hidden in the test object. Thus, the verification and evaluation of each test case can be very expensive.

- Evaluate the state transition diagram from a testing point of view from the beginning when writing the specification. If there are a high number of states and transitions, indicate the higher test effort and push for simplification if possible.
- Check in the specification, as well, that the different states are easy to identify and that they are not the result of a broad combination of values of different variables.
- Check in the specification that the state variables are easy to access from the outside. It is a good idea to include functions that set or reset, and, read the state for use during testing.

Hint

Definition of the Test Completion Criteria

Criteria for test intensity and for completion can also be defined for the state transition testing:

- Every state has been reached at least once
- Every transition has been executed at least once
- Every transition violating the specification has been checked

Percentages can be defined using the proportion of actually executed test requirements to possible ones analogous to the earlier described coverage measures.

Higher-level criteria

For highly critical applications even more intensified state transition test completion criteria can be declared as follows:

- All combination of transitions
- All transitions in any order with all possible states, including multiple instances in succession

But, achieving sufficient coverage is often not possible due to the large number of necessary test cases. Therefore, a limit to the number of combinations or sequences that must be verified may then be reasonable.

The value of the technique

State transition testing should be applied where states are important and where the functionality is influenced by the state of the test object. The other testing techniques that have been introduced do not support these aspects because they do not respond to the different behavior of the functions depending on the state.

Especially useful for test of OO systems

In object-oriented systems, objects can have different states. The appropriate methods to manipulate the objects must then react according to the different states. State transition testing is of greater importance for object-oriented testing because it takes into account the special aspects of the object orientation.

5.1.4   Cause-Effect Graphing and Decision Table Technique

The previously introduced techniques regard the different input data as independent, and the input values are each considered separately for generating the test cases. Dependencies among the different inputs and their effects on the outputs are not explicitly considered for test case design.

Cause-effect graphing

[Myers 79] describes a technique that uses the dependencies for identification of the test cases known as →cause-effect graphing. The logical relationships between the causes and their effects in a component or a system are displayed in a so-called →cause-effect graph. It must be possible to find the causes and effects from the specification. Every cause is described as a condition that consists of input conditions (or combinations of those). The conditions are connected with logical operators (e.g., AND,

OR and NOT). A condition, and therefore a cause, can be `true` or `false`. The effects are treated in the same way and noted in the graph (figure 5-7).

In the following example, withdrawing money at an automated teller machine (ATM) shall illustrate how to prepare a cause-effect graph. In order to get money from the machine, the following conditions must be fulfilled[48]:

Example: Cause-effect graph analysis for an ATM

- The bankcard is valid
- The PIN must be correctly entered
- The maximum number of PIN inputs is three
- There is money in the machine, and in the account

The following actions are possible at the machine:

- Reject card
- Ask for another PIN input
- "Eat" the card
- Ask for an alternate dollar amount
- Pay the requested amount of money

Figure 5-7 shows the cause-effect graph of the example.

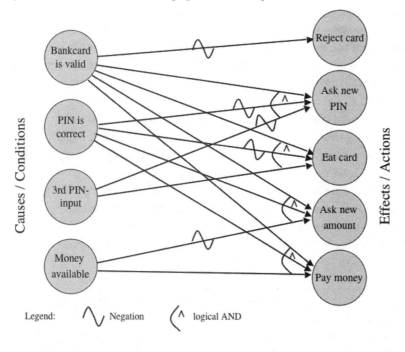

Figure 5–7
Cause-effect graph of the ATM

---

48.   Hint: This is not a complete description of a real automated teller machine, but is just an example to illustrate the technique.

The graph makes clear which conditions must be combined in order to achieve the corresponding effects.

The graph must be transformed into a →decision table from which the test cases can be taken. The steps to transform a graph into a table are as follows:

1. Choose an effect
2. Looking in the graph, find combinations of causes that have this effect and combinations that do not have this effect
3. Add one column into the table for every one of these cause-combinations and the caused states of the remaining effects
4. Check if decision table entries occur several times and, if yes, delete them

Test with decision tables   The test based on decision tables has the objective to design tests for executing "interesting" combinations of inputs. Interesting in the sense that possible failures can be detected. Besides the causes and effects, intermediate results may be included in the decision table.

A decision table has two parts. In the upper half, the inputs (causes) are listed; the lower half contains the effects. Every column is a test case, i.e., the combination of conditions and the expected effects or outputs for this combination.

In the least optimized case, every combination of causes is considered as a test case. However, conditions may influence or exclude each other in such a way that not all combinations make sense. The fulfillment of every cause and effect is noted with a "yes" or "no". Each cause and effect should occur at least once with "yes" and "no" in the table.

From a decision table, a decision tree may be derived. The decision tree may be used analogous to the transition tree in state transition testing. Every path from the root of the tree to a leaf corresponds to a test case. Every node on the way to a leaf contains a condition that determines the further path, depending on its truth-value.

As there are four conditions (from "bank card is valid" to "there is no money"), there are, theoretically, 16 (2^4) possible combinations. However, not all dependencies are taken into account here. For example, if the bankcard is invalid, the other conditions are not interesting, as the machine should reject the card.

An optimized decision table does not contain all possible combinations, but the impossible or unnecessary combinations are not entered any more. As there are dependencies between the inputs and the results (actions, outputs), the following optimized decision table shows the result (table 5-10).

Condition / Cause	1	2	3	4	5
Bankcard is valid	N	Y	Y	Y	Y
PIN is correct	-	N	N	Y	Y
3 incorrect PIN	-	N (exit)	Y	-	-
Money available	-	-	-	N	Y
Effect / Action					
Reject card	Y	N	N	N	N
Ask new PIN	N	Y	N	N	N
Eat card	N	N	Y	N	N
Ask new amount	N	N	N	Y	N
Pay money	N	N	N	N	Y

Table 5–10
Optimized decision table for the ATM

Every column of this table should be interpreted as a test case. From the table, the necessary input conditions and expected actions can be directly found. Test case 5 shows the following condition: The money is delivered only if the card is valid, the PIN is correct after maximum three tries, and there is money available both in the machine and in the account.

This relatively small example shows how more conditions or dependencies can soon result in large and unwieldy graphs or tables.

Test cases

In a decision table the conditions and dependencies for the inputs, and the corresponding outputs and results for this combination of inputs can be read directly from every column. The table defines logical test cases. They

Every column is a test case

must be fed with concrete data values in order to execute them, and necessary preconditions and post-conditions must be annotated.

Definition of the Test Completion Criteria

Simple criteria for test completion

As with the previous methods, criteria for test completion can be defined relatively easily. A minimum requirement is to execute every column in the decision table by at least one test case. This verifies all sensible combinations of conditions and their corresponding effects.

The value of the technique

The systematic and very formal approach in defining a decision table with all possible combinations may reveal combinations which are not included when using other test case design techniques. However, errors can result from optimization of the decision table, for example when the input and condition combinations to be considered are left out.

As mentioned above, the graph and the table may grow very quickly and lose readability when the number of conditions and dependent actions increases. Without adequate support by tools, the technique is not easily applicable.

5.1.5   Use Case Testing

UML widely used

With the increasing use of object-oriented methods for software development, the Unified Modeling Language (UML) ([URL: UML]) is used more frequently. UML defines more than ten graphical notations, which may be used in software development, not only if it is object-oriented. There exist quite a number of (research) results and approaches to directly derive test cases from UML diagrams and to generate these tests more or less automatically. This chapter will only describe the use of use cases or use case diagrams.

Identification of the requirements

In order to detect requirements, use cases or business cases are described. These are then compiled into use case diagrams. The diagrams serve the purpose of defining requirements on a relatively abstract level and describing typical user system interactions. Figure 5-8 shows a use case diagram for a part of the dialog when using an ATM for getting money.

The individual use cases in this example are "Get money", "PIN query", and "Eat card." Relationships between use cases may be "include" and "extend." "Include" conditions are always involved, and "extend" connections can lead to extensions of a use case under certain conditions at a certain point (*extension point*). Thus, the "extend" conditions are not always executed as there are alternatives.

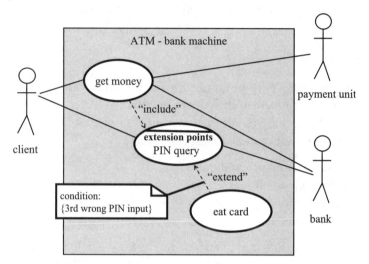

Figure 5–8
Use case diagram for ATM

Use case diagrams mainly serve to show the external view of a system. It shall explain the external view of the system from the viewpoint of the user or the relation to neighboring systems. Such external connections are shown as lines to "actors" (for example the man symbol in the figure). There are further elements in a use case diagram that are not further discussed here.

Showing an external view

For every use case, there exist certain preconditions that must be fulfilled to make it possible to execute the use case. A precondition for getting money at the ATM is, for example, that the bankcard is valid. After executing a use case there exist post-conditions. For example, after successfully entering the correct PIN, it is possible to get money. However, first the amount must be entered and it must be confirmed that the money is available. Preconditions and post-conditions are also applicable for the flow of use cases in a diagram, i.e., the path through the diagram.

Pre- and postconditions

Use cases and use case diagrams serve as the basis for determining test cases in use case based testing. As the external view is modeled, the technique is useful for both system testing and acceptance testing. If the diagrams are used to model the interactions between different subsystems, test cases can also be derived for integration testing.

Useful for system and acceptance testing

Typical system use is tested   The diagrams show the "normal", "typical", or "probable" flows and often their alternatives. Thus, the use case based test checks typical use of a system. It is especially important for acceptance of a system that it runs relatively stable in "normal" use. Thus, use case based testing has a high relevance for the customer, and therefore for the developer and tester as well.

Test Cases

Every use case has a purpose and shall achieve a certain result. Events may occur that lead to further alternatives or activities. After the execution, there are post-conditions. All the following information is necessary for determining the test cases and must be available:

- Start situation and preconditions
- Other possible conditions
- Expected results
- Post-conditions

However, the concrete input data and results for the individual test cases cannot be derived directly for the use cases. Analysis of the concrete conditions for the individual input and output data is necessary. However, each alternative contained in the diagram ("extend" relation) must be covered by a test case.

Definition of the test completion criteria

A possible criterion is that every use case and every possible sequence of use cases in the diagram is tested at least once by a test case. Since alternatives and extensions are use cases too, this criterion also requires their execution.

The value of the technique

Use case based testing is very useful for testing typical user system interactions. Thus, it is best to apply it in acceptance testing and in system testing. Additionally, test specification tools are available to support this approach (section 7.1.4). "Expected" exceptions and special treatment of cases can be shown in the diagram and included in the test cases (figure 5-8). However, no systematic method exists to determine further test cases to test facts that are not shown in the use case diagram. The other test techniques, such as boundary value analysis, are helpful for this.

5.1.6   Further Black Box Techniques

This chapter contained a description of some black box techniques, but this is far from complete. Below, a few more practical techniques are briefly described in order to offer some hints about their selection. Further techniques can be found in [Myers 79], [Beizer 90], [Beizer 95], and [Pol 98].

→Syntax testing describes a technique for identification of the test *Syntax test* cases that may be applied if a formal specification of the syntax of the inputs is available. This may be the case for testing interpreters of command languages, compilers, and protocol analyzers. The rules of the syntax definition are used to specify test cases that cover both the compliance to and violation of the syntax rules for the inputs [Beizer 90].

→Random testing generates values for the test cases by random selec- *Random test* tion. If a statistical distribution of the input values is given (e.g., normal distribution), then it can be used for the selection of test values. This ensures the derivation of test cases that are preferably close to reality, making it possible to use statistical models for predicting or certifying system reliability [IEEE 982], [Musa 87].

The term →smoke test is often used. A smoke test is commonly *Smoke test* understood as a "quick and dirty" test that is primarily aimed at verifying a minimum reliability of the test object. The test is concentrated on the main functions of the test object. The output of the test is not evaluated in detail. The main outcome of interest is a crash or serious misbehavior of the test object. A test oracle is not used, which contributes to making this test inexpensive and easy. The term "smoke test" is derived from testing electrical circuits in which short circuits lead to smoke rising. A smoke test is often used to decide if the test object is mature enough to proceed with further testing by the more comprehensive test techniques. A further use of smoke tests is the first test and the fast test of software updates.

5.1.7   General Discussion of the Black Box Technique

The basis of all black box techniques are the requirements or the specifi- *Faults in specification not* cation of the system, or its components and their collaboration. Black box *detected* testing, when applied carelessly, will not find problems where the implementation is based on incorrect requirements or a faulty design specification, because there will be no deviation between the faulty specification or design and the program under execution. The test object executes, as the requirements or specification require it, even when they are wrong. If the tester is critical towards the requirements or specifications, and uses "common sense", wrong requirements can be found during test design. Otherwise, to find inconsistencies and problems in the specifications, reviews must be used (section 4.1.2).

Not required functionality is not detected

In addition, black box testing cannot reveal extra functionality that exceeds the specification. (Such extra functionality is often the cause of security problems). Such additional functions are neither specified nor required by the client. Test cases that execute those additional functions are, if at all, performed by pure chance. The coverage criteria, which serve as condition for test completion, are exclusively identified on the basis of the specification or requirements. They are not identified on the basis of unmentioned or just assumed functions.

Verification of the functionality

The center of attention for all black box techniques is the verification of the functionality of the test object. It is indisputable that the correct working of a software system has the highest priority. Thus, black box techniques should always be applied.

5.2   White Box Testing Techniques

Code-based testing techniques

The basis for white box techniques is the source code of the test object. Therefore, these techniques are often called →code-based testing techniques or structural testing techniques. The source code must be available, and in certain cases, it must be possible to manipulate it, i.e., to add code.

All code should be executed

The generic idea of white box techniques is to execute every part of code of the test object at least once. Flow-oriented test cases are identified, analyzing the program logic and then executed. However, the expected results should be determined using the requirements or specifications, not the code. This is done in order to decide if execution resulted in a failure.

The focus of examination of a white box technique can, for example, be the statements of the test object. The primary goal of the technique is then to achieve a previously defined coverage of the statements while testing, for example, to execute all possible statements in the program.

The basic white box test case design techniques are as follows:

- →Statement coverage
- →Branch coverage

- Test of conditions
  - branch condition testing[49] (→branch condition coverage)
  - →branch condition combination testing
  - condition determination testing
- →Path coverage

The following sections describe these techniques in more detail.

5.2.1 Statement Coverage

This analysis focuses on each statement of the test object. The test cases shall execute a predefined minimum quota or even all statements of the test object. The first step is to translate the source code into a control flow graph. The graph makes it easier to specify in detail the control elements that must be covered. In the graph, the statements are represented as nodes and the control flow between the statements are represented as edges (connections). If sequences of unconditional statements appear in the program fragment, then they are illustrated as one single node, because execution of the first statement of the sequence guarantees that all following statements will be executed. Conditional statements (IF, CASE) and loops (WHILE, FOR) have more than one edge going out from them.

Control flow graph necessary

After execution of the test cases it must be verified which of the statements have been executed (section 5.2.7). When the previously defined coverage level has been achieved, the test is considered to be sufficient and will therefore be terminated.

The following example should clarify the proceeding. A very simple program fragment is chosen for this example. It only consists of two decisions and one loop (figure 5-9).

Example

---

49. A related technique is called "modified condition decision coverage" (MCDC). For the differences between both techniques see the glossary.

Figure 5–9

Control flow of a program
fragment

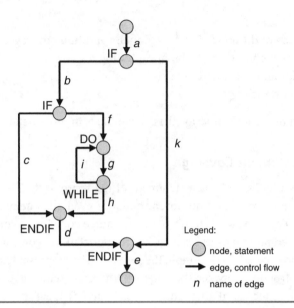

Test Cases

Coverage of the nodes
of the control flow

In the example, all statements (all nodes) can be reached by a single test case. In this test case the edges of the graph must be traversed in the following order:

a, b, f, g, h, d, e

One test case is enough

After traversing the edges in this way, all statements have been executed once. Other combinations of edges of the graph can also achieve complete coverage. But, the cost of testing should always be minimized, which means reaching the goal with the least possible number of test cases.

The expected results and the expected behavior of the test object should be identified in advance from the specification. After execution, the expected and actual results, and the behavior of the test object, must be compared to detect any difference or failure.

Definition of the Test Completion Criteria

The completion criteria for the tests can be clearly defined:

Statement coverage =
(number of executed statements / total number of statements) *100 %

Statement coverage is also known as C0-coverage. It is a very weak criterion. However, sometimes 100% statement coverage is difficult to achieve,
for instance, if exception conditions appear in the program, which can be
triggered only with great trouble or not at all during test execution.

C0-measure

The Value of the Technique

If complete coverage of all statements is required, and some statements
cannot be executed by any test cases, then this may be an indication for
unreachable source code (dead statements).

Unreachable code can be detected

   If a condition statement (IF) has statements only after it is fulfilled,
i.e., after the THEN clause, and there is no ELSE, then the control flow
graph has a (THEN-) edge, starting at the condition, with (at least) one
node and a second outgoing (ELSE-) edge without nodes. The control flow
of both these edges is reunited at the terminating (ENDIF-) node. For
statement coverage an empty (ELSE-) edge (between IF and ENDIF) is
irrelevant, such as when there is no requirement to cover it during the test.
Possible missing statements after ELSE are not detected by a test using this
criterion!

Empty ELSE-parts are not considered

   Coverage is measured using test tools (section 7.1.4).

5.2.2   Branch Coverage

A more advanced criterion for white box testing is →branch coverage of
the control flow graph; for example, the edges in the graph are the center
of attention. The execution of each statement is not considered, but rather
the execution of decisions. The result of the decision determines which
statement is executed next. Testing should make sure every decision is executed with both possible outcomes (TRUE and FALSE – →decision coverage is another name for this criterion).

   Thus, contrary to statement coverage, for branch coverage it is not
interesting if, for instance, an IF-statement has no ELSE-part. It must be
executed anyway. Branch coverage requires the test of every decision outcome: both THEN and ELSE in the IF-statement; all possibilities for the
CASE-statement and the fall-through case; for loops, both execution of
the loop body, i.e., and the bypassing of the loop body and a return to the
beginning of the loop.

Empty ELSE-parts are considered

Test Cases

Additional test cases necessary

In the example (figure 5-9) additional test cases are necessary if all branches of the control flow graph must be executed during the test. For 100% statement coverage a test case executing the following order of edges was sufficient:

a, b, f, g, h, d, e

The edges c, i, and k have not been executed in this test case. The edges c and k are empty branches of a condition, while the edge i is the return to the beginning of the loop. Additionally, three further test cases are necessary:

a, b, c, d, e
a, b, f, g, i, g, h, d, e
a, k, e

Connection (edge) coverage of the control flow graph

Together, all four test cases result in a complete coverage of the edges of the control flow graph. With that, all possible branches of the control flow in the source code of the test object have been tested.

Some edges have been executed more than once. This seems to be redundant, however, it cannot always be avoided. In the example, the edges a and e are executed in every test case because there is no alternative to these edges.

For each test case, other than the precondition and post-condition, the expected result and expected behavior must be determined and then compared to the actual result and behavior. Furthermore, it is reasonable to record which of the branches have been executed in which test case. This helps to find faults, especially missing code in empty branches.

Definition of the Test Completion Criteria

Analogous to the statement coverage, the degree of coverage for branch coverage is defined as follows:

$$\text{Branch coverage} =$$
$$(\text{number of executed branches / total number of branches}) * 100\%$$

C1-measure

Branch coverage is also called C1-coverage. The calculation counts only if a branch has been executed. The frequency of execution is not relevant. In the example, the edges a and e are each passed four times, once for each test case.

If we execute only the first three test cases in our example (not the fourth one), edge k will not be executed. This gives a branch coverage of 9 executed branches out of 10 total, i.e.,

9/10 *100% = 90%.

For comparison: 100% statement coverage has already been reached after the first test case.

Depending on the criticality of the test object, and depending on the expected failure risk, the test completion criterion can be defined differently. For instance, 85% branch coverage can be sufficient for a component of one project, whereas for a different project, another component must be tested with 100% coverage. The example shows that the test cost is higher for higher coverage requirements.

The Value of the Technique

Branch coverage usually requires the execution of more test cases than statement coverage. How much more depends on the structure of the test object. In contrast to statement coverage, branch coverage makes it possible to detect missing statements in empty branches. 100% branch coverage guarantees 100% statement coverage, but not vice versa. Thus, branch coverage is a stronger criterion.

More test cases necessary

Each of the branches is regarded separately with no particular combination of single branches required.

▨ A branch coverage of 100% should be aimed for.
▨ The test can be categorized as sufficient only if, in addition to all statements, every possible branch of the control flow is considered during test execution.

Hint

For object-oriented systems, statement coverage, as well as branch coverage, is inadequate, because the control flow of the functions in the classes is usually short and not very complex. Yet, the required coverage can be achieved with little effort. The complexity in object-oriented systems lies mostly in the relationship between the classes. Thus, additional coverage criteria are necessary in this case. As tools often support determining coverage, coverage data can be used to detect uncalled methods or program parts.

Inadequate for object-oriented systems

5.2.3 Test of Conditions

Considering the complexity
of combined conditions

Branch coverage exclusively considers the logical value of the result of a condition ("true" or "false"). Using this value, it is then decided which branch in the control flow graph is chosen, and accordingly, which statement is the next to be executed in the program. If a decision is based on several (part) conditions connected by logical operators, then the complexity of the condition should be considered in the test. The following sections describe different requirements, and thence degrees of test intensity under consideration of the composed conditions.

Branch condition testing

The goal of the branch condition testing is that each →atomic (partial) condition in the test shall adopt the values TRUE or FALSE.

Definition of an
atomic condition part

An atomic part of a condition is a condition that has no logical operators such as AND, OR, and NOT, but at the most, includes relation symbols such as ">" or "=". A condition in the source code of the test object can consist of multiple atomic partial conditions.

Example for combined
conditions

An example for a composed condition is: $x > 3$ OR $y < 5$. The condition consists of two atomic partial conditions ($x>3$; $y<5$) connected by the logical operator OR. The goal of the branch condition testing is that every atomic part of conditions is evaluated once for each of the logical values. The test data x=6 and y=8 result in the logical value true for the first part of condition ($x>3$) and the logical value false for the second part of the conditions ($y<5$). The logical value of the complete condition is true (true OR false = true). The second pair of test data with the values x=2 and y=3 results in false for the first part of condition and true for the second part of condition. The value of the complete condition results in true again (false OR true = true). Both parts of the condition have each resulted in both logical values. The result of the complete condition, however, is equal for both combinations.

Weak criterion

Branch condition testing is therefore a weaker criterion than statement or branch coverage because it is not required that different logical values for the result of the complete condition are included in the test.

Branch Condition Combination Testing

All combinations of the
logical values

Branch condition combination testing, also called multiple-condition coverage [Myers 79], requires that all true-false combinations of the atomic partial conditions be exercised at least once. All variations should be built, if possible.

For the example above four combinations of test cases are possible with the test data from above for the two atomic parts of conditions (x>3, y<5):

Continuation of the example

> x=6 (T), y=3 (T), x>3 OR y<5 (T)
> x=6 (T), y=8 (F), x>3 OR y<5 (T)
> x=2 (F), y=3 (T), x>3 OR y<5 (T)
> x=2 (F), y=8 (F), x>3 OR y<5 (F)

The complete condition gives both logical values as results. Thus, branch condition combination testing meets the criteria of statement, as well as branch coverage. It is a more comprehensive criterion that also takes into account the complexity of composed conditions. But it is a very expensive technique due to the growing number of atomic conditions which make the number of possible combinations grow exponentially (to 2^n with n atomic parts of conditions).

Branch condition combination testing includes statement and branch coverage

A problem results from the fact that all combinations cannot always be implemented by test data.

All combinations are not always possible

An example should clarify this. For the combined condition of 3<=x AND x<5 not all combinations with the according values for the variable x can be produced because the parts of conditions depend on each other:

Example for not feasible combinations of condition parts

> x=4: 3<=x (T), x<5 (T), 3<=x AND x<5 (T)
> x=8: 3<=x (T), x<5 (F), 3<=x AND x<5 (F)
> x=1: 3<=x (F), x<5 (T), 3<=x AND x<5 (F)
> x=?: 3<=x (F), x<5 (F), combination not possible because the value x shall be smaller than 3 and greater or equal to 5 at the same time.

Condition Determination Testing

Condition determination testing eliminates the problems that have just been discussed. Not all combinations must be considered; however, consideration should be given to every possible combination of logical values where the modification of the logical value of an atomic condition can change the logical value of the whole. Stated in another way, for a test case, every atomic condition has a meaningful impact on the result. Test cases in which the result does not depend on a change of an atomic condition need not be designed.

Restriction of the combinations

Continuation of the
example

For clarification we revisit the example with the two atomic condition parts (x>3, y<5). Four combinations are possible (2^2):

1) x=6 (T), y=3 (T), x>3 OR y<5 (T)
2) x=6 (T), y=8 (F), x>3 OR y<5 (T)
3) x=2 (F), y=3 (T), x>3 OR y<5 (T)
4) x=2 (F), y=8 (F), x>3 OR y<5 (F)

Changing a partial condition
without changing the result

For the first combination the following applies: If the logical value is calculated wrong for the first condition part (i.e., an incorrect condition is implemented) then the fault can change the logical value of the first condition part from true (T) to false (F). But the result of the complete condition stays unchanged (T). The same applies for the second condition part.

For the first combination incorrect results of each condition part are masked because they have no effect on the result of the complete condition and thus failures will not become visible. Consequently the test with the first combination can be left out.

If the logical value of the first condition part in the second test case is calculated wrongly as false, then the result value of the total condition changes from true (T) to false (F). A failure then becomes visible because the value of the complete condition has also changed. The same applies for the second condition part in the third test case. In the fourth test case an incorrect implementation is detected as well because the logical value of the complete condition changes.

Small number of test cases

For every logical combination of the conditions, it must be decided which test cases are sensitive to faults and for which combinations faults can be masked. Combinations where faults are masked need not be considered in the test. The number of test cases is considerably smaller compared to the branch condition combination testing. The amount lies between n+1 and 2n with n = number of the Boolean operands of the condition.

Test Cases

For designing the test cases, it must be considered which input data lead to which result of the condition or condition part, and which parts of the program will be executed after the decision. The expected output and expected behavior of the test object should also be defined in advance, in order to detect whether the program behaves correctly or not.

- Because of the weak significance, branch condition testing should be abandoned for complex conditions.
- For complex conditions, condition determination testing should be applied for test case design, because the complexity of the conditional expression is taken into account. The method also leads to statement and branch coverage, which means they need not be used additionally.

Hint

However, it may be very expensive to choose the input values in such a way that a certain part of the condition gets the logical value required by the test case.

Definition of the Test Completion Criteria

Analogous to the previous techniques, the proportion between the executed and all the required logical values of the condition (parts) can be calculated. This can serve as criteria for termination of the tests. For the techniques, which concentrate attention to the complexity of the conditions in the source code, it is reasonable to try to achieve a complete verification (100 % coverage). If there are no complex condition expressions, branch coverage can be seen as sufficient.

The Value of the Technique

If complex conditions are present in the source code, they must be tested intensively to uncover possible failures. Combinations of logical expressions are especially defect-prone. Thus, a comprehensive test is very important. Admittedly, condition determination testing is a very expensive technique for test case design.

Complex conditions are often defect-prone

- It can be reasonable to split combined complex conditions into a tree-structure of nested simple conditions, and then execute a branch coverage test for these sequences of conditions.
- The intensive test of complex conditions can possibly be omitted if they have been subjected to a review (section 4.1.2) in which the correctness is verified.

Hint

A disadvantage of condition coverage is that it checks Boolean expressions only inside a statement (for example, IF-statement). In the following example of a program fragment, it is not detected that the IF-condition is combined of multiple condition parts and that modified branch condition determination testing should be applied.

Excursion

If all Boolean expressions that appear in the program are analyzed for construction of combined conditional test cases then this disadvantage can be prevented.

```
...
Flag = (A || (B && C));
If (Flag)
      ...;
else  ...;
...
```

Compiler terminates evaluation of expressions

Another problem occurs in connection with measuring the coverage of condition parts. Some compilers shortcut the evaluation of the Boolean expression as soon as the total result will not change any more. For instance, if the value FALSE has been detected for one of two condition parts of an AND-concatenation then the complete condition is FALSE regardless of what the second condition part will result in. Some compilers even change the order of the evaluation, depending on the Boolean operators, in order to receive the final result as fast as possible and to be able to disregard any other condition part. Test cases that are supposed to reach coverage of 100 % can be executed, but because of the shortened evaluation, the coverage cannot be verified.

5.2.4   Path Coverage

All possible paths through the test object

Until now, test case determination focused on the statements or branches of the control flow, as well as the complexity of conditions. If the test object includes loops or repetitions, the previous deliberations are not sufficient for an adequate test. Path coverage requires the execution of all different paths through the test object.

Example for a path test

Considering the control flow graph (figure 5-9), we try to clarify the term "path". The program fragment represented by the graph includes a loop. This DO-WHILE loop is executed at least once. In the WHILE-condition it is decided at the end of the loop whether the loop must be repeated, i.e., if a jump to the start of the loop is necessary. When using branch coverage for test design the loop has been considered in two test cases:

■ Loop without repetition:
a, b, f, g, h, d, e
■ Loop with single return (i) and a single repetition:
a, b, f, g, i, g, h, d, e

Usually a loop is repeated more than once. Further possible sequences of branches through the graph of the program are

a, b, f, g, i, g, i, g, h, d, e
a, b, f, g, i, g, i, g, i, g, h, d, e
a, b, f, g, i, g, i, g, i, g, i, g, h, d, e
etc.

This shows that there is an indefinite number of paths in the control flow graph. Even with restrictions on the number of loop repetitions, the number of paths increases indefinitely (see also section 2.1.4).

A path describes the possible order of single program parts in a program fragment. Contrary to this, branches are viewed independently, each for itself. The paths consider dependencies between the branches, as with loops for example, at which one branch leads back to the beginning of another branch.

Combination of program parts

In section 5.1.1 for the function `calculate_price` () of the VSR subsystem *DreamCar* test cases from valid and invalid equivalence classes of the parameters have been chosen. In the following, test cases are evaluated by their ability to cover the source code, i.e., accordingly execute fragments of the method. 100 % coverage should be achieved in order to ensure that during test execution all branch have been passed at least once.

Example: Statement and branch coverage VCR

For better understanding the source code of the function from section 3.2.3 is displayed again:

```
double calculate_price (
        double baseprice, double specialprice,
        double extraprice, int extras, double discount)
{
        double addon_discount;
        double result;

        if (extras >= 3) addon_discount = 10;
        else if (extras >= 5) addon_discount = 15;
        else addon_discount = 0;
        if (discount > addon_discount)
                addon_discount = discount;
        result  = baseprice /100.0*(100-discount)
                + specialprice
                + extraprice/100.0*(100-addon_discount);
        return (result);
}
```

The control flow graph of the function `calculate_price()` is shown in figure 5-10.

Figure 5-10
Control flow graph of the
function
calculate_price()

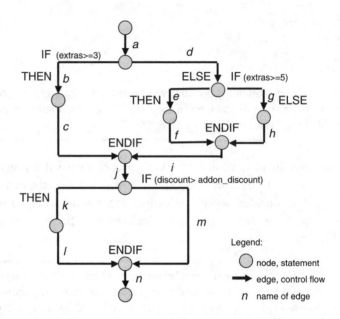

In section 3.2.3 the following two test cases have been chosen:

```
// testcase 01
price = calculate_price(10000.00,2000.00,1000.00,3,0);
test_ok = test_ok && (abs(price–12900.00) < 0.01);
```

```
// testcase 02
price = calculate_price(25500.00,3450.00,6000.00,6,0);
test_ok = test_ok && (abs(price-34050.00) < 0.01);
```

The test cases cause the execution of the following edges of the graph:

Test case 01: a, b, c, j, m, n
Test case 02: a, b, c, j, m, n

43 % branch coverage
achieved

The edges d, e, f, g, h, i, k, l have not been executed. The two test cases covered only 43 % of the branches (6 out of 14). Test case 02 gives no improvement of the coverage and is not necessary for branch coverage. However, considering the specification test case 02 should have led to execution of more statements because a different discount was supposed to be calculated (with five or more pieces of extra equipment).

In order to increase the coverage the following additional test cases are specified:

```
// testcase 03
price = calculate_price(10000.00,2000.00,1000.00,0,10);
test_ok = test_ok && (abs(price−12000.00) < 0.01);

// testcase 04
price = calculate_price(25500.00,3450.00,6000.00,6,15);
test_ok = test_ok && (abs(price−30225.00) < 0.01);
```

These test cases cause the execution of the following edges of the graph:

Test case 03: a, d, g, h, i, j, k, l, n
Test case 04: a, b, c, j, k, l, n

The test cases lead to execution of further edges (d, g, h, i, k and l) and thus increase branch coverage to 86%. Edges e and f have not yet been executed.

86 % path coverage achieved

Before trying to reach the missing edges by further test cases the conditions of the IF-statements are analyzed more closely, i.e., the source code is analyzed in order to define further test cases. To reach the edges e and f the condition of the first condition (extras >= 3) must be false in order to execute the ELSE-part. In this ELSE-part the condition (extras >= 5) must be true. Therefore a value has to be found that meets the following condition:

Evaluation of the conditions

```
¬(extras >=3) AND (extras >=5)
```

There is no such value and the missing edges can never be reached. Here is a defect in the source code.

This example shall clarify the relationship between statement, branch and path coverage as well. The test object consists of altogether three IF-statements whereof two are nested and the third is placed separately from the others (figure 5-10).

Example: Relationship between the measures

All statements (nodes) are reached by the following sequence of edges in the graph:

a, b, c, j, k, l, n
a, d, e, f, i, j, k, l, n
a, d, g, h, i, j, k, l, n

These sequences are sufficient to achieve 100% statement coverage. But not all branches (edges) have been covered yet. The edge m is still missing. A sequence might look as follows:

a, b, c, j, m, n

This additional sequence should have replaced the first sequence (test case) above. With the resulting three test cases, branch coverage of 100% is achieved.

Further paths through   But, even for this simple program fragment, there are still possibilities to
the graph   traverse the graph differently, and thus consider all paths of the graph. Until now, the following paths have not been executed:

a, d, e, f, i, j, m, n
a, d, g, h, i, j, m, n

Altogether, six different paths through the source code result (the three possible paths through the graph before edge j multiplied with the two possible paths after edge j). There is the precondition that the conditions are independent from each other and the edges can be combined freely.

If there are loops in the source code, then every possible number of repetitions is counted as one possible path through the program fragment. It is obvious that 100% path coverage is not feasible in a program as soon as the program is not trivial.

5.2.5   Further White Box Techniques

There are a number of additional white box test techniques. However, these are not described here. This chapter described the most common techniques. Further techniques are explained in [Myers 79], [Beizer 90], and [Pol 98]. The following section describes one technique a little closer.

Data flow based techniques   A number of techniques use the data flow through the test object as the basis for identifying the test cases. Primarily the data usages in the test object are verified. The use of every variable is analyzed. The definitions of variables, and the read and write accesses of variables, are distinguished. These techniques may find faults where a value given to a variable in one place leads to failure at another place where it is used. Furthermore, it is analyzed if the value of the variable is used for calculation of another variable or for identification of the logical value of a condition. By means of this information, different criteria in relation to the data flow can be defined. These should then be covered by test cases. A detailed description of the data flow based techniques can be found in [Clarke et al. 85] .

5.2.6   General Discussion of the White Box Technique

Determine test intensity   The basis for all white box techniques is the source code. Adequate test case design techniques can be chosen and applied depending on the complexity of the program structure. Considering the source code and the selected technique, the intensity of the test is defined.

White box techniques are suited for the lower test levels. For example, it is not very reasonable to require coverage of single statements or branches at system test, because system testing is not the right method to check single statements or conditions in the code.

Useful for lower test levels

Missing implementation of requirements is impossible to find for white box techniques. White box techniques can only verify code that exists, i.e., requirements that are implemented in the program, not code that should be there but isn't. Thus, to find omissions requires other test design techniques.

"Not existing source code" is not considered

5.2.7   Instrumentation and Tool Support

White box techniques require that different program fragments are executed, and conditions get different logical values. In order to be able to evaluate the test, it must be determined which program fragments have already been executed and which fragments have not yet been executed. For that purpose, the test object must be instrumented at strategic relevant spots of the test execution. →Instrumentation often works this way: The tool inserts counters in the program and initializes them with zero. During program execution, the counters are incremented when they are passed. At the end of the test execution, the counters contain the number of passes through the according program fragments. If a counter stayed at zero during the test, then the according program fragment has not been executed.

Determination of the executed program parts

The instrumentation, the evaluation of the test runs, and the calculation of the achieved coverage should not be done manually, because this would require too many resources, and a manual instrumentation is error-prone. Numerous tools perform these tasks (section 7.1.4). These tools are very important for white box testing because they increase the productivity and indirectly improve the quality of the test object.

Use tools

5.3   Intuitive and Experience Based Test Case Determination

Besides the methodical approach, intuitive determination of test cases should be performed. The systematically identified test cases may be complemented by intuitive test cases. Intuitive testing can uncover faults overlooked by systematic testing.

Intuitive skill and experience of the tester

Basis of this method is the skill, experience, and knowledge of the tester. The tester selects test cases to uncover expected problems and their symptoms. A more systematic approach for this cannot be described. The test cases are based on the experience of where faults have occurred in the past or the tester's assumptions where faults might occur in the future. This type of test case design is also called →"error guessing" and is used very often in practice.

Knowledge in developing similar applications and using similar technologies should also be used when designing test cases, in addition to experience in testing. If, for example, there exist experiences with a new programming language in previous projects, it is reasonable to apply the failures found, as well as their cause in using the programming language for designing the tests in the actual project. One technique for intuitive testing, exploratory testing, will be discussed in more detail in the following.

Exploratory Testing

If the documents, which form the basis for test design, are of very low quality or do not exist at all, so-called "exploratory testing" may help. In the extreme case only the program exists. The technique is also applicable when time is severely restricted because it uses much less time than other techniques. The approach is mainly based on the intuition and experience of the tester.

The approach in "exploratory testing"

The test activities in exploratory testing are executed nearly in "parallel". There is no application of a structured test process. An explicit previous planning of the test activities is not done. The possible elements of the test object (its specific tasks and functions) are "explored". It is then decided which parts will be tested. Few test cases are executed and their results are analyzed. After executing them, the "unknown" behavior of the test object will be determined further. Anything considered special, as well as other information, are then used to determine the next test cases. In this step-by-step way, knowledge about the test object under test is collected. It increasingly becomes clearer what the test object does and how it works, which quality problems there could be, and which expectations to the program should be fulfilled. One result of exploratory testing may be that it becomes clear which test techniques can be applied if there is time left.

"Test charter"

It makes sense to restrict exploratory testing to certain elements of the program (certain tasks or functions). The elements are further broken down. The term "test charter" is used for such smaller parts. The test of a "*charter*" should not take more than one or two hours of uninterrupted test time. When executing test charters, the following questions are of interest:

- Why? With which goal, is the test run?
- What is to be tested?
- How? Which testing method should be used?
- Which problems should be found?

The generic ideas of exploratory testing are:

Main features of exploratory testing

- Results of one test case influence the design and execution of further test cases.
- During testing, a "mental" model of the program under test is created. The model contains how the program works and how it behaves or how it should behave.
- The test is run against this model. The focus is to find further aspects and behavior of the program, which are still not part of the mental model or are differing from aspects found before.

The approaches for intuitive test case determination cannot be associated explicitly with white box or black box techniques because neither the requirements nor the source code are exclusively the basis for the considerations. Its range of application is in the higher test levels. In the lower ones, usually sufficient information such as source code or detailed specification is accessible for applying systematic techniques.

Neither black box nor white box

   The intuitive test case determination should not be applied as the primary testing technique. Instead, this technique should be used to support and complete the choice of test cases through systematic testing techniques.

Not to be used as first or only technique

Test Cases

Knowledge from experience of the tester for determination of additional test cases can be drawn from many sources.

In case of the development project for the *CarConfigurator*, the testers are very familiar with the previous system. Many of them have tested this system as well. They know which weaknesses the system had and they know the problems the car dealers had with the operation of the old software (from hotline data and from discussions with car dealers). Employees from the companies' marketing department know for the business-process-based test which vehicles in which configurations are sold often and what theoretically possible combinations of extra equipment

Example:
Tester knowledge for the
CarConfigurator

might not even be shippable. They use this experience to intuitively prioritize the systematically identified test cases and to complete them by additional test cases. The test manager knows which of the developer teams act under the most severe time pressure and even work on weekends. Hence, she will test the components from these teams more intensively.

Using all knowledge   The tester is supposed to use all their knowledge to find additional test cases. Naturally, the pre- and post-conditions, the expected outcome, and the expected behavior of the test object must be defined in advance for intuitive testing, as well.

Hint   ▪ Because extensive experience is often only available in the minds of the experienced testers, maintaining a list with possible errors, faults, and suspicious situations might be very helpful. Frequently occurring errors, faults, and failures are noted in the list and are thus available to all the testers. With the help of the identified possible trouble and critical situations, additional test cases can be determined.

▪ The list may even be beneficial to developers because it is indicated in advance what potential problems and difficulties might occur. Those can be considered during implementation and thus serve for error prevention.

Definition of the Test Completion Criteria

The test exit criterion is not definable   Contrary to the systematic techniques, a criterion for termination cannot be specified. If the above-mentioned list exists, then a certain completeness can be verified against the list.

The Value of the Technique

Mostly successful in finding more defects   Intuitive test case determination and exploratory testing can often be used with good success. However, they should only be used in addition to systematic techniques. The success and effectiveness of this approach depend very much on tester skill, intuition, and their previous experience with applications like the test object and the technologies used. Such approaches can also contribute to find holes and errors in the risk analysis. If intuitive testing is executed in addition to systematic testing, hitherto no detected inconsistencies in the test specification can be found. Intensity and completeness of intuitive and exploratory test design cannot be measured.

5.4 Summary

This chapter has introduced quite a number of techniques for testing of software.[50] The question is: When each of the techniques should be applied? The following gives advice and shows a reasonable procedure for answering this question. The general goal is to identify sufficiently different test cases, using any available method, in order to be able to find existing faults with a certain probability and with as little effort as possible. The techniques for test design should therefore be chosen "appropriately".

Which technique and when to use it

However, before doing the work some factors should be checked, which have considerable influence on the selection or even prescribe the application of certain test methods. The selection of techniques should be based on different kinds of information:

- **The kind of test object** – The complexity of the program text can vary considerably. Adequate test techniques should be chosen. If, for example, conditions in the program are combined from atomic subconditions, branch coverage is not sufficient. A suitable technique to check the conditions should be chosen. Which one to choose depends on the risk in case of failure and the criticality.
- **Formal documentation and the availability of tools** – If specification or model information is available in a formal notation, this can be fed directly into test design tools, which then derive test cases. This will very much decrease the effort required to design the tests.
- **Conformance to standards** – Industry and regulatory standards may require use of certain test techniques and coverage criteria, especially for safety critical software or software with a high integrity level.
- **Tester experience** – Tester experience may lead to choice of special techniques. A tester will, for example, reuse techniques which have led to finding serious faults earlier.
- **Customer wishes** – The customer may require specific test techniques to be used and test coverage to be achieved (when using white box test design techniques). This is a good idea, as it generally leads to at least a minimum thoroughness of supplier testing, which may lead to fewer faults to be detected in customer or acceptance testing.

---

50. There exist other techniques not described in this book. The reader should check further literature in case of need. This applies especially to integration testing, test of distributed applications and test of real time and embedded programs. Such techniques are part of the Advanced Level Tester Certification Scheme.

■ **Risk analysis** – The expectation of risk dictates more or less thorough testing, i.e., the choice of techniques and the intensity of the execution. Risk prone areas should be tested more thoroughly.

■ **Further factors** – Finally there are factors like the availability of the specification and other documentation, the knowledge and skill of the test personnel, time and budget, the test level and previous experience with what kind of defects occur most often and with which test techniques these have been found. They can all have a large influence on selecting the testing techniques.

Test design techniques should never be chosen by default. Their selection should always be based on a thoughtful decision. The following list should help in choosing the most useful test technique.

Testing functionality ■ Correct functioning of the system is certainly of great relevance. A sufficient verification of the functionality of the test object has to be guaranteed, in any case. Developing all test cases, regardless by which technique or procedure, includes determination of the expected results and reactions of the test object. This ensures a verification of the functionality for every executed test case. It may be distinguished if a failure exists or the correct functioning has been implemented.

Equivalence class partition combined with boundary value analysis ■ Equivalence class partitioning in combination with boundary value analysis should be applied for every test object to determine the test cases. When executing these test cases, the according tools for measuring code coverage should be used in order to find the already achieved test coverage (see section 7.1.4).

Consider execution history ■ If different states have an influence on the operating sequence in the test object, state transition testing must be applied. Only state transition testing verifies the cooperation of the states, transitions, and the according behavior of the functions in an adequate way.

■ If dependencies between the input data are given, which must be considered in the test, these dependencies can be modeled using cause-effect graphs or decision tables. The corresponding test cases can be taken from the decision table.

■ Testing a whole system's use cases (displayed in use case diagrams) can be applied as a basis for designing test cases.

■ In component and integration testing, coverage measurements should be included with these black box techniques. The parts of the test object still not executed should then be specifically considered for a white box test. Depending on the criticality and nature of the test object, an accordingly expensive white box technique must be selected.

- As minimum criterion, branch coverage should be used. If complex conditions exist in the test object, then condition determination testing is the appropriate technique.

Minimum criterion: branch coverage

- While measuring coverage, loops should be repeated more than once. At critical parts of the system, verification of the loops must be done using the according methods (*boundary interior*-path test and structured path test [Howden 75]).

- Path coverage has to be seen as a mere theoretical measure and is of little importance in practice because of the great cost and because it is impossible to achieve for programs with loops.

- It is reasonable to apply white box techniques at lower test levels while black box techniques offer an adequate solution for all test levels, especially the higher ones.

- Intuitive determination of test cases should not be ignored. It is a good supplement to systematic test design methods. It is reasonable to use the experience of the testers to find further faults.

- Testing always contains the combination of different techniques because no testing technique exists that covers all aspects to be considered in testing equally well.

Hint

- The criticality and the expected risk in case of failure guide the selection of the testing techniques and the intensity of the execution.

- Basis for the selection of the white box technique is the structure of the test object. If for example no complex conditions are included in the test object, the usage of condition determination testing makes no sense.

---

6 Test Management

This chapter describes how to organize test teams, which team member qualifications are important, the tasks of a test manager, and which supporting processes must be present for efficient testing.

6.1 Test Organization

6.1.1 Test Teams

Testing activities must be executed during the entire software product life cycle (see chapter 3). These testing related tasks should be coordinated and planned in close cooperation with development activities. The easiest solution is for the developer to perform the testing, but the individual developer or development team tends to be blind to their own errors. Therefore it is much more effective to have different people develop and test, and to organize testing as independently as possible from development.

The benefits of independent testing include:

- Independent testers are unbiased and see different defects than developers.
- An independent tester can verify (implicit) assumptions made by developers during specification and implementation of the system.

Benefits of independent testing

But there can also be some drawbacks to independent testing:

- There might be a lack of communication due to too much isolation from the development team.
- Independent testing may become a bottleneck if the testers are not equipped with the necessary resources.
- Developers may lose a sense of responsibility for quality, as they may think, "the testers will find the trouble anyway".

Possible drawbacks of independent testing

Models of independent
testing

The following models or options for independence are possible:

1. The development team is responsible for testing, but developers test each other's programs[51], instead of their own, i.e., a developer tests the program of a colleague.
2. There are testers within the development team; these testers do all test work on their team.
3. One or more dedicated testing teams exist within the project team (these teams are not responsible for development tasks). Such independent testers may belong to the business organization, user community, or an IT operations group.
4. There are independent test specialists for specific testing tasks (such as performance test, usability test, security test, or compatibility test).
5. A separate organization (testing department, external testing facility (contractor), test laboratory) is responsible for testing (on specific test levels, e.g., system test).

When to choose which
model

For each of these models, having testing consultants available would be advantageous. These consultants could support several projects and could offer methodical assistance in areas such as training, coaching, test automation, etc. Which of the above-mentioned models is appropriate depends – among other things – on the actual test level.

Component testing: Testing should be performed in close conjunction with the development activities. Although often implemented, it is definitely the worst choice to allow developers to test their own programs. Independent testing organized like model 1 would certainly improve testing quality. Testing like model 2 is useful, if a sufficient number of testing staff relative to the number of development staff can be made available for testing. However, with both testing models, there is the risk that the participating people essentially consider themselves developers, and thus will neglect their testing responsibilities. To prevent this, the following measures are recommended:

Hint

- Project or test management sets testing standards and rules, prepares testing schedules, and requires test logs from the developers.
- To provide method support, testing specialists should, at least temporarily, be called in as coaches.

---

51. Often called "buddy testing".

Integration testing: When the same team that developed the components also performs integration and integration testing, this testing can be organized analogous to component testing (models 1, 2).

If components originating from several teams are integrated, then a mixed integration team with representatives from the involved development groups, or an independent integration team should be responsible. The individual development team may have their own view about their own component, and therefore may overlook faults. Depending on the size of the development project and the number of components, models 3 to 5 should be considered here.

System testing: The final product shall be considered from the point of view of the customer and the end user. Therefore, independence from the development is crucial. This leaves only models 3, 4, and 5 as professionally acceptable choices.

In the VSR project, each respective development team is responsible for component testing. These teams are individually organized according to the above-mentioned models 1 and 2. In parallel to these development teams, an independent testing group is established. This testing group is responsible for integration and system testing. Figure 6-1 depicts the project organization.

Example: VSR testing organization

Figure 6–1
VSR project organization

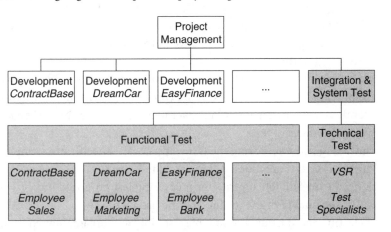

Two or three employees from each responsible user department (sales, marketing, etc.) will be made available for the functional or business-process based testing of every subsystem (*ContractBase, DreamCar* etc.). These people are familiar with the business processes to be supported by the particular subsystem and are aware of the requirements "their" test object should fulfill from the users' point of view. They are experienced PC users, but not IT experts. It is their task to support the test specialists in specifying functional test cases and to perform these tests.

Upon starting the testing activities, they will receive training in basic testing procedures (test process, specification, execution, and logging).

Additionally, test personnel consists of three to five IT and test specialists, responsible for integration activities, nonfunctional tests, test automation, and the support of test tools ("technical test").

A test manager, responsible for test planning and test control, will be in charge of the test team. The manager's tasks also comprise coaching of the test personnel, especially instruction of the staff on the subject of testing the business requirements.

6.1.2   Tasks and Qualifications

Specialists with knowledge covering the full scope of activities in the test process should be available. The following roles should be assigned, ideally to specifically qualified employees:

Roles and qualification profiles

■ **Test manager** (test leader): Test planning and test control expert, possessing knowledge and experience in the fields of software testing, quality management, project management, and personnel management. Typical tasks may include:
  - Writing or reviewing the test policy for the organization
  - Writing the test strategy and test plan as described in section 6.2.2
  - Representing the testing perspective in the project
  - Procuring testing resources
  - Selecting suitable test strategies and methods, and introducing or improving testing related processes (problem management, suitable configuration management) in order to be able to trace back changes and reproduce all tests
  - Initiating and monitoring the test work, i.e., the specification, implementation, and execution of tests at all test levels
  - Introducing suitable metrics for measuring test progress, and evaluating the quality of the testing and the product
  - Selecting and introducing suitable test tools, and organizing required training in tool use for testers. Deciding the type and extent of the test environment and test automation.
  - Planning the test runs and regular adaptation of the test plans based on test results and project and test progress
  - Writing →test reports and communicating them

▦ **Test designer** (test analyst): Expert(s) in test methods and test specification, having knowledge and experience in the fields of software testing, software engineering, and (formal) specification methods. Typical tasks may include:

- Analyzing, reviewing, and assessing user requirements, specifications, designs, and models for testability and in order to design test cases
- Creating test specifications
- Preparing and acquiring test data

▦ **Test automator**: Test automation expert(s) with knowledge of testing basics, programming experience, and excellent knowledge of the testing tools and script languages. Automates tests as required, making use of the test tools available for the project, including scripting languages.

▦ **Test administrator**: Expert(s) for installing and operating the test environment (system administrator knowledge). Sets up and supports the test environment (often coordinating with system administration and network management).

▦ **Tester**[52]: Expert(s) in executing tests and incident reporting (IT basics, testing basics, applying the test tools, understanding of the test object). Typical tester tasks may include:

- Reviewing test plans and test cases
- Using test tools and test monitoring tools (for example tools for performance measurement)
- Executing and logging tests, evaluating the results, and documenting the results and the deviations

In this context, what does the Certified Tester training offer? The basic training (Foundation Level) qualifies for the "tester" role (without covering the required IT basics). This means that a Certified Tester knows why discipline and structured work procedures are necessary. Under the supervision of a test manager, a Certified Tester can manually perform tests and document them. They are familiar with basic techniques from the field of test specification and test management. Every software developer should also know these basics of software testing in order to be able to adequately execute the testing tasks required by organizational models 1 and 2. Before being able to fulfill the role of a test designer or test manager, appropriate

Certified Tester

---

52. The term "tester" often is also used as generic term for all above-mentioned roles.

experience as a tester should be gathered. The second educational level (Advanced Level) offers training for the tasks of the designer and manager.

Even social competence is
important

■ To be successful, in addition to technical and test specific skills, a tester also needs social skills: ability to work in a team, and political and diplomatic aptitude

■ Skepticism: willingness to question apparent facts

■ Persistence and poise

■ Accuracy and creativity

■ Ability to get quickly acquainted with (complex fields of) application

Multi-disciplinary team

Especially when performing system tests, it is often necessary to extend the test team by additional IT specialists, at least temporarily, to perform work for the test team. For example, these might be database administrators, database designers, or network specialists. Professional specialists from the application field of the software system currently being tested are often indispensable. Managing such a multi-disciplinary test team can be a challenge even for experienced test managers.

Specialized software test
service providers

If appropriate resources are not available within the company, test activities can also be assigned to external service providers, specializing in software testing or in certain test areas (such as performance, security, or usability testing). This is similar to placing a contract for software development with an external software house. Based on their experience and their use of predefined solutions and procedures, these test specialists are able to rapidly deploy the optimal test for the project at hand. They can also provide any missing specialist skills from each of the above mentioned qualification profiles for application in the project.

6.2   Test Planning

Testing should not be the only measure for quality assurance (QA). It should be used in combination with other quality assurance measures. Therefore, an overall plan for quality assurance measures is needed that will be documented in the quality assurance plan.

6.2.1   Quality Assurance Plan

Guidelines for structuring the quality assurance plan can be found in the standard [IEEE 730]. The following subjects shall be considered (additional sections may be added as required. Some of the material may also appear in other documents).

> **Quality Assurance Plan according to IEEE 730**
>
> 1. Purpose
> 2. Reference documents
> 3. Management
> 4. Documentation
> 5. Standards, practices, conventions, and metrics
> 6. Software reviews
> 7. Test
> 8. Problem reporting and corrective action
> 9. Tools, techniques, and methodologies
> 10. Media control
> 11. Supplier control
> 12. Records collection, maintenance, and retention
> 13. Training
> 14. Risk management
> 15. Glossary
> 16. SQAP Change Procedure and History

During this quality assurance planning, the role the tests play as special, analytical measures of quality control is roughly defined. The details are then determined during test planning and documented in the test plan.

6.2.2   Test Plan

A task as extensive as testing requires careful planning. This planning starts as early as possible in the software project and is influenced by the test policy of the organization, the scope of testing, objectives, risks, constraints, and product criticality. The test manager's planning activities may include:

- Defining the overall approach to and strategy for testing (see section 6.4)   *Test planning activities*
- Deciding about the test environment
- Definition of the test levels, as well as their cooperation and integrating and coordinating the testing activities with other project activities
- Deciding how to evaluate the test results

- Selecting metrics for monitoring and controlling test work, as well as defining test exit criteria
- Determining how much test documentation shall be prepared and deciding about templates
- Writing the test plan and deciding on what, who, when, and how much testing
- Estimating test effort and test costs ; (Re)estimating and (re)planning the testing tasks.

The results are documented in the test plan[53]. Standard [IEEE 829] provides a reference structure:

Test Plan according to IEEE 829

1. Test plan identifier
2. Introduction
3. Test items
4. Features to be tested
5. Features not to be tested
6. Approach
7. Item pass/fail criteria (test exit criteria)
8. Suspension criteria and resumption requirements
9. Test deliverables
10. Testing tasks
11. Environmental needs
12. Responsibilities
13. Staffing and training needs
14. Schedule
15. Risk and contingencies
16. Approvals

This structure[54] works well in practice. A detailed description of the listed points can be found in appendix A. The sections listed will be found in

---

53. "Test plan" must not be confused with the "test schedule" which means the "detailed time planning".
54. The current draft of the new IEEE 829 standard (2005, [IEEE 829]) shows an outline for a master test plan and a level test plan. IEEE Standard 1012 ([IEEE 1012]) gives another reference structure for a verification and validation plan. This standard can be used for planning the test strategy for more complex projects.

many projects in this same, or slightly modified, form. For example, separate test plans for system testing or other specific test levels are possible. Test planning is a continuous activity for the test manager throughout all phases of the development project. The test strategy and related plans must be updated regularly, considering feedback from test activities and recognizing changing risks.

6.2.3   Prioritizing Tests

Even with good planning and control it is possible that time and budget for the total test, or in a certain test level, are not sufficient to execute all planned test cases. In this case, it is necessary to select test cases in a sensible way. Even with a reduced test, it must be assured that as many critical faults are found as possible. This means test cases must be prioritized.

Test case prioritization should happen in such a way that a premature end of testing still assures the best possible test result at that actual point in time.

Prioritization rule

A prioritization also has the advantage that the most important test cases are executed first. This way important problems can be found early.

The most important test cases first

Below, criteria for prioritization, and thus for determining the order of execution of the test cases are outlined. It depends on the project, the application area, and the customer requirements which criteria are used.

Criteria for prioritization of test cases may be:

Criteria for prioritization

- The **usage frequency** of a function or the **probability** of failure in software use: If certain functions of the system are used often and they contain a fault, then the probability of this fault leading to a failure is high. Thus, test cases for this function should have a higher priority than test cases for a less often used function.
- **Risk** of failure: Risk is the combination (mathematic product) of severity and failure probability. The severity is the expected damage. Such risks may be, for example, that the business of the customer using the software is impacted, thus leading to financial losses for the customer. Tests which may find failures with a high risk get higher priority than tests which may find failures with low risks (see also section 6.4.3).
- The **visibility** of a failure for the end user is a further criterion for prioritization of test cases. This is especially important in interactive systems. For example, a user of a city information service will feel unsafe if

there are problems in the user interface, and will lose confidence in the other information output.

- Test cases can be chosen depending on the **priority of the requirements**. The different functions delivered by a system have different levels of importance for the customer. The customer may be able to accept the loss of some of the functionality, if it cannot be made to work. For other parts, this may not be possible.
- Besides the functional requirements, the **quality characteristics** may have differing importance for the customer. Correct implementation of the important quality characteristics must be tested. Test cases for verifying conformance to required quality characteristics get a high priority.
- Prioritization can also be done from the perspective of the developer of the system architecture. Components which lead to severe consequences when they fail, for example a crash of the system, should be tested more intensively.
- The **complexity** of the individual components and system parts can be used to prioritize test cases. Complex program parts should be tested more intensively, because developers probably introduced more faults. However, it may happen that program parts seen as easy contain many faults, because development was not done with the necessary care. Therefore, prioritization in this area should be done using data from experience gained from earlier projects run within the organization.
- Failures having a high **project risk** should be found early. These are failures that require considerable correction work which monopolizes resources and leads to considerable delays of the project (see section 6.4.3).

The project manager should define adequate priority criteria and priority classes for the project. Every test case in the test plan should get a priority class using these criteria. This helps in deciding which test cases must be run and which can be left out if resource problems occur.

Where there are many defects, there are probably more

The following phenomenon often occurs in projects: where many faults were found before, more are present. In order to react in such circumstances, it must be possible to change test case priority. In the next test cycle (see section 6.3), additional test cases should be executed for such defect-prone test objects. Without prioritizing test cases it is not possible to find an adequate allocation of limited test resources. The concentration of resources to high priority test cases is a must.

6.2.4   Test Exit Criteria

An important part of test planning is the definition of test exit criteria. The purpose of test exit criteria is to define when testing can be stopped (totally or within a test level). As test execution is generally at the end of a project, time restraints and resource shortage can easily lead to random, premature decisions about the end of testing. Deciding clear exit criteria during test planning helps mitigate this risk. Typical test exit criteria are:

- Test coverage: how many test cases have been run (successfully), how many requirements are covered, and how much code is covered?
- Product quality: number of faults found, criticality of failures, failure rates, reliability etc.
- Residual risk: not executed tests, not repaired defects, incomplete coverage of requirements or code, etc.
- Economic constraints: allowed cost, project risks, delivery dates, and market chances

The test manager defines the project-specific test exit criteria in the test strategy. During test execution, these criteria are then regularly measured and serve as the basis for decisions by test and project management (section 6.3.1).

6.3   Cost and Economy Aspects

Testing can be very costly and can constitute a significant cost factor in software development. The question is: How much effort is adequate for testing a specific software product? When does the testing effort overweigh the possible benefit? In order to answer these questions, one must understand the potential defect costs due to lack of testing. Then, one has to weigh defect costs against testing costs.

6.3.1   Costs of Defects

If verification and testing activities are reduced or cut out completely, the consequence is a higher number of unrevealed faults and deficiencies in the product. These remain in the product and may lead to the following costs:

Costs due to product
deficiencies

■ **Direct defect costs**: Costs that arise for the customer due to failures during operation of the software product (and that the vendor may be obliged to pay for). Examples for such costs are costs due to calculation mistakes (data loss, wrong orders, damage of hardware or parts of the technical installation, damage to personnel); costs because of the failure of software controlled machines, installations, or business processes; and costs due to installation of new versions, which might also require training of employees etc. Very few people think of these costs, but they can be huge. Just the time it takes to install a new version at all customer sites can be enormous.

■ **Indirect defect costs**: Costs or loss of sales for the vendor that occur because the customer is dissatisfied with the product. Some examples include penalties or reduction of payment for not meeting contractual requirements, increased costs for the customer hotline, service, and support, bad publicity, loss of goodwill, loss of customers, even legal costs such as loss of license (for example, for safety critical software) etc.

■ **Costs for defect correction**: Costs for vendor work caused by fault correction. For example, time needed for failure analysis, correction[55], test and regression test, redistribution and reinstallation, repeated customer and user training, delay of new products due to tying up the developers while they maintain the existing product, decreasing competitiveness, etc.

Risk analysis

It is hard to determine which types of costs will actually occur, how likely this is, and how expensive this will be, i.e., how high the defect risk is for a project. This risk, of course, depends on the kind and size of the software product, the type of customer, the business or application area, as well as the design of the contract, judicial framework, etc. It also depends on the type and number of failures, on the number of product installations, as well as the number of users. There are certainly big differences between software developed specifically for a customer and commercial off-the-shelf products. In case of doubt, all these influencing factors must be evaluated in a project-specific risk analysis.

Finding faults as early as
possible lowers the costs

■ Independent of how high the risk of a fault actually is, it is crucial to find faults as early as possible after their creation. Defect costs grow

---

55. For example, for medical devices there are regulating agencies like FDA [URL: FDA] requiring more extensive documentation of the testing.

rapidly the longer a fault remains in the product. A fault that is created very early, e.g., an error in the requirements definition, can, if not detected, produce many subsequent defects during the following development phases ("multiplication" of the original defect).

- The later a fault is detected, the more corrections are necessary. Previous phases of the development (requirements definition, design, and programming) may even have to be partly repeated. A reasonable, typical assumption is: with every test level, the correction costs for a fault double with respect to the previous level. Investigations on this subject can be found in [URL: NIST Report]. If the customer has already installed the software product, there is added the risk of direct and indirect defect costs. In the case of safety critical software (control of technical installations, vehicles, aircraft, medical devices, etc.), the potential consequences and costs can be disastrous.

6.3.2   Costs of Testing

The most important action to reduce or limit risk is to plan verification and test activities. But, the factors that influence costs[56] of such testing activities are manifold, and in practice it is very hard to quantify them. The following list shows the most important factors that a test manager should take into account when estimating the costs of testing:

- **Maturity** of the development process
  - Stability of the organization
  - Developer's error rate
  - Frequency of changes in the software
  - Time pressure from unrealistic plans
  - Validity, level of detail, and consistency of plans
  - Maturity of the test process, and the discipline in configuration, change, and incident management

- **Quality and testability of the software**
  - Number, severity, and distribution of defects in the system being tested
  - Quality, expressiveness, and relevance of the documentation and other information used as test basis
  - Size and type of the software and its system environment

---

56.   A detailed discussion can also be found in [Pol 98] and [Pol 02].

- Complexity of the problem domain and of the software (e.g., cyclomatic number, see section 4.2.5)

■ **Test infrastructure**
  - Availability of testing tools
  - Availability of test platforms, test environment, and infrastructure
  - Availability of and experience with testing processes, standards, and procedures

■ **Qualification of employees**
  - Testing experience and knowledge of the testers
  - Test tool and test environment experience of the testers
  - Application (test object) experience and knowledge of the testers
  - Collaboration of tester-developer-management-customer

■ **Quality requirements**
  - Intended test coverage
  - Intended reliability or maximum number of remaining defects after testing
  - Requirements for security and safety
  - Requirements for test documentation

■ **Test strategy**
  - The testing objectives (themselves driven by quality requirements) and means to achieve them, such as number and content of test levels (component, integration, system test …)
  - Selection of the test techniques (black box or white box)
  - Schedule of the tests (start and execution of the test work in the project or in the software life cycle)

The test manager can directly influence only a few of these factors. The manager's perspective looks like this:

The test manager's influence

■ **Maturity** of the software development process: This is an item that cannot be influenced in the short run; it must be accepted as is. Influence in this area can only be exercised in the long run, through a process improvement program.

■ **Testability** of the software: This strongly depends on the maturity of the development process. A well-structured process with the corresponding reviews leads to better-structured software that is easier to test. That is why it can only be influenced in the long run through a process improvement program.

- **Test infrastructure**: This usually exists from before, but if planned for, can be improved during the course of the project. Thus, there is some potential for saving time and cost.
- **Qualification of employees:** This can be partly influenced in the short-run by the choice of test personnel, and can be improved over time with training and coaching.
- **Quality requirements**: These are given by the customer and other stakeholders, and can be partly influenced by priority setting.
- **Test approach and strategy**: This is the only aspect the test manager can influence and control in the short term, because it can be chosen freely.

6.3.3   Test Effort Estimation

Before defining a schedule and assigning resources, the testing effort and the amount of resources needed must be estimated. For small projects this estimation can be done in one step. For larger projects separate estimations per test level and per test cycle might be necessary.

In general, two approaches for estimation of test effort are possible[57]:

- Listing all testing tasks, then letting either the task owner or experts who have estimation experience estimate each task.
- Estimating the testing effort based on effort data of former or similar projects, or based on typical values (e.g., average number of test cases run per hour).

General test effort estimation approaches

The effort per testing task depends on the factors described in the above section on testing costs. Most of these factors influence each other and it is nearly impossible to analyze them completely. Even if no testing task is overlooked, task driven test effort estimation tends to underestimate the testing effort. Estimating based on effort data of similar projects or typical values usually leads to better results.

If no data are at hand, a commonly used rule of thumb can be helpful: testing tasks (including all test levels) in typical business application development takes about 50 % of the overall project resources.

Rule of thumb

---

57.   For more information and articles about test estimation see [URL: RBS].

6.4   Definition of Test Strategy

A test strategy defines the project's testing objectives and the means to achieve them. The test strategy therefore determines testing effort and costs. Selecting an appropriate test strategy is one of the most important planning task decisions the test manager has. The goal is to choose a test approach that optimizes the relation between costs of testing and costs of defects.

Cost-benefit relation   The test costs should, of course, be less than the costs that would be caused by defects and deficiencies in the final product. But, very few software development organizations possess or bother to collect data material that makes it possible to quantify the relation between costs and benefits. This often leads to intuitive, rather than rational decisions about how much testing is enough.

6.4.1   Preventative vs. Reactive Approach

The point in time at which testers become involved has a high influence on the strategy. We can distinguish two typical situations:

- **Preventive approaches** are those in which testers are involved from the beginning: test planning and design start as early as possible. The test manager can really optimize testing and reduce testing costs. The use of the general V-model (see figure 3-1), with emphasis on design reviews, will contribute a lot to prevent defects. Early test specification and preparation, as well as application of reviews and static analysis, contribute to early defect finding, and thus lead to reduced defect density during test execution. Especially, in safety critical software, a preventive approach may be mandatory.
- **Reactive approaches** are those in which testers are involved (too) late and a preventive approach cannot be chosen: test planning and design starts after the software or system has already been produced. Nevertheless, the test manager must react appropriately. One very successful strategy in such a situation is called "exploratory testing". This is a heuristic approach in which the tester "explores" the test object and the test design, with execution and evaluation occurring nearly concurrently (see also section 5.3).

Preventative approaches should be chosen whenever possible. The analysis of the costs clearly shows:

When should testing be started?

- The testing process should start as early as possible in the project.
- Testing should continuously accompany all phases of the project.

In project VSR, test planning and test documentation started immediately after the approval of the requirements document. For each requirement, at least one test case was designed. The draft test specification created using this approach was subjected to a review. Customer representatives, the development staff, and the later system test staff were involved in this review. The result was that many requirements were identified as "unclear" or "incomplete". Additionally, staff found wrong or insufficient test cases.

Example:
VSR test planning

Therefore, simply by preparing reasonable tests and discussing them with the developers and stakeholders helped to find many problems long before the first test was actually run.

6.4.2   Analytical vs. Heuristic Approach

During test planning and test design the test manager may use different sources of information. Two extreme approaches are possible:

- **Analytical approach:** Test planning is founded on data and (mathematical) analysis of these data. The criteria discussed in section 6.3 will be quantified (at least partially) and their correlation will be modeled. Amount and intensity of testing are then chosen such that individual or multiple parameters (costs, time, coverage, etc.) are optimized.
- **Heuristic approach:** Test planning is founded on experience of experts (from inside or outside the project) and/or on rules of thumb. Reasons might be that no data are available, mathematical modeling is too complicated, or because know-how is missing.

The approaches used in practice are often between these extremes and use (to different degrees) both analytical and heuristic elements:

- **Model-based testing** uses abstract functional models of the software under test for test case design to find test exit criteria, and to measure test coverage (against the model).
- **Statistical or stochastic (model-based) testing** uses statistical models about fault distribution in the test object, failure rates during use of the software (such as reliability growth models), or statistical distribution

of use cases (such as operational profiles); based on these distribution data the test effort is allocated.

- **Risk-based testing** uses information on project and product risks and directs testing to areas of greatest risk (see section 6.4.3).
- **Process- or standard-compliant approaches** use rules, recommendations, and standards[58] (e.g., the V-model or IEEE 829) as a "cookbook".
- **Reuse-oriented approaches** reuse existing test environments and test material. The goal is to set up testing quickly by maximal reuse.
- **Checklist-based (methodical) approaches** use failure and defect lists from earlier test cycles[59], lists of potential defects or risks[60], or prioritized quality criteria and other less formal methods.
- **Expert-oriented approaches** use the expertise and "gut feeling" of involved experts (for the used technology or the application domain).

The above-mentioned approaches are seldom used stand-alone. Generally, the test manager uses a combination of several approaches to develop the testing strategy.

6.4.3   Testing and Risk

When looking for criteria to select and prioritize testing objectives, test methods, and test cases, one of the best criteria is "risk".

*Risk = damage * probability*

Risk is defined as the loss or damage due to failure and the probability (or frequency) of failure. Damage comprises any consequences or loss due to failure (see section 6.3.1). The probability of occurrence of a product failure depends on the way the software product is used. The software's operational profile must be considered here. Detailed estimation of risks is therefore difficult[61]. Risk factors to be considered may arise from the project, as well as from the product to be delivered.

Project risks

Project risks are the risks that threaten the project's capability to deliver the product, such as:

---

58. Such patterns and standards themselves include best practices and heuristics.
59. Where many faults were found, there are often more. Faults often cling together and are a symptom of more faults. Extra test cases should be run through such defect-prone areas during the next test cycles.
60. A standard method here is "Failure Mode and Effects Analysis" (FMEA) [URL: FMEA].
61. A spreadsheet-based method for estimating risks or risk classes can be found at [URL: Schaefer].

- Supplier-side risks are, for example, the risk that a subcontractor fails to deliver. Project delays or even legal action may result from these risks.
- Often underestimated are the resources that are necessary (total or partial lack of personnel with the necessary skills), problems of human interaction (e.g., if testers or test results do not get adequate attention), or internal political struggling (i.e., lack of cooperation between different departments).
- Technical problems are a further project risk. Wrong, incomplete, or infeasible requirements may easily lead to a total collapse of the entire project. If new technologies, tools, programming languages, or methods are employed without sufficient experience, the expected results – getting better results faster – can easily turn into the opposite. Another technical project risk is intermediate results (design documents, program code, or test cases) of too low quality that have not been detected and corrected.

Product risks are risks resulting from problems with the delivered product, for example:

Product risks

- The delivered product has inadequate functional quality or is nonfunctional. The product is not fit for its intended use and is thus unusable.
- The use of the product causes harm to equipment or even endangers human life.

The [IEEE 730] and [IEEE 829] standards for quality assurance and test plans demand systematic risk management. This comprises:

Risk management

- Assessing (and reassessing on a regular basis) what can go wrong (risks)
- Prioritizing identified risks
- Implementing actions to mitigate or fight those risks

An important risk mitigation activity is testing; testing provides information about existing problems and the success or failure of problem correction. Testing decreases uncertainty about risks, helps to estimate risks, and identifies new risks.

Risk-based testing helps to minimize and fight product risks from the beginning of the project. Risk-based testing uses information about identified risks for planning, specification, preparation, and execution of the

Risk-based Testing

tests. All major elements of the test strategy are determined on the basis of risk:

- The test techniques to be employed
- The extent of testing
- The priority of test cases

Even other risk minimizing measures, such as training for inexperienced software developers, are considered as alternatives or supplements.

Risk-based test prioritization   Risk based prioritization of the tests ensures that risky product parts are tested more intensively and earlier than parts with lower risk. Severe problems (causing much corrective work or serious delays) are found as early as possible. Opposed to this, distributing scarce test resources equally throughout all test objects does not make much sense, as this approach will test critical and uncritical product parts with the same intensity. Critical parts are then not adequately tested and test resources are wasted on uncritical parts.

6.5   Test Activity Management

Test manager tasks   Every cycle through the test process (section 2.2, figure 2-4) commonly generates change requests or fault correction requests to the developers. If faults are corrected or changes are implemented, a new version of the software emerges, and it must be tested again. Thus, in every test level the test process is executed repeatedly or cyclically. The test manager is responsible for initiating, supervising, and controlling these test cycles. Depending on the project size, a separate test manager might be responsible for each test level.

6.5.1   Test Cycle Planning

Section 6.2 showed the initial test planning (test strategy and overall schedule). It should be drawn up as early as possible in the project and documented in a test plan.

Detailed planning   This general planning must be supplemented by detailed planning for
for each test cycle   each upcoming concrete test cycle. At regular intervals, it must then be adapted to the current project situation, considering the following aspects:

- **Development status**: Compared to the original plans, the software actually available at the beginning of a test cycle may have restricted or altered functionality. This may require adaptation of test specifications or test cases.

■ **Test results**: Problems revealed by previous test cycles may necessitate a change in test priorities. Corrected faults require additional retests, which also need to be planned; additional tests may also be needed when problems cannot be completely reproduced and analyzed.

■ **Resources**: Planning the current test cycle must be consistent with the current project plan; consequences of current personnel and holiday planning, current availability of the test environment and of special test tools, etc. should be considered.

Taking these items into consideration, the test manager estimates effort and time requirements for the test activities, and defines in detail what test cases should be performed at what time by which tester, and in which order. The result of this detailed planning is the (regression) test plan for the upcoming test cycle.

Planning test effort

6.5.2   Test Cycle Monitoring

To measure and monitor the results of the ongoing tests, objective →test metrics should be used. They are defined in the test strategy. Only reliable, regular, and simply measurable[62] metrics should be used. The following approaches can be distinguished:

■ **Fault-based and failure-based metrics:** Number of encountered faults respectively generated →incident reports (per test object) in the particular release. This should also include the problem class and status, and, if possible, a relation to the size of the test object (lines of code), test duration, or other measures (section 6.6).

■ **Test case based metrics:** Number of test cases specified or planned, number of test cases still →blocked (e.g., because of a fault not eliminated), number of test cases run (successful and unsuccessful).

■ **Test object based metrics**: Coverage of code, dialogues, possible installation variants, platforms, etc.

■ **Cost based metrics**: Already incurred test cost, cost of the next test cycle in relation to expected benefit (prevented failure cost or reduced project risk or product risk).

Metrics for monitoring the test process

---

62. This is the case when the applied test tools yield such data.

Test status report   The test manager lists the respective current measurement results in their reports. After each test cycle a test status report is written, specifying the following information about the status of the test activities:

- Test object(s), test level, test cycle date from … to …
- Test progress: tests planned/run/blocked
- Incident status: new/open/corrected
- Risks: new/changed/known
- Outlook: planning of the next test cycle
- Assessment: (subjective) assessment of the test object with respect to its maturity, possibility for release, or the current degree of trust in the test object.

Test exit criteria   A template for such a report can be found in [IEEE 829]. On the one hand, the measured data serve as a means to determine the current situation, and to answer the question, "How far progressed is the test?" On the other hand, the data serve as exit criterion and for answering the question, "Can the test be finished and the product be delivered?" The quality requirements to be met (thus the product's criticality), and the available test resources (time, personnel, test tools), determine which criteria are appropriate for determining the end of the test. These test completion criteria are also documented in the test strategy or test plan. For every test completion criterion chosen it should be possible to calculate its value from the continuously collected test metrics.

Example:
Test completion criteria for
the VSR-System test

The test cases in the VSR project are divided into three priority levels:

Priority	Meaning
1	Test case **must** be executed
2	Test case **should** be executed
3	Test case **may** be executed

Based on this prioritization, the following test case based completion criteria for the VSR-System test were decided upon:

- All test cases with priority 1 have been executed successfully
- At least 60% of the test cases with priority 2 have been run

Product release   If the defined test exit criteria are met, project management (receiving advice from the test manager) decides whether the corresponding test object should be released and delivered. For component and integration testing, "delivery" means passing the test object onto the next test level. The system test precedes the release of the software for delivery to the customer. Finally, the customer's acceptance test releases the system for operation in the actual application environment.

Release does not mean "bug free". The product will surely contain some undiscovered faults, as well as some known ones which were rated as "not preventing release" and were therefore not corrected. The latter faults are recorded in the →incident database and will be corrected later, in the course of software maintenance (section 3.6.1).

6.5.3 Test Cycle Control

If testing is delayed with respect to the project and test planning, the test manager must take suitable countermeasures. This is called test (cycle) control. These actions may relate to the test or any other development activity.

React on deviations from the plan

It may be necessary to request and deploy additional test resources (personnel, workstations, equipment, and tools) in order to make up for the delay and catch up on the schedule in the remaining cycles.

If additional resources are not available, the test plan itself must be adapted. Test cases with low priority will be omitted. If test cases are planned in several variants, a further option is to only run them in a single variant and omit all further variants. (e.g., tests are performed on one operating system instead of several). Although these adjustments lead to omission of some interesting tests, the available resources at least can ensure the execution of the high priority test cases.

Depending on the severity of the faults and problems found, the test duration may be extended. This happens because additional test cycles become necessary, as the corrected software must be retested after each correction cycle (section 3.7.4). This could mean that the product release must be postponed.

It is important that the test manager documents and communicates every change in the plans, because the change in the test plan may increase the release risk. The test manager is responsible for communicating this risk openly and clearly, whenever necessary, to the people responsible for the project.

Changes to test plan must be communicated clearly

6.6   Incident Management

To ensure reliable and fast elimination of failures detected by the various test levels, a well-functioning procedure for communication and administration of those incident reports is indispensable. Incident management starts during test execution, or upon test run completion by evaluating the test log.

6.6.1   Test Log

Test log analysis

After each test run, or at the latest upon completion of a test cycle, all test logs are evaluated. Actual results are compared to the expected results. Each significant, unexpected event that occurred during testing could be an indication of a test object's malfunctioning. Corresponding passages in the test log are analyzed. The testers ascertain whether a deviation from the predicted outcome really has occurred, or whether an incorrectly designed test case, a faulty test automation, or an erroneous test execution caused the deviation (testers, too, can make mistakes).

Documenting incidents

If the problem[63] was caused by the test object, an incident report is initiated. This is done for every unexpected behavior or observed deviation from the predicted outcome documented in the test log. Possibly, an observation may be a recurrence of an observation recorded earlier. In this case, it should be examined whether the second observation yields additional information, which may make it possible to narrow down the search for the cause of the problem. Otherwise, to prevent incident record duplication, a second recording of the same incident should not take place.

Cause-analysis is developers' task

However, the testers do not have to investigate the cause of a recorded incident. This *debugging* is the developers' responsibility.

6.6.2   Incident Reporting

In general, a central database should be established for each project, in which all incidents[64] and failures discovered during testing (and possibly

---

63. Should the problem be caused by the tester, creating an incident report may of course also be sensible; for example if the problem calls for further analyses. In this case, the incident will be reported to the tester and not to the developers.
64. The ISTQB syllabus uses the term "incident". IEEE Standard 1044 uses the term "anomaly". In industry, the term "problem" or "issue" is often used.

during operation) are registered and administered. Personnel involved in development, as well as customers and users[65] can report incidents.

These reports can refer to problems in the tested (parts of) programs, as well as to errors or faults in specifications, user manuals, or other documents.

Incident reporting is also referred to as problem, anomaly, or failure reporting. But, incident reporting sounds less like an "accusation". All open problems are reported, however, not every reported incident turns out to be a developer's error.

Incident reporting is not a one-way-street, as every developer can comment on reports, for example, by requesting comments or clarification from a tester, or by rejecting an unjustified report. Should a developer undertake corrections on a test object, these corrections will also be documented in the incident repository. This enables the responsible tester to understand this correction's implications in order to retest it in the following test cycle.

At any point in time, the incident repository enables the test manager and the project manager to get an up-to-date and complete picture about the number and status of problems, and on the progress of corrections. For this purpose, the repository should offer appropriate reporting and analysis tools.

One of the first steps when introducing a systematic test process for a project should be implementing disciplined incident management. An efficient incident database, giving role related access to all staff involved in the project, is essential.

Hint: Use an incident database

To allow for smooth communication and to enable statistical analysis of the incident reports, every report shall be derived from a report template valid for the whole project. This template and reporting structure must be defined, for example, in the test strategy. In addition to the actual problem description, the incident report typically contains further information identifying the tested software, test environment, name of the tester, defects class and prioritization, as well as other information important for reproducing and localizing the fault. Table 6-1 shows an example for an incident report template:

Standardized reporting Format

---

65. To simplify the following explanations, we assume that only developers and testers communicate using the problem report repository.

Table 6–1

Incident report template

	Attribute	Meaning
Identification	Id / Number	Unique identifier/number for each report
	Test object	Identifier or name of the test object
	Version	Identification of the exact version of the test object
	Platform	Identification of the HW/SW platform or the test environment where the problem occurs
	Reporting person	Identification of the reporting tester (possibly with test level)
	Responsible developer	Name of the developer or the team responsible for the test object
	Reporting date	Date and possibly time when the problem was observed
Classification	Status	The current state (and complete history) of processing for the report (section 6.6.4)
	Severity	Classification of the severity of the problem (section 6.6.3)
	Priority	Classification of the priority of correction (section 6.6.3)
	Requirement	Pointer to the (customer-) requirements which are not fulfilled due to the problem
	Problem source	The project phase, where the defect was introduced (analysis, design, programming); useful for planning process improvement measures
Problem description	Test case	Description of the test case (name, number) or the steps necessary to reproduce the problem
	Problem description	Description of the problem or failure occurred; expected vs. actual observed results or behavior
	Comments	List of comments on the report from developers and other staff involved
	Defect correction	Description of the changes made to correct the defect
	References	Reference to other related reports

A similar, slightly less complex structure can be found in [IEEE 829]. Many attributes can be more sophisticated and split up as shown in [IEEE 1044]. For example, if the incident repository is used in acceptance testing or product support, additional customer data must be collected. The test manager has to develop a template or scheme suitable for the particular project.

Document all information relevant to reproduction and correction

In doing so, it is important to collect all information necessary for reproducing and localizing a potential fault, as well as information enabling analysis of product quality and correction progress. Irrespective of the scheme agreed upon, the following rule must be observed: Each report must be written in such a way that the responsible developer will understand the problem and can identify its cause with minimal effort. Localizing the cause of problems and repairing faults is extra work for developers who normally have enough to do from previous assignments. Thus, the tester has the task of "selling" the incident report to the developers. In this situation, it is very tempting for developers to ignore or postpone analysis and repair of problems, which are unclear or difficult to understand.

6.6.3 Incident Classification

An important criterion when judging a reported problem is its "severity", meaning the degree of impact on the operation of the system (see [IEEE 610.12]). Of course, it makes a major difference whether one hundred uncorrected problems in the incident database represent system breakdowns or just cosmetic mistakes in some screen layouts. A severity classification is needed and could, for example, look like table 6-2:

Class	Description
1 – FATAL	System breakdown, possibly with loss of data. The test object cannot be released in this form.
2 – VERY SERIOUS	Essential malfunctioning; requirements not adhered to or incorrectly implemented; substantial impairment to many stakeholders. The test object can only be used with severe restrictions (difficult or expensive workaround).
3 – SERIOUS	Functional deviation or restriction ("normal" failure); requirement incorrectly or only partially implemented; substantial impairment to some stakeholders. The test object can be used with restrictions.
4 – MODERATE	Minor deviation; modest impairment to few stakeholders. System can be used without restrictions.
5 – MILD	Mild impairment to few stakeholders; system can be used without restrictions. For example, spelling errors or wrong screen layout.

Table 6–2
Failure severity

The severity of a problem should be assigned from the point of view of all stakeholders, especially that of the user or future user of the test object. The above classification does not indicate how quickly the particular problem should be corrected. Priority of handling the problem is a different category and should not be blended with severity! When determining priority of corrections, additional requirements defined by product or project management (for example correction complexity, risk in use), as well as requirements with respect to further test execution (blocked tests), are to be taken into account. Therefore, the question of how quickly a fault should be corrected is answered by an additional attribute, "fault priority" (or rather "correction priority"). Table 6-3 presents a possible classification:

Table 6–3

Fault priority

Priority	Description
1 – IMMEDIATE	The user's business or working process is blocked or the running tests cannot be continued. The problem requires immediate, or if necessary, provisional repair (→"patch").
2 – NEXT RELEASE	The correction will be implemented in the next regular product release or with the delivery of the next (internal) test object version.
3 – ON OCCASION	The correction will take place, when the affected system parts are due for a revision anyway.
4 – OPEN	Correction planning has not taken place yet.

Incident analysis for monitoring the test process

Analyzing the severity and priority of reported incidents allow the test manager to make statements regarding product robustness or deliverability. Apart from test status determination and clarification of questions such as, "How many faults were found?", "How many of these are corrected?", "How many are still to be corrected?", trend analyses are important. This means making predictions based on the analysis of the trend of incoming incident reports over the course of time. In this context, the most important question is, "Does the volume of product problems still increase or does the situation seem to improve?"

Incident analysis for improving the test process

Data from incident reports can also be used to improve the test process; e.g., a comparison of data from several test objects can demonstrate which test objects show an especially small number of faults. This could mean that certain test cases have not yet been defined or executed, or, on the other hand, that the program has been implemented with special care and skill.

6.6.4 Incident Status

Test management has the responsibility to not only make sure that incidents are collected and documented properly, but is also responsible (in cooperation with project management) for enabling and supporting rapid fault correction and delivery of improved versions of the test object. This necessitates continuous monitoring of the defect analysis and correction process in all its phases. For this purpose the incident status is used. Every incident report (see table 6-1) passes a series of predefined states, covering all steps from original reporting to successful defect resolution. Table 6-4 shows an example for an incident status scheme.

Status (set by)	Description
New (Tester)	A new report was written. The person reporting has included a sensible description and classification.
Open (Test manager)	The test manager regularly checks the new reports on comprehensibility and complete description of all necessary attributes. If necessary, attributes will be adjusted to ensure a project-wide uniform assessment. Duplicates or obviously useless reports are adjusted or rejected. The report is assigned to a responsible developer and its status is set to "Open".
Rejected (Test manager)	The report is deemed unjustified and rejected (no fault in the test object, request for change not taken into account).
Analysis (Developer)	As soon as the responsible developer starts processing this report, the status is set to "Analysis". The result of the analysis (cause, possible remedies, estimated correction effort, etc.) will be documented in comments.
Observation (Developer)	The incident described can neither be reconstructed nor be eliminated. The report remains outstanding until further information/insights are available.
Correction (Project manager)	Based on the analysis, the project manager decides correction should take place and therefore sets the status to "Correction". The responsible developer performs the corrections and documents the kind of corrections done using comments.
Test (Developer)	As soon as the responsible developer has corrected the problem from his point of view, the report is set to "Test" status. The new software version containing this correction is identified.
Closed (Tester)	Reports carrying the status "Test" are verified in the next test cycle. For this purpose, at least the test cases, which discovered the problem, are repeated. Should the test confirm that the repair was successful, the tester finishes the report-history by setting the final status "Closed".
Failed (Tester)	Should the repeated test show that the attempt to repair was unsuccessful or insufficient, the status is set to "Failed" and a repeated analysis becomes necessary.

Table 6–4

Incident status scheme

Figure 6-2 demonstrates this procedure:

Figure 6–2
Incident status model

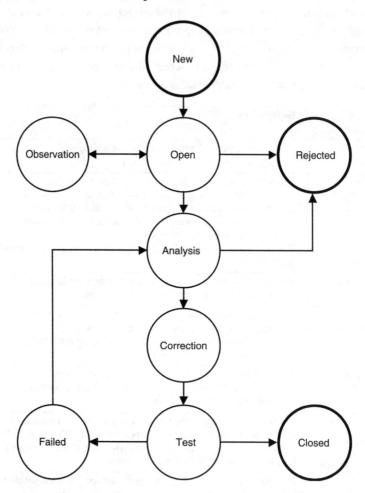

A crucial fact that is often ignored is that the status "Closed" may only be set by the tester, and not by the developer! And this should only happen after the repeated test has proven that the problem described in the problem report does not occur anymore. Should new failures occur as side effects after bug fixing, these failures are to be reported in new incident reports.

The test exit criteria for the VSR-System test shall not only reflect test progress, but also the accomplished product quality. Therefore, the test manager enhances the test exit criteria with metrics as follows:

Example for extended test exit criteria for the VSR-System test

- All faults of severity "1 – FATAL" are "Closed".
- All faults of severity "2 – IMMEDIATE" are "Closed".
- The number of "new" incident reports per test week is stable or falling.

The scheme described above can be applied to many projects. However, the model must be tailored to cover existing or necessary project decision processes. In the above-described basic model, all decisions lie with the single person. In larger scale projects, boards make these decisions because representatives of many stakeholders must be heard. The decision making process becomes more complex.

In many cases, changes to be performed by the developers are not really bug fixes, but functional enhancements. As the distinction between "incident report" and "enhancement request" and the rating as "justified" or "not justified" is often a matter of opinion, an institution accepting or rejecting incident reports and change requests is needed. This institution, called the *change control board*, usually consists of representatives from the following stakeholders: product management, project management, test management, and the customer.

Change control board

6.7   Requirements to Configuration Management

A software system consists of a multitude of individual components which must fit together to ensure the functionality of the system as a whole. In the course of the system's development, new, corrected, or improved versions, or variants of each of these components evolve. As several developers and testers take part in this process simultaneously, it is far from easy to keep an overview of the current related components. If configuration management is not done properly in a project, the following typical symptoms may be observed:

- Developers mutually overwrite each other's modifications in the source code or other documents, as simultaneous access to shared files is not avoided.

Typical symptoms of insufficient configuration management

- Integration activities are impeded:
  - Because it is unclear which code versions of a specific component exist in the development team and which ones are the current versions
  - Because it is unclear which versions of several components belong together and can be integrated to a larger subsystem
  - Because different versions of compilers and other development tools are used
- Problem analysis, fault correction, and regression tests are complicated:
  - Because it is unknown where and why a component's code was changed with respect to a previous version
  - Because it is unknown from which code files a particular integrated subsystem (object code) originates
- Tests and →test evaluation are impeded, because it is unclear:
  - Which test cases belong to which version of a test object
  - Which test cycle of which version of the test object gave which test results

Testing relies on configuration management

Insufficient configuration management leads to a number of possible problems disturbing the development and test process. If, for example, it is unclear during a →test phase whether the test objects being examined are the latest version, the tests rapidly lose their significance. A test process cannot be properly executed without reliable configuration management.

Configuration management requirements

From the perspective of the test, the following requirements should be met:

- **Version management:** This is the cataloging, filing, and retrieval of different versions of a →configuration item (for example version 1.0 and 1.1 of a system). This also includes comments on the reason for the particular change.
- **Configuration identification:** This is the identification and management of all files (configuration objects) in the particular version, which together comprise a subsystem (configuration). The prerequisite for this is version management.
- **Incident status and change status accounting**: This is the documenting of incident reports and change requests and the possibility to reconstruct their application on the configuration objects.
- To check the effectiveness of configuration management, it is useful to organize **configuration audits**. Such an →audit offers the possibility to check whether all software components were documented by the con-

figuration management, whether configurations can be correctly identified, etc.

The software developed in the VSR project is available in different languages (for example English, German, Chinese, and French) and must be compatible with several hardware and software platforms. Several components must be compatible with particular external software versions (e.g., the mainframe's current communication software). Furthermore, data from miscellaneous sources must be imported at regular intervals (e.g., product catalogues, price lists, and contract data) with changing content and format during the system's life cycle. The VSR configuration management must ensure that development and testing always take place with consistent, valid product configurations. Similar requirements exist during system operation at the customer.

Example for configuration management in the VSR project

In order to implement configuration management fulfilling the above-mentioned requirements, differing processes and tools should be chosen depending on project characteristics. A configuration management plan must therefore determine a process tailored to the project situation. A standard for configuration management and respective plans can be found in [IEEE 828].

6.8   Relevant Standards

Today, a multitude of standards exist which set constraints and define the "state-of-the-art" for software development. This is especially true for the area of software quality management and software testing, as the standards quoted in this book prove. One of the tasks for a quality manager or test manager is defining, in this context, which standards, rules, or possibly legal directives are relevant for the product to be tested (product standards) or for the project (project standards), and to ensure these are adhered to. Possible sources are:

- **Company standards**: These are company internal directives, procedure and guidelines (also possibly set by the customer), such as the quality management handbook, a test plan template or programming guidelines.
- **Best practices**: These are not standardized, but professionally developed and widely accepted methods and procedures representing the state-of-the-art in a particular field of application.

▧ **Quality management standards**: These are standards spanning several industrial sectors, specifying minimal process requirements, yet not stating specific requirements for process implementation. A well known example is [ISO 9000], which requires appropriate (intermediate) tests during the production process (also in the special case of the software development process), without indicating when and how these tests are to be performed.

▧ **Standards for particular industrial sectors**: An example is standard [RTC-DO 178B] for airborne software products, defining the minimum extent to which tests must be performed, or documented for a particular product category or application field. Another example is [EN 50128] for railway signaling applications.

▧ **Software test standards**: These are process or documentation standards, defining independently of the product how software tests should be performed or documented. For example the standards [BS 7925-2], [IEEE 829], [IEEE 1028].

The standards that are important and relevant for software testing are covered in this book. The test concept according to [IEEE 829] is described in detail in Appendix A. Following such standards also makes sense, even when compliance is not mandatory. At least when encountering legal disputes, demonstrating that development has been done according to the "state of best industry practice" is helpful. This also includes compliance to standards.

6.9   Summary

Development activities and testing activities should be independently organized. The more clear this separation is, the more effective the testing which can be performed.

▧ Depending on the task to be executed within the test process, staff with role-specific test skills are needed. In addition to professional skills, social competence is required.

▧ The test manager's tasks comprise the initial planning of the tests, as well as further planning, monitoring, and controlling of the different test cycles.

- In the test plan, the test manager describes and explains the test strategy (test objectives, test measures, tools, etc.). The international standard [IEEE 829] provides a checklist for format and content.

- Faults and deficiencies that are not found by the testing and thus remain in the product, can lead to very high costs. The testing strategy has to balance testing costs, available resources, and possible defect costs.

- If lack of test resources occurs, it is important to quickly decide which tests can be left out. Thus, the tests should be prioritized.

- Risk assessment is one of the best criteria for prioritizing. Risk-based testing uses information about identified risks for planning, specification, preparation, and execution of the tests. All major elements of the test strategy are determined on the basis of risk.

- Measurable test exit criteria define when testing can be stopped. Without given test exit criteria, testing might stop randomly.

- Incident management and configuration management, together, form the basis for an efficient test process.

- Incident reports must be collected in a project-wide standardized method and used and updated throughout all stages of the incident analysis and fault resolution process.

- Standards contain specifications and recommendations for professional software testing. Following such standards makes sense, even when compliance is not mandatory.

7 Test Tools

This chapter gives an overview of the miscellaneous test tools supporting a tester executing his tasks. Also, prerequisites for the application of such tools, tool selection, and implementation are discussed.

7.1 Types of Test Tools

A multitude of test tools exists for supporting or automating test activities. Analogous to the term →CASE tools (Computer Aided Software Engineering) the term →CAST tools (Computer Aided Software Testing) is used. Miscellaneous tool categories exist to support the different test process phases and activities. They are classified by the phases or activities they support (section 2.2)[66]. Inside one class of tools there are often specialized versions for specific platforms or application areas (for example performance test tools specialized for web applications). All available test tool categories are rarely applied in a project. However, the available types of tools should be known in order to decide when and where to apply them efficiently in a project. A list of commercial tools can be found at [URL: Tool-List].

CAST tools

Tool list

The functions offered by the different tool classes are described in the following sections.

7.1.1 Tools for Test Management and Control

Test management tools offer mechanisms for easy capturing, cataloging, and administration of test cases and their priorities. They allow status tracking of the test cases, i.e., to document and evaluate if, when, how

Test management

---

66. Especially commercially available tools often support several activities or phases and can then be classified to more than one class of tools mentioned below.

often, and with which result ("passed", "failed") a test case has been executed. Some tools additionally support project management aspects during testing (i.e., resource and schedule planning for the tests).

They help the test manager to plan the tests and to remain informed
about the status of hundreds or thousands of test cases.

Advanced test management tools support requirements-based testing.
For this purpose, they allow the capture of requirements (or to import
them from requirements management tools) and the linking of them with
the test cases needed for validation. Various consistency checks can be
executed, for example, if there is at least one test case for each requirement.
Figure 7-1 shows, using the example of the CarConfigurator test plan, how
this can look:

Figure 7–1

Requirements-based test
planning using TestBench
[URL: TestBench]

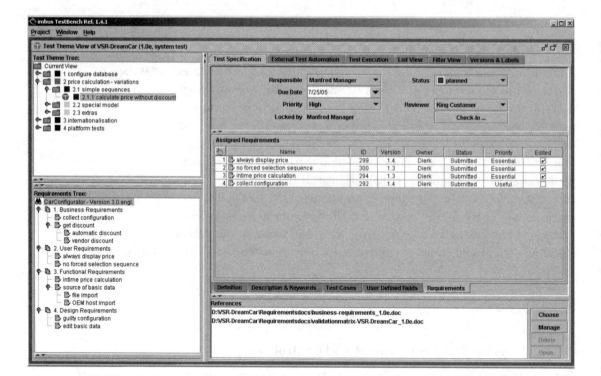

Requirements management

Tools for requirements management store and administer information
about requirements. They allow prioritizing requirements and tracing
their implementation status.

In the narrow sense, they are not test tools, nevertheless, they are of
great help to derive tests from the requirements (see section 3.7.1) and to

plan the tests relative to the implementation status of every requirement. In order to support this, requirements management tools can usually exchange data with test management tools. This allows a direct and complete connection between requirements, test cases, and test results, and assures a traceable validation of every requirement.

A tool for documenting incident reports is practically indispensable to the test manager. As described in section 6.6, →incident management tools (also called problem tracking or defect tracking tools) are used for documentation, administration, prioritization, allocation, and statistical analysis of incident reports. Advanced tools of this class include individually parameterizable incident status models. The complete workflow, from problem detection via bug fixing to regression testing, can be determined and supported. Every project team member will be guided through this workflow according to his role in the team.

Incident management

Configuration management tools (see section 6.7) also are, strictly speaking, not testing tools in the narrow sense. They make it possible to keep track of different versions and builds of the software, as well as different versions of documentation and testware. Using such tools makes it easier, or at least possible, to trace the test results of a test run on a certain test object version.

Configuration management

Integration of test tools, as well as between test tools and other tools, is becoming more and more important. The test management tool is the key for this:

Tool integration

- Requirements are imported from the requirements management tool and used for test planning. The test status of every requirement can be watched and traced in the requirements management tool or the test management tool.
- From the test management tool, test execution tools (for example test robots) are started and supplied with test procedures. The test results are automatically sent back and archived.
- The test management tool is coupled with the incident management tool. Thus, a plan for retest can be generated, i.e., a list of all test cases necessary to verify which defects have been successfully corrected in the latest test object version.
- Through configuration management every code change is connected to the incident or to the change request causing it.

Such a tool chain makes it possible to completely trace the test status from the requirements, through the test cases and test results, to the incident reports and code changes.

Generating test reports and test documentation

Both test management and incident management tools may include extensive analysis and reporting features, including the possibility to generate the complete test documentation (test plan, test specification, test report) from the contained data. The format and contents of such documents can usually be individually adjusted. Thus the documents will be easy to integrate into the existing documentation workflow. The collected data can be evaluated quantitatively in many ways. For example it is very easy to determine how many test cases have been run and how many of them were successful, or how often the tests have found failures of a certain incident class. Such information helps to assess the progress of the testing and to manage the test process.

7.1.2   Tools for Test Specification

In order to make test cases reproducible, the pre- and post-conditions as well as test input data and expected results must be specified.

Test data generators

So-called test (data) generators can support the test designer in generating test data. According to [Fewster 99], several approaches can be distinguished depending on the test basis used for deriving the test data:

- **Database-based test data generators** process database schemas and are able to produce test databases from these schemas. Alternatively, they perform dedicated filtering of database contents and thus produce test data. A similar process is the generation of test data from files in different data formats.
- **Code-based test data generators** produce test data by analyzing the test object's source code. Drawbacks and limitations are that no expected results can be generated (a test oracle is needed for this), and the ability to only consider existing code (as with all white box methods). Faults caused by missing program instructions (code) remain undetected. Using code as a test basis for testing the code itself is, in general, a very poor foundation.
- **Interface-based test data generators** analyze the test object's interface, identify the interface parameter domains, and use equivalence class partitioning and boundary value analysis to derive test data from these domains. Tools are available for different kinds of interfaces, ranging

from programming interfaces (Application Programming Interface, API) to Graphical User Interface (GUI) analysis. The tool is able to identify what data fields are available in a screen (e.g., numeric field, date) and generate test data covering the respective value range (e.g., by applying boundary value analysis). Here, too, the problem is that no expected results can be generated. However, the tools are very well suited for automatic generation of negative tests (see also robustness test), as specific target values are of no importance here.

- **Specification-based test data generators** use a specification to derive test data and appropriate expected results. A precondition is, of course, that the specification is available in a formal notation. For example, a method calling sequence may be given by an UML message sequence chart. The UML model is designed using a CASE tool and is then imported by the test generator. The test generator generates test procedures, which are then passed on to a test execution tool. This approach is called model based testing (MBT).

Such test tools cannot work miracles. Specifying tests is a very challenging task, which requires a comprehensive understanding of the test object, as well as creativity and intuition. A test data generator can apply certain rules (e.g., boundary value analysis) for systematic test generation. However, it cannot judge whether the generated test cases are suitable, important, or irrelevant. The test designer must still perform this creative-analytical task. The corresponding expected result must be determined manually, as well.

Test designer's creativity cannot be replaced

7.1.3 Tools for Static Testing

Static analysis can be executed on source code or on specifications before there are executable programs. Tools for static testing can therefore be helpful to find faults in early phases of the development cycle (i.e., the left branch of the general V-model in figure 3-1). As faults can be detected and fixed soon after being introduced, this decreases costs and development time.

Reviews are structured, manual examinations using the principle that four eyes find more defects than two (see section 4.1). Review support tools help to plan, execute, and evaluate reviews. They store information about planned and executed review meetings, participants, findings and their resolution, and results. Even review aids such as checklists can be included online and maintained. The collected data of many reviews can

Review support tools

be evaluated and compared. This not only helps to better estimate review resources and to plan reviews, but also to uncover typical weaknesses in the development process and prevent them.

Static analysis

Static analyzers provide measures of miscellaneous characteristics of the program code, such as the cyclomatic number and other code metrics (see section 4.2). Such data can be used in order to identify complex, and therefore defect-prone or risky, code sections. Such areas can then be reviewed.

Static analyzers are also used for detecting discrepancies and mistakes in the source code early in the development process. These discrepancies and mistakes are, for example, data flow and control flow anomalies. Analyzers are further used to enforce coding standards or link checkers for finding broken or invalid links in web site contents.

The analyzers will list all "strange" places, and the list of results can grow very long. These tools are, in most cases, configurable, thus making it possible to choose the breadth and depth of analysis. When using the tool for the first time, the warning level should be chosen with a weak setting. Later, a stronger setting can be chosen. It is very important that the setting is chosen according to project specific needs. This is crucial for the acceptance of such tools.

Model checking tools

The source code is not the only document that can be analyzed automatically for certain characteristics. Specifications can also be analyzed if they are written in a formal notation or as a formal model. Analysis tools for this purpose are called "model checkers". They "read" the structure of a model and check the different static characteristics. For example, they can find missing states, missing transitions, or other inconsistencies in the model to be checked. The specification based test generators discussed in section 7.1.2 are often extensions of such static "model checkers".

7.1.4   Tools for Dynamic Test

Tools take the burden of mechanical test tasks

When speaking of test tools in general, we often mean tools for automating test execution, i.e., tools for automating dynamic tests. The tester is thus released from the necessary mechanical tasks for the test execution. The tools supply the test object with test data, log the test object's reactions, and record the test execution. In most cases, the tools must run on the same hardware platform as the test object itself. This, however, can have an influence on the run time behavior (like memory and processor usage) of the test object and influence the test results. This must be remembered when using such tools and evaluating test results. Since such tools need to be connected to the particular test object's test interface, they vary greatly depending on the test level (component, integration, system test) in which they are applied.

A debugger allows the execution of a program, or part of a program line by line, halting the execution at any line of code, and setting and reading program variables. Primarily, debuggers are developers' analysis tools for reproducing program failures and analyzing their causes. Additionally, during testing, debuggers are useful for enforcing certain, special test situations, such as simulating faults, data storage overflow, etc. Faulty conditions like that are usually impossible to create, or can only be created with disproportionately great effort. Debuggers can also serve as test interfaces during component or integration tests.

Debuggers

Test drivers or test harnesses are either commercial products or individually developed tools, offering mechanisms for executing test objects through their programming interface. Alternatively, they can be used with test objects without a user interface that are not directly accessible for a manual test. Test harnesses are mainly required during component and integration testing, or for special tasks during system testing. Generic test drivers or test bed generators are also available. They perform an analysis of the programming interface of the test object and generate a test harness. Hence, such tools are tailored for specific programming languages or development environments. The generated test harnesses comprise the necessary initializations and calling sequences to drive the test object. If necessary, the tool also creates dummies or stubs, as well as functions for documenting target reactions and →test logging. Thus, test harness (generators) significantly reduce the programming effort for the test environment. Some generic solutions (test frameworks) are available on the internet as freeware [URL: xunit].

Test drivers

If performing a system test in its operational environment, or using the final system is not possible or demands a disproportionally great effort (e.g., airplane control robustness test in the airplane itself), simulators can be used. The simulator simulates the actual application environment as comprehensively and realistically as possible.

Simulators

Should the user interface of a software system directly serve as the test interface, so-called →test robots can be used. These tools have traditionally been called →*capture/replay* or →*capture/playback tools*, which almost completely explains their way of functioning. A test robot works in a similar way as a video recorder: The tool logs all manual inputs by the tester

Test robots

(keyboard inputs and mouse clicks). These inputs are then saved as a test script. This test script can be repeated automatically by "playing it back". This principle sounds very tempting and easy, however, in practice, there are traps.

In capture mode the capture/playback tool logs keyboard inputs and mouse clicks. Not only the x/y coordinates of the mouse clicks are recorded, but also the events (e.g., pressButton("Start")) triggered in the Graphical User Interface (GUI), as well as the object's attributes (object name, color, text, position, etc.) which are necessary to recognize the selected object.

In order to determine if the program under test is performing correctly, the tester can include checkpoints, i.e., comparisons between expected and actual results (either during test recording or during script editing).

Thus, layout properties of user interface controls (e.g., color, position, and button size) can be verified, as well as functional properties of the test object (value of a screen field, contents of an alert box, output values and texts, etc.).

The captured test scripts can be replayed and therefore, in principle, be repeated as often as desired. Should a discrepancy in values occur when reaching a checkpoint, "the test fails". The test robot then writes an appropriate notice in the test log file. Because of their capability to perform automated comparisons of actual and expected values, test robot tools are extraordinarily well suited for regression test automation.

However, one problem exists: Should, in the course of program correction or program extension, the test object's GUI be changed between two test runs, it is possible that the original script will not "suit" the new GUI layout. Under these circumstances the script, no longer being synchronized to the application, may come to a halt and abort the automated test run. Test robot tools offer a certain robustness with respect to such GUI layout changes, as they recognize the object itself and its properties, instead of just x/y positions on the screen. This is why, for example, during replay of the test script, buttons will be recognized again, even if their position has moved.

Test scripts are usually written in scripting languages. These scripting languages are similar to common programming languages (BASIC-, C- or Java-like) and offer their well-known general language properties (decisions, loops, procedure calls, etc.). With these properties it is possible to implement even complex test runs or to edit and enhance captured scripts. In practice, this editing of captured scripts is nearly always necessary, as capturing usually does not deliver scripts with full regression test capability. The following example illustrates this:

In testing the VSR-subsystem for contract documentation, it shall be examined whether sales contracts are properly filed and retrieved. For test automation purposes, the tester may record the following interaction-sequence:

```
Call screen "contract data';
Enter data for customer "Miller",
Set checkpoint;
Store "Miller" contract in contract database;
Clear screen "contract data";
Read "Miller" contract back from contract database;
Compare checkpoint with screen contents;
```

A successful check indicates that the contract read from the database corresponds to the contract previously filed, which leads to the conclusion that the system correctly files contracts.

But, when replaying this script, the tester is surprised to find that the script has halted unexpectedly. What happened?

When the script is played a second time, upon trying to store the "Miller" contract the test object reacts in a different way than during the first run. The "Miller" contract already exists in the contract database, and the test object ends the attempt to file the contract for the second time by reporting:

Problem:
Regression test capability

```
"Contract already exists.
Overwrite the contract Y/N ?"
```

The test object now expects a keystroke. As this keystroke is missing in the captured test script, the automated test halts.

The two test runs have different preconditions. As the captured script relies on a certain precondition ("Miller" contract not in the database), the test case is not regression test capable. This problem can be corrected by programming a case decision or by deleting the contract from the database as the final "cleaning-up action" of the test case.

As seen in the example, it is crucial to edit the scripts, i.e., to do programming. This requires programmer know-how. When comprehensive and long-lived automation is required, a well-founded test architecture must be chosen, i.e., the test scripts must be modularized.

A good structure for the test scripts is helpful to minimize the expense for creating and maintaining automated tests. A good structure also supports dividing workload between test automators (knowing the test tool) and testers (knowing the application/ business domain).

Excursion: Test
automation architectures

Often, a test procedure (test script) will be repeated many times with different data. In the previous example, not only the contract of Mr. "Miller" was loaded and executed, but the contracts of many other customers were loaded, as well.

Data driven testing

An obvious step to structure the test script and minimize the effort is to separate test data and test procedure. Usually the test data are exported into a table or spreadsheet file. Naturally, expected results must also be stored. The test script reads a test data line, executes the test procedure with the test data, and repeats this process with the next test data line. If additional test data are necessary, they are just added to the test data table without changing the script. Even testers without programmer know-how can extend these tests and maintain them to a certain degree. This approach is called *data driven testing*.

Command or keyword driven testing

In extensive test automation projects an enhanced requirement is reusing test procedures. For example, if contract handling should be tested, not only for buying new cars, but also for buying used cars, it would be useful to run the script from the example without changes for both areas. Thus, the test steps are encapsulated in a procedure named, for example, check_contract(customer). The procedure can then be called via its name and reused anywhere.

With correct granularity and correspondingly well chosen test procedure names, it is possible to achieve a situation where every execution sequence available for the system user is mapped to such a procedure or command. In order to make it possible to use such procedures without programmer know-how, the architecture is implemented to make the procedures callable through spreadsheet tables. The (business) tester will then (analogous to the data driven test) only work with commands or keywords and test data in tables. Specialized test automation programmers have to implement each of the commands. This approach is called command-, keyword- or action-word driven testing.

The spreadsheet-based approach is only partly scalable. With large lists of keywords and complex test runs, the tables become incomprehensible. Dependencies between commands, and between commands and their parameters, are difficult to trace. The effort to maintain the tables grows disproportionally as the tables grow.

Interaction method

The newest generation of test tools (for example [URL: TestBench]) implements an object-oriented management of test modules in a database. Test modules (so called *interactions*) can be retrieved from the database by dragging and dropping them into new test sequences. The necessary test data (even complex data structures) are then automatically included. If any module is changed, every area using this module is easy to find and can be selected. This considerably reduces the test maintenance effort. Even very large repositories can be used efficiently and without losing overview.

Comparators

→Comparators (another tool class) are used in order to identify differences between expected and actual results. Comparators typically function with standard file and database formats, detecting differences between data files containing expected and actual data. Test robots usually include integrated comparator functions, operating with terminal contents, GUI objects, or screen content copies. These tools usually offer filtering mechanisms that skip data or data fields that are irrelevant to the comparison. For example, this is necessary when date/time information is contained in the test object's file or screen output. As this information differs from test run to test run, the comparator would wrongly interpret this change as a difference between expected and actual outcome.

During test execution, dynamic analysis tools acquire additional
information on the internal state of the software being tested (e.g., information on allocation, usage, and release of memory). Thus, memory leaks,
pointer allocation, or pointer arithmetic problems can be detected.

Dynamic analysis

Coverage analyzers provide structural test coverage values that are
measured during test execution (see section 5.2). For this purpose an
instrumentation component of the analysis tool inserts measurement code
into the test object prior to test execution (instrumentation). If such measurement code is executed during a test run, the corresponding program
fragment is logged as "covered". After test execution, the coverage log is
analyzed and a coverage report is created. Most tools provide just simple
coverage metrics, such as statement coverage and branch coverage (sections 5.2.1 and 5.2.2).

Coverage analysis

7.1.5   Tools for Nonfunctional Tests

Even for nonfunctional tests there is tool support, especially for load and
performance tests.

Load test tools generate a synthetic load (i.e., parallel database que-
ries, user transactions, or network traffic). They are used for executing
volume-, stress-, or performance tests. Tools for performance tests measure and log the response time behavior, depending on the load input of
the system being tested. In order to successfully use such tools and evaluate the test results, experience with performance tests is crucial.

*Tools for load and
performance test*

The necessary "measurement elements" are called "monitors".

Monitors

Load/performance tests are necessary when a software system has to execute a
large number of parallel requests or transactions within a certain maximum response
time. Real-time systems and, normally, client/server systems as well as web-based
applications must fulfill such requirements. By doing performance tests, the increase
in response time correlated to increasing load (for example increasing number of
users) can be measured, as well as the system's maximum capacity, when the
increased load leads to unacceptable latency due to overload. Used as an analysis
resource, performance test tools generally supply the tester with extensive charts,
reports, and diagrams representing the system's response time and transaction
behavior relative to the load applied, as well as information on performance bottlenecks. Should the performance test indicate that overload already occurs under everyday load-conditions, system-tuning measures (hardware extension, optimization of
performance-critical software components) must be utilized.

Excursion

Checking security   Tools for checking access and data security examine a system for the possibility that unauthorized persons can break into the system. Even virus scanners and firewalls can be seen as part of this tool category, as the protocols generated by such tools deliver hints about security deficiencies.

7.2   Selection and Introduction of Test Tools

Some elementary tools (e.g., comparators, coverage analyzers, primitive test drivers) are already available in several operating system environments (e.g., UNIX) as a standard feature. In these cases, the tester can get the necessary tool support using simple, available means. Naturally, the capabilities of such standard tools are limited, so it is sometimes necessary to buy more advanced test tools available on the market.

As described above, special tools are commercially available for each phase in the test process, supporting the tester in executing the phase-specific tasks or performing these tasks themselves. The tools range from test planning and test specification tools, supporting the tester when they are creating the test development process, to test drivers and test robots, which are able to automate the mechanical test execution tasks.

When contemplating the acquisition of test tools, automation tools for test execution should not be the only choice taken into consideration.

Automating chaos   The realm in which tool support may be advantageous strongly
just gives faster chaos   depends on the respective project environment and the maturity level of the development and test process. In a chaotic project environment, where "programming on the fly" is common practice, documentation does not exist or is inconsistent, and tests are performed in an unstructured manner (if at all), automating test execution is not a very good idea. A tool can never replace a nonexistent process or compensate for a sloppy procedure. "It is far better to improve the effectiveness of testing first than to improve the efficiency of poor testing. Automating chaos just gives faster chaos" [Fewster 99, p. 11].

In those situations, testing must first be organized. This means, initially, that a systematic test process must be defined, introduced, and adhered to. Next, thought can be given to the question; Which process steps tools can be used? What can be done to enhance the productivity or quality of each process step? When introducing testing tools, it is recommended to adhere to the following order of introduction:

Order of tool introduction

1. Incident management
2. Configuration management
3. Test planning
4. Test execution
5. Test specification

Some time is necessary to learn a new tool and to establish its use, and this must be taken into account. Given the learning curve, instead of the desired productivity increase, productivity may even decline for some amount of time. It is, therefore, risky to introduce a new tool during "hot" project phases, hoping to solve bottlenecks then and there by introducing automation.

Take into account the learning curve

7.2.1   Cost Effectiveness of Tool Introduction

Introducing a new tool brings with it selection, acquisition, and maintenance costs. In addition, costs may arise for hardware acquisition or updates and employee training. Depending on tool complexity and the number of workstations to be equipped with the tool, the amount invested can rapidly grow large. As with every investment, it is also important to consider the time frame in which the new test tool will start to pay back.

Test execution automation tools offer a good possibility for estimating the amount of effort saved when comparing an automated test to a manually run test. The extra test programming effort must, of course, be taken into account, resulting in a negative cost-benefit balance after only one automated test run. Only after further automated regression test runs have been performed (figure 7-2) may achieved savings accumulate.

Make a cost-benefit analysis

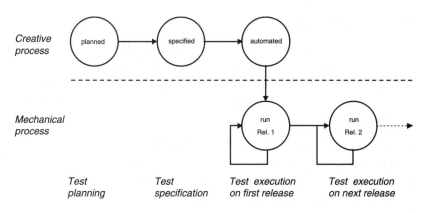

Figure 7–2
Test case life cycle

After a certain number of regression test runs, the balance will become positive. It is difficult to give an exact estimate of the time for pay back. The break-even point will only be reached if the tests are designed and programmed for easy use in regression testing, and easy maintenance. If tests are easy to repeat and maintain, a favorable balance is definitely possible from the third test cycle onwards for test robot tools (see [URL: imbus 98]). Of course, this kind of calculation only makes sense when manual execution is possible at all. However, there are many tests which cannot be run in a purely manual way (e.g., performance tests). They *have to* be run automatically.

Evaluate the influence on test quality

Merely discussing the level of test effort does not suffice. The extent of test quality improvement by applying a new test tool that results in detection and elimination of more faults, or results in more trustworthiness of the test, must also be taken into account. Development-, support- and maintenance-expenses will decrease as a result of the new tool. Even though this savings will not occur before the medium-term, the savings potential is significantly higher and therefore more interesting. To summarize, we observe that:

- The creative test activities can be supported by tools. This helps the tester improve test quality.
- The mechanical test execution can be automated, reducing test effort or allowing for more tests with the same effort. More tests do not necessarily mean better tests, though.

In both cases, without good test procedures or well-established test methods, tools do not lead to the desired cost reduction.

7.2.2   Tool Selection

The actual selection (and evaluation) of the tool starts as soon as it has been clarified which test task a tool shall support. As explained earlier, the investment can become very large. It is, therefore, advisable to proceed carefully and in a well-planned way. The selection process consists of the following five steps:

1. Requirement specification for the tool application
2. Market research (creating an overview of possible candidates)
3. Tool demonstrations and creation of a short list
4. Evaluating the tools on the short list
5. Reviewing of the results and selection of the tool

For the first step, requirement specification, the following criteria may be relevant:

Selection criteria

- Quality of interaction with the potential test objects
- Tester know-how regarding the tool or method
- Ease of integration into the existing development environment
- Ease of integration with other testing tools or tools from the same supplier
- Platform on which the tool will be deployed
- Manufacturer's service, reliability, and market position
- License conditions, price, maintenance costs

These and possible further individual criteria are compiled into a list and weighted according to their relative importance. Absolutely indispensable criteria are identified and marked as knock-out criteria[67].

Parallel to creating a catalog of criteria, market research takes place: a list is created, listing the available products of the interesting tool category. Product information is requested from suppliers or collected from the internet. Based on these materials, the suppliers of the preferred candidates are invited to demonstrate their respective tools. At least some impression of the company at hand and its service philosophy can be gained from these demonstrations. The best vendors will then be taken into the final evaluation process, where primarily the following points need to be verified:

Market research and short-listing

- Does the tool work with the test objects and the development environment?
- Are the features and quality characteristics that caused the respective tool to be considered for the final evaluation fulfilled in reality? (Advertising can promise a lot).
- Can the supplier's support staff provide qualified information and help with nonstandard questions (before and after purchase[68])?

---

67. An example of such a criteria catalogue can be downloaded under [URL: imbusdownloads].
68. Many suppliers just refer to the general hot line after purchase.

7.2.3   Tool Introduction

After a selection has been made, the tool shall be introduced to the company. Usually, for this purpose, a pilot project is run to verify whether the expected benefits can actually be achieved in the context of a real project environment. The pilot project should not be run by the same people that have been involved in the evaluation in order to prevent a possible conflict of interest when interpreting the evaluation results.

Pilot operation   Pilot operation should deliver additional knowledge of the technical details of the tool, as well as experiences with the practical use of the tool and experiences about the usage environment. It should become apparent whether, and to what extent, there exists a need for training, and where, if necessary, changes should be made to the test process. Furthermore, rules and conventions for extensive use should be developed, such as naming conventions for files and test cases, rules for modularizing the tests, etc. If test drivers or test robots are introduced, it can be determined during the pilot project if it is reasonable to build test libraries in order to facilitate reuse of certain tests and test modules outside the project.

Because the new tool will generate additional workload in the beginning, tool introduction requires the strong and ongoing commitment of the tool users and stakeholders. Thus, it would be wrong to proceed with a company-wide introduction with excessive promises. Coaching and training will help to motivate the future tool users.

Success factors   Important success factors during rollout are:

- Stepwise introduction
- Integrate the tool support with the processes
- Implement user training and continuous coaching
- Make available rules and suggestions for applying the tool
- Collect usage experiences and make them available to all users (hints, tricks, FAQs, etc.)
- Monitor tool acceptance and gather and evaluate cost-benefit data

Successful tool introduction follows these six steps:

1. Execute a pilot project
2. Evaluate the pilot project experiences
3. Adapt the processes and implement rules for usage
4. Train the users
5. Introduce the tool in a stepwise fashion
6. Offer accompanying coaching

This chapter pointed out many of the difficulties and the additional effort involved when selecting and introducing tools for supporting the test process. This is not meant to create the impression that using tools is not worthwhile. On the contrary, in larger projects, testing without the support of appropriate tools is not feasible. A careful tool introduction, however, is necessary, otherwise the wrong tool quickly becomes "shelfware" lying unused on the bookshelf.

7.3   Summary

- Tools are available for every phase of the test process, helping the tester to automate test activities or improve the quality of these activities.
- Use of a test tool is only beneficial when the test process is defined and controlled.
- Test tool selection must be a careful and well-managed process, as introducing a test tool may incur large investments.
- Information, training, and coaching must support the introduction of the selected tool. This helps to assure the future users' acceptance and hence the regular application of the tool.

Appendix

A   Test Plan According to IEEE Std. 829

This appendix describes the contents of a test plan according to IEEE Standard 829. It can be used as a guide to prepare a test plan[69].

1. Test Plan Identifier

Specify uniquely the name and version of the test plan. The identifier must make it possible to refer to this document from other project documents in a clear and precise way. A standard for document identification is often given by rules set by the project manager or by the organization's central document management. Depending on the size of the project organization, the identifier may be more or less complicated. The minimum components to be used are the name of the test plan, its version, and its status.

2. Introduction

The introduction should give a short summary of the project background. Its intent is to help those involved in the project (customer, management, developer, and tester) to better understand the contents of the test plan.

Included in this chapter should be a list of documents used. These typically include policies and standards, such as industry standards, company standards, project standards, customer standards, the project authorization (possibly the contract), project plan and other plans, and the specification.

In multi-level test plans, each lower level test plan must reference the next higher-level test plan.

---

69. The standard is going to change in 2006 and probably a master test plan and a level test plan will replace this outline.

3. Test Objects or Items

This section should contain a short overview of the parts and components of the product to be tested; identify the test items including their version/ revision level; and specify characteristics of their transmittal media and their specification. In order to avoid misunderstanding, there should be a list of what is not subject to testing.

4. Features to be tested

This section should identify all functions or characteristics of the system, which should be tested. The test specification and more detailed descriptions, as well as an assignment to test levels or phases, should be referenced.

5. Features not to be tested

In order to avoid misunderstanding and prevent unrealistic expectations, it should be defined which aspects of the product shall not or cannot be tested. (This may be due to resource constraints or technical reasons). There may also be different levels of testing for different features.

Hint
- Because the test plan is prepared early in the project, this list will be incomplete. Later it may be found that some components or features cannot be tested anyway. The test manager should then issue warnings in the status reports.

6. Test Approach or Strategy

Describe the test objectives, if possible, based on risk analysis. The analysis shows which risks are imminent if faults are not found due to lack of testing. From this it can be derived which tests must be executed and which are more or less important. This assures that the test is concentrated on important topics.

Building on this, choose and describe the test methods to be used. It must be clearly visible, if and why the chosen methods are able to achieve the test objectives, considering the identified risks and the available resources.

7. Acceptance Criteria

After all tests for a test object have been executed, it must be determined, based on the test results, if the test object can be released[70] and delivered[71]. Acceptance criteria or test exit criteria are defined to achieve this.

The criterion "defect free" is, in this context, a rather less useful criterion, because testing cannot show that a product has no faults. Usually, criteria therefore include a combination of "number of tests executed", "number of faults found " and "severity of problems found".

For example: At least 90% of the planned tests are executed correctly and no class 1 problems (crashes) have been found.

Such acceptance criteria can vary between the test objects. The thoroughness of the criteria should be oriented depending on the risk analysis, i.e. for uncritical test objects, acceptance criteria can be weaker than for e.g. safety critical test objects. Thus, the test resources are concentrated on important system parts.

8. Suspension Criteria and Resumption Requirements

Aside from acceptance criteria, there is also a need for criteria to indicate a suspension or termination of the tests.

It may be that a test object is in such a bad shape that it has no chance to be accepted, even after an enormous amount of testing. In order to avoid such wasteful testing we need criteria which will lead to termination of such useless testing at an early enough stage. The test object will then be returned to the developer without the need to execute all tests.

Analogous to this there is the need for criteria for resumption or continuation of the tests. The responsible testers will typically execute an entry test. After this is executed without trouble, the real test begins.

▪ Criteria should only involve measurements, which can be measured regularly, easy and reliably, for example because they are automatically collected by the used test tools. The test manager should then list and interpret these data in every test report.   *Hint*

---

70. Release: A management decision in which the test object is decided to be "ready".
71. Delivery may also mean: transfer to the next test level.

9. Test Deliverables

In this section we describe which data and results every test activity will deliver and in which form these results are communicated. This not only means the test results in a narrow sense (for example incident reports and test protocols), but it also includes planning and preparation documents such as test plans, test specifications, schedules, documents describing the transmittal of test objects, and test summary reports.

Hint
- In a test plan, only formal documentation is mentioned. However, informal communication should not be forgotten. Especially in projects which are already in trouble, or in very stressful phases (for example the release week), an experienced test manager should try to directly communicate with the involved people. This is not in order to reveal bad news, but it should be used to assure that the right consequences are chosen after possible bad news.

10. Testing Tasks

This section is a list of all tasks necessary for the planning and execution of the tests, including assignment of responsibilities. The status of the tasks (open, in progress, delayed, done) must be followed up. This point is rather part of the normal project planning and follow-up, and is therefore reported in the regular project or test status reports.

11. Test Infrastructure and Environmental Needs

This section lists the elements of the test infrastructure necessary to execute the planned tests. This typically includes test platform(s), tester work places and their equipment, test tools, development environment or parts thereof necessary for the testers, and other tools (email, WWW, Office packages etc.).

Hint
- The test manager should consider the following aspects: Acquisition of the not available parts of the before mentioned "wish list", questions about budget, administration and operation of the test infrastructure, the test objects and tools. Often, this requires specialists, at least for some time. Such specialists may be in other departments or must be recruited from external providers.

12. Responsibilities

How is testing organized with respect to the project? Who has what authority and responsibility? Possibly the test personnel must be divided into different test groups or levels. Which people have which tasks?

▨ Responsibilities and authorities may change during the course of the project. Therefore the list of responsibilities should be a table, maybe as an appendix to the test plan.	*Hint*

13. Staffing and Training Needs

This section specifies the staffing needs (roles, qualifications, capacity, and when they are needed, as well as planning vacations, etc.) This planning is not only for the test personnel, but should also include personnel for administrating the test infrastructure, developers, and customers and consultants for every tool, software product (for example, database systems) and interfacing product necessary during the testing effort. Training for providing necessary skills should be included.

14. Schedule

An overall schedule for the test activities is described here, with the major milestones. This plan must be coordinated with the project plan and maintained there. Regular consultation between the project manager and the test manager must be implemented. The test manager should be informed about delays during development and must react by changing the detailed test plan. The project manager must react on test results and, if necessary, delay milestones because extra correction and testing cycles must be executed. If any test resources are shared with others, for example a test lab, this must be clearly visible in the schedule.

▨ The test manager must assure that the test activities are included in the project plan. They must not be an independent "state in the state".	*Hint*

15. Risks and Contingencies

In the section about test strategy, risks in the test object or its use are addressed. This section, however, addresses risks within the testing project itself, i.e. risks when implementing the test concept, and risks resulting from not implementing reasonable activities, because there are no resources for them in the concrete project. The minimum should be a list of risks, which will then be monitored at certain points in time, in order to find measures to minimize them.

Hint   These risks should definitely be addressed:

- Delays in development
- Too low quality in the system under test
- Problems with the test infrastructure
- Lack of qualified or other key personnel

16. Approvals

This section should contain a list of people or organizations that approve the test plan, review it, or at least should be informed about it. Signatures should document approval. Information to other parties should also be documented after major changes, especially changes of test strategy or changes of key personnel.

Hint   - Relevant persons or organizations are typically development group(s), project management, project steering committee, user and operator of the software system, customer or client, and, naturally, the testing group(s).

Depending on the project situation, the intention of the approval documented here can vary.

The ideal situation is: "You approve that the here-mentioned resources will be financed and used, in order to test this system appropriately as described here."

However, the most commonly occurring practical situation is: "Because of the lack of resources, tests can only be done in an inappropriate/minimal way. Only the most important tests are executed. You approve this way of testing and accept that release decisions based on this test bear a high risk."

17. Glossary

Testing has no tradition for using standardized terminology. Thus, the test plan should contain an explanation of the testing terms used. There is a high danger that different people will have different interpretations of test terminology. For example, just ask several people for the definition of the term "load testing".

B Important Information on the Curriculum and on the Certified Tester Exam

The "Certified Tester Foundation Level" curriculum forms the basis of this textbook, in accordance with the ISTQB 2005-curriculum. The respective national boards create and maintain additional national versions of the curriculum. The national boards coordinate and guarantee mutual compatibility of their curricula and exams. In this context, the responsible board is the "International Software Testing Qualifications Board" [URL: ISTQB].

The exams are based on the current version of the curriculum in its corresponding examination language at the time of examination. The exams are offered and executed by the respective national board or by the appointed certification body. Further information on the curricula and the exams can be found under [URL: ISTQB]. The ISTQB web page provides links to the national boards.

For didactic reasons, the subjects contained in this book may be addressed in a different order than presented in the curriculum. The size of the individual chapters does not indicate the relevance of the presented contents for the exam. Some subjects are covered in more detail in the book. Some passages, marked as excursion, go beyond the scope of the curriculum. In any case, the exams are based on the official curricula.

The exercises and questions contained in this book should be regarded solely as practice material and examples. They are not representative of the official examination questions.

9 Exercises

Exercises to Chapter 2

2.1 Define the terms *failure*, *fault*, and *error*.
2.2 What is defect masking?
2.3 Explain the difference between testing and debugging.
2.4 Explain why each test is a random sampling.
2.5 List the main characteristics of software quality according to ISO 9126.
2.6 Define the term *system reliability*.
2.7 Explain the phases of the fundamental test process.
2.8 What is a test oracle?
2.9 Why should a developer not test her own programs?

Exercises to Chapter 3

3.1 Explain the different phases of the general V-model.
3.2 Define the terms *verification* and *validation*.
3.3 Explain why verification makes sense, even when a careful validation is performed, too (and vice versa).
3.4 Characterize typical test objects in component testing.
3.5 Discuss the idea of "test-first".
3.6 List the goals of the integration test.
3.7 What integration strategies exist and how do they differ?
3.8 Name the reasons for executing tests in a separate test infrastructure.
3.9 Describe four typical forms of acceptance tests.
3.10 Explain requirements-based testing.
3.11 Define *load test*, *performance test*, and *stress test*, and describe the differences between them.
3.12 How do retest and regression tests differ?
3.13 Why are regression tests especially important in incremental development?
3.14 According to the general V-model, during which project phase should the test concept be defined?

Exercises to chapter 4

4.1   Describe the basic steps for running a review.
4.2   What different kinds of review exist?
4.3   Which roles participate in a technical review?
4.4   What makes reviews an efficient means for quality assurance?
4.5   Explain the term *static analysis*.
4.6   How are static analysis and reviews related?
4.7   Static analysis cannot uncover all program faults. Why?
4.8   What different kinds of data flow anomalies exist?

Exercises to chapter 5

5.1   What is a dynamic test?
5.2   What is the purpose of a test harness?
5.3   Describe the difference(s) between black box and white box test procedures.
5.4   Explain the equivalence class partition technique.
5.5   Define the test completeness criterion for equivalence class coverage.
5.6   Why is boundary value analysis a good supplement to equivalence class partitioning?
5.7   List further black box techniques.
5.8   Explain the term *statement coverage*.
5.9   What is the difference between statement and branch coverage?
5.10 What is the purpose of instrumentation?

Exercises to chapter 6

6.1   What basic models for division of responsibility for testing tasks between development and test can be distinguished?
6.2   Discuss the benefits and drawbacks of independent testing.
6.3   Which roles are necessary in testing? Which qualifications are necessary?
6.4   State the typical tasks of a test manager.
6.5   Discuss why test cases are prioritized and mention criteria for prioritizing.
6.6   What purpose do test exit criteria serve?
6.7   Define the term *test strategy*.
6.8   Discuss four typical approaches to determine a test strategy.
6.9   Define the term *risk* and mention risk factors relevant for testing.
6.10 Which idea is served by risk-based testing?

6.11 What different kinds of metrics can be distinguished for monitoring test progress?

6.12 What information should be contained in a test status report?

6.13 What data should be contained in an incident report?

6.14 What is the difference between defect priority and defect severity?

6.15 What is the purpose of a incident status model?

6.16 What is the task of a change control board?

6.17 From the point of view of testing, what are the requirements for configuration management?

6.18 What basic different kinds of standards exist?

Exercises to chapter 7

7.1 What main functions do test management tools offer?

7.2 Why is it reasonable to couple requirements and test management tools and exchange data?

7.3 What different types of test data generators exist?

7.4 What type of test data generator can also generate expected output values? Why can't other types of test data generators do the same?

7.5 What is a test driver?

7.6 Explain the general way of working for a capture/playback tool.

7.7 Describe the principle of data driven testing.

7.8 What steps should be taken when selecting a test tool?

7.9 What steps should be taken when introducing a tool?

Glossary

The definition of most of the following terms are taken from in the "Standard Glossary of Terms used in Software Testing" Version 1.1 (September 2005), produced by the "Glossary Working Party" of the International Software Testing Qualifications Board. You can find the current version of the glossary here: [URL: ISTQB].

This glossary presents terms and definitions in software testing and related disciplines. The related terms are flagged by an <u>underline</u>.

abstract test case
    See high level test case.

acceptance testing
Formal testing with respect to user needs, requirements, and business processes conducted to determine whether or not a system satisfies the acceptance criteria and to enable the user, customers, or other authorized entity to determine whether or not to accept the system. [IEEE 610.12]

actual result
The behavior produced/observed when a component or system is tested under specified conditions.

ad hoc review
    See informal review.

ad hoc testing
Testing carried out informally; no formal test preparation takes place, no recognized test design technique is used, there are no expectations for results and arbitrariness guides the test execution activity.
    See also exploratory testing.

alpha testing

Simulated or actual operational testing by potential customers/users or an independent test team at the software developers' site, but outside the development organization.

Note: Alpha testing is employed for off-the-shelf software as a form of internal acceptance testing.

analytical quality assurance

Diagnostic based measures, for example testing, to measure or evaluate the quality of a product.

anomaly

Any condition that deviates from expectation based on requirements specifications, design documents, user documents, standards, etc. or from someone's perception or experience. Anomalies may be found during, but not limited to, reviewing, testing, analysis, compilation, or use of software products or applicable documentation. [IEEE 1044] See also defect, deviation, error, fault, failure, incident, problem, bug.

atomic (partial) condition

Boolean expression containing no Boolean operators.

EXAMPLE: "A < B" is an atomic condition but "A and B" is not.
[BS 7925-1]

audit

1. An independent evaluation of software products or processes to ascertain compliance to standards, guidelines, specifications, and/or procedures based on objective criteria, including documents that specify:
2. The form or content of the products to be produced
3. The process by which the products shall be produced
4. How compliance to standards or guidelines shall be measured.
   [IEEE 1028]

back-to-back testing

Testing in which two or more variants of a component or system are executed with the same inputs, the outputs compared, and analyzed in cases of discrepancies. [IEEE 610.12]

bespoke software

Software developed specifically for a set of users or customers. The opposite of off-the-shelf software.

beta testing

Operational testing by potential and/or existing customers/users at an external site not otherwise involved with the developers, to determine whether or not a component or system satisfies the user needs and fits within the business processes.

Note: Beta testing is employed as a form of external acceptance testing in order to acquire feedback from the market.

big-bang testing

A type of integration testing in which software elements, hardware elements, or both are combined all at once into a component or an overall system, rather than in stages. [IEEE 610.12]

See also integration testing.

black box test design techniques

Documented procedure to derive and select test cases based on an analysis of the specification, either functional or nonfunctional, of a component or system without reference to its internal structure.

black box testing

Testing, either functional or nonfunctional, without reference to the internal structure of the component or system.

See also functional test design technique, requirements-based testing.

blocked test case

A test case that cannot be executed because the preconditions for its execution are not fulfilled.

bottom-up testing

An incremental approach to integration testing where the lowest level components are tested first, and then used to facilitate the testing of higher level components. This process is repeated until the component at the top of the hierarchy is tested.

See also integration testing.

boundary value

An input value or output value which is on the edge of an equivalence partition or at the smallest incremental distance on either side of an edge, for example the minimum and maximum value of a range.

boundary value analysis

A black box test design technique in which test cases are designed based on boundary values.

See also boundary value.

branch

A basic block that can be selected for execution based on a program construct in which one of two or more alternative program paths are available, e.g., case, if-then-else.

branch condition

See condition.

branch condition combination coverage

See multiple condition coverage.

branch condition combination testing

See multiple condition testing.

branch condition coverage

See condition coverage.

branch coverage

The percentage of branches that have been exercised by a test suite. 100% branch coverage implies both 100% decision coverage and 100% statement coverage.

branch testing

A white box test design technique in which test cases are designed to execute branches.

bug

See defect.

business-process-based testing

An approach to testing in which test design is based on descriptions and/or knowledge of business processes.

capture/playback tool

A type of test execution tool where inputs are recorded during manual testing in order to generate automated test scripts that can be executed later (i.e., replayed). These tools are often used to support automated regression testing.

capture/replay tool

See capture/playback tool.

CASE

Acronym for Computer Aided Software Engineering.

CAST

Acronym for Computer Aided Software Testing.

See also test automation.

cause-effect graph

A graphical representation of inputs and/or stimuli (causes) with their associated outputs (effects), which can be used to design test cases.

cause-effect graphing

A black box test design technique in which test cases are designed from cause-effect graphs. [BS 7925-2]

change

Rewrite or new development of a released development product (document, source code)

change order

Order or permission to perform a change of a development product.

change request

1. Written request or proposal to perform a specific change for a development product or to allow it being performed.
2. A request to change some software artifact due to a change in requirements.

class test

Test of one or several classes of an object-oriented system.

See also component testing.

code-based testing

See white box testing.

comparator

See test comparator.

complete testing

See exhaustive testing.

component
A minimal software item that can be tested in isolation.

component integration testing
Testing performed to expose defects in the interfaces and in the interaction between integrated components.

component testing
The testing of individual software components. [IEEE 610.12]

concrete test case
Test case with concrete values for its data.
> See low level test case and logical test case, abstract test case.

condition
A logical expression that can be evaluated as True or False, e.g., A>B.

condition coverage
The percentage of condition outcomes that have been exercised by a test suite. 100% condition coverage requires each single condition in every decision statement to be tested as True and False.

condition determination coverage
The percentage of all single condition outcomes that independently affect a decision outcome that have been exercised by a test suite. 100% condition determination coverage implies 100% decision coverage.

condition determination testing
A white box test design technique in which test cases are designed to execute single condition outcomes that independently affect a decision outcome.

configuration
The composition of a component or system as defined by the number, nature, and interconnections of its constituent parts.

configuration item
An aggregation of hardware, software or both, that is designated for configuration management and treated as a single entity in the configuration management process. [IEEE 610.12]

configuration management

A discipline applying technical and administrative direction and surveillance to: identify and document the functional and physical characteristics of a configuration item, control changes to those characteristics, record and report change processing and implementation status, and verify compliance with specified requirements. [IEEE 610.12]

control flow

An abstract representation of all possible sequences of events (paths) in the execution of a component or system.

control flow anomaly

Statically detectable anomaly in the control flow of a test object (for example a not reachable statement).

control flow based test

Dynamic test, whose test cases are derived using the control flow of the test object and whose test coverage is determined against the control flow.

See also white box testing

control flow graph

A sequence of events (paths) in the execution through a component or system.

coverage

The degree, expressed as a percentage, to which a specified coverage item has been exercised by a test suite.

cyclomatic complexity

The number of independent paths through a program. Cyclomatic complexity is defined as: $L - N + 2P$, where L = the number of links in a graph N = the number of nodes in a graph P = the number of disconnected parts of the graph (e.g., a calling graph and a subroutine) [McCabe 76]

cyclomatic number

See cyclomatic complexity.

data flow

An abstract representation of the sequence and possible changes of the state of data objects, where the state of an object is any of: creation, usage, or destruction. [Beizer 90]

data flow analysis

A form of static analysis based on the definition and usage of variables.

data flow anomaly

Unintended or unexpected sequence of operations on a variable.

Note: The following data flow anomalies are being distinguished: ur-anomaly is the referencing an undefined variable; dd-anomaly is two subsequent writings to a variable without referencing this variable in between; du-anomalyis the writing (defining) of a variable followed by undefining it without referencing this variable in between.

data flow coverage

The percentage of definition-use pairs that have been exercised by a test case suite.

data flow test

A white box test design technique in which test cases are designed to execute definition and use pairs of variables.

dead code

See unreachable code.

debugger

See debugging tool.

debugging

The process of finding, analyzing and removing the causes of failures in software.

debugging tool

A tool used by programmers to reproduce failures, investigate the state of programs, and find the corresponding defect. Debuggers enable programmers to execute programs step by step, to halt a program at any program statement, and to set and examine program variables.

decision

A program point at which the control flow has two or more alternative routes. A node with two or more links to separate branches.

decision condition coverage

The percentage of all condition outcomes and decision outcomes that have been exercised by a test suite. 100% decision condition coverage implies both 100% condition coverage and 100% decision coverage.

decision condition testing

A white box test design technique in which test cases are designed to execute condition outcomes and decision outcomes.

decision coverage

The percentage of decision outcomes that have been exercised by a test suite. 100% decision coverage implies both 100% branch coverage and 100% statement coverage.

decision table

A table showing combinations of inputs and/or stimuli (causes) with their associated outputs and/or actions (effects), which can be used to design test cases.

decision table testing

A black box test design techniques in which test cases are designed to execute the combinations of inputs and/or stimuli (causes) shown in a decision table. [van Veenendaal 04]

defect

A flaw in a component or system that can cause the component or system to fail to perform its required function, e.g., an incorrect statement or data definition. A defect, if encountered during execution, may cause a failure of the component or system.

defect detection percentage (DDP)

The number of defects found by a test phase, divided by the number found by that test phase and any other means afterwards.

defect management

The process of recognizing, investigating, taking action and disposing of defects. It involves recording defects, classifying them and identifying the impact. [IEEE 1044]

defect management tool

A tool that facilitates the recording and status tracking of defects. They often have workflow-oriented facilities to track and control the allocation, correction, and retesting of defects and provide reporting facilities.

   See also incident management tool.

defect masking

An occurrence in which one defect prevents the detection of another. [IEEE 610.12]

deficiency

Nonfulfillment of a requirement related to an intended or specified use. [ISO 9000] Synonym: defect

development process

See iterative development model and incremental development model.

development specification

1. A document that specifies the requirements for a system or component. Typically included are functional requirements, performance requirements, interface requirements, design requirements, and development standards. [IEEE 610.12]
2. Development phase (of the general V-model) in which the requirements for the system to be developed are collected, specified, and approved.
    See also requirement and specification.

development testing

Formal or informal testing conducted during the implementation of a component or system, usually in the development environment by developers. [IEEE 610.12]

See also component testing.

deviation

1. difference between a value assigned to a characteristic and a reference value.
2. Deviation of the software from its expected delivery or service.
    See also incident.

driver

A software component or test tool that replaces a program that takes care of the control and/or the calling of a component or system. [Pol 02]

dummy

A special program, normally restricted in its functionality, to replace the real program during testing.

dynamic analysis

The process of evaluating the behavior, e.g., memory performance and/or CPU usage, of a system or component during execution. [IEEE 610.12]

dynamic testing

Testing that involves the execution of the software of the component or system.

efficiency

The capability of the software product to provide appropriate performance relative to the amount of resources used under stated condition.
[ISO 9126]

efficiency testing

The process of testing to determine the efficiency of a software product.

emulator

A device, computer program, or system that accepts the same inputs and produces the same outputs as a given system. [IEEE 610.12]

See also simulator.

equivalence class

See equivalence partition.

equivalence (class) partition

A portion of an input or output domain for which the behavior of a component or system is assumed to be the same, based on the specification.

equivalence (class) partition coverage

The percentage of equivalence partitions that have been exercised by a test suite.

equivalence (class) partitioning

A black box test design technique in which test cases are designed to execute representatives from equivalence partitions. In principle test cases are designed to cover each partition at least once.

error (erroneous action)

Human action that produces an incorrect result. [IEEE 610.12]

error guessing

A test design technique where the experience of the tester is used to anticipate what defects might be present in the component or system under test as a result of errors made, and to design tests specifically to expose them.

error tolerance

The ability of a system or component to continue normal operation despite the presence of erroneous inputs. [IEEE 610.12]

See also robustness.

exception handling

Behavior of a component or system in response to erroneous input, from either a human user or from another component or system, or to an internal failure.

exhaustive testing

A test approach in which the test suite comprises all combinations of input values and preconditions.

Synonym: complete testing.

exit criteria

The set of generic and specific conditions, agreed upon with the stakeholders, for permitting a process to be officially completed. The purpose of exit criteria is to prevent a task from being considered completed when there are still outstanding parts of the task which have not been finished.

Note: Exit criteria are used by testing to report against and to plan when to stop testing. [Gilb 96]

expected result

The behavior predicted by the specification, or another source, of a component or system under specified conditions.

See also test oracle.

exploratory testing

An informal test design technique where that the tester actively controls the design of the tests as those tests are performed and uses information gained while testing to design new and better tests. [Bach 04]

extreme programming

Agile development process, which propagates, amongst other things, the test-first approach.

See also test-first programming.

failure

Actual deviation of the component or system from its expected delivery, service, or result. [Fenton 91]

failure priority
Determination of how pressing it is to correct the cause of a failure by taking into account failure severity, necessary correction work, and the effects on the whole development and test process.

fault
See defect.

fault tolerance
The capability of the software product to maintain a specified level of performance in cases of software faults (defects) or of infringement of its specified interface. [ISO 9126]
See also reliability.

field testing
See beta testing.

finite state machine
A computational model consisting of a finite number of states and transitions between those states, possibly with accompanying actions.
[IEEE 610.12]

finite state testing
See state transition testing.

functional requirement
A requirement that specifies a function that a system or system component must be able to perform. [IEEE 610.12]
See also functionality.

functional test design technique
Documented procedure to derive and select test cases based on an analysis of the specification of the functionality of a component or system without reference to its internal structure.
See also black box test design technique.

functional testing
Testing based on an analysis of the specification of the functionality of a component or system.
See also black box testing.

functionality

The capability of the software product to provide functions which meet stated and implied needs when the software is used under specified conditions. Subcharacteristics of functionality are suitability, accuracy, interoperability, security, and compliance. [ISO 9126]

functionality testing

The process of testing to determine the functionality of a software product.

high level test case

A test case without concrete (implementation level) values for the input data and expected results. Logical operators are used, instances of the actual values are not yet defined and/or available.

See also low level test case.

incident

Any event occurring during testing that requires investigation.
[IEEE 1008]

incident management

The process of recognizing, investigating, taking action and disposing of incidents. It involves recording incidents, classifying them, and identifying the impact. [IEEE 1044]

incident management tool

A tool that facilitates the recording and status tracking of incidents found during testing. They often have workflow-oriented facilities to track and control the allocation, correction, and retesting of incidents and provide reporting facilities.

See also defect management tool.

incident report

A document reporting on any event that occurs during the testing which requires investigation.

incremental development model

A development life cycle where a project is broken into a series of increments, each of which delivers a portion of the functionality in the overall project requirements. The requirements are prioritized and delivered in priority order in the appropriate increment. In some (but not all) versions of this life cycle model, each subproject follows a 'mini V-model' with its own design, coding, and testing phases.

informal review

A review not based on a formal (documented) procedure.

inspection

A type of review that relies on visual examination of documents to detect defects, e.g., violations of development standards and nonconformance to higher level documentation. The most formal review technique and therefore always based on a documented procedure. [IEEE 610.12], [IEEE 1028]

instrumentation

The insertion of additional code into the program in order to collect information about program behavior during execution, e.g., for measuring code coverage.

intake test

A special instance of a smoke test to decide if the component or system is ready for detailed and further testing. An intake test is typically carried out at the start of the test execution phase.

See also smoke test.

<u>integration</u>

The process of combining components into larger assemblies.

integration testing

Testing performed to expose defects in the interfaces and in the interactions between integrated components or systems.

See also component integration testing, system integration testing.

<u>iterative development model</u>

A development life cycle where a project is broken into , usually, large numbers of iterations. An interaction is a complete development loop resulting in a release (internal or external) of an executable product, a subset of the final product under development, which grows from iteration to iteration to become the final product.

load testing

A test type concerned with measuring the behavior of a component or system with increasing load, e.g., number of parallel users and/or numbers of transactions to determine what load can be handled by the component or system.

See also stress testing.

logical test case

A test case without concrete values for the inputs and outputs. In most cases, conditions or equivalence classes are specified.

See high level test case.

low level test case

A test case with concrete (implementation level) values for the input data and expected results. Logical operators from high level test cases are replaced by actual values that correspond to the objectives of the logical operators.

See also high level test case.

maintainability

The ease with which a software product can be modified to correct defects, modified to meet new requirements, modified to make future maintenance easier, or adapted to a changed environment. [ISO 9126]

maintenance

Modification of a software product after delivery to correct defects, to improve performance or other attributes, or to adapt the product to a modified environment. [IEEE 1219]

management review

A systematic evaluation of software acquisition, supply, development, operation, or maintenance process, performed by or on behalf of management that monitors progress, determines the status of plans and schedules, confirms requirements and their system allocation, or evaluates the effectiveness of management approaches to achieve fitness for purpose. [IEEE 610.12], [IEEE 1028]

metric

A measurement scale and the method used for measurement. [ISO 14598]

milestone

A point in time in a project at which defined (intermediate) deliverables and results should be ready.

minimal multicondition coverage

See modified condition decision coverage.

mock-up

A program in the test environment that takes the place of a stub or dummy, but that contains more functionality. This makes it possible to trigger desired results or behavior.

See also dummy.

moderator

The leader and main person responsible for an inspection or review process.

modified condition decision coverage

1. See condition determination coverage.
2. Coverage percentage defined as the number of Boolean operands values shown to independently affect the decision outcome, divided by the total number of Boolean operands (atomic part conditions), multiplied by 100.

Note: RTCA-DO 178B defines Modified Condition/Decision Coverage (MC/DC) as follows – Every point of entry and exit in the program has been invoked at least once, every condition in a decision in the program has taken all possible outcomes at least once, every decision in the program has taken on all possible outcomes at least once, and each condition in a decision has been shown to independently affect that decision's outcome.

module testing

See component testing.

monitor

A software tool or hardware device that runs concurrently with the component or system under test and supervises, records and/or analyses the behavior of the component or system. [IEEE 610.12]

multiple condition coverage

The percentage of combinations of all single condition outcomes within one statement that have been exercised by a test suite. 100 % multiple condition coverage implies 100 % condition determination coverage.

multiple condition testing

A white box test design technique in which test cases are designed to execute combinations of single condition outcomes (within one statement).

negative testing

Tests aimed at showing that a component or system does not work. Negative testing is related to the testers' attitude rather than a specific test approach or test design technique, e.g., testing with invalid input values or exceptions. [Beizer 90]

nonfunctional requirement

A requirement that does not relate to functionality, but to attributes such as reliability, efficiency, usability, maintainability, and portability.

See also quality objective.

nonfunctional testing

Testing the attributes of a component or system that do not relate to functionality, e.g., reliability, efficiency, usability, maintainability and portability.

N-switch testing

A form of state transition testing in which test cases are designed to execute all valid sequences of N+1 transitions. [Chow 78]

See also state transition testing.

off-the-shelf software

A software product that is developed for the general market, i.e., for a large number of customers, and that is delivered to many customers in identical format.

operational environment

Hardware and software products installed at users' or customers' sites where the component or system under test will be used. The software may include operating systems, database management systems, and other applications.

patch

1. A modification made directly to an object program without reassembling or recompiling from the source program.
2. A modification made to a source program as a last minute fix or afterthought.
3. Any modification to a source or object program.
4. To perform a modification as in (1), (2), or (3).
5. Unplanned release of a software product with corrected files in order to, possibly in a preliminary way, correct special (often blocking) faults. [IEEE 610.12]

path

A sequence of events, e.g., executable statements, of a component or system from an entry point to an exit point.

path coverage

The percentage of paths that have been exercised by a test suite.

path testing

A white box test design technique in which test cases are designed to execute paths.

peer review

A review of a software work product by colleagues of the producer of the product for the purpose of identifying defects and improvements. Examples are inspection, technical review, and walkthrough.

<u>performance</u>

The degree to which a system or component accomplishes its designated functions within given constraints regarding processing time and throughput rate. [IEEE 610.12]

See also efficiency.

performance testing

The process of testing to determine the performance of a software product.

See efficiency testing.

Point of Control (PoC)

Interface used to send inputs and stimuli to the test object.

Point of Observation (PoO)

Interface used to observe and log the reactions and outputs of the test object.

postcondition

Environmental and state conditions that must be fulfilled after the execution of a test or test procedure.

precondition

Environmental and state conditions that must be fulfilled before the component or system can be executed with a particular test or test procedure.

predicted outcome

See expected result.

preventive software quality assurance

Use of methods, tools, and procedures contributing to designing quality into the product. As a result of their application, the product should then have certain desired characteristics, and faults are prevented or their effects minimized.

Note: Preventive (constructive) software quality assurance is especially used in early stages of software development. Many defects can be avoided when the software is developed in a thorough and systematic manner.

problem

See defect.

problem database

1. A list of known failures or defects/faults in a system or component, and their state of repair.
2. Contains current and complete information about all identified defects.

See also incident management tool.

quality

1. The degree to which a component, system or process meets specified requirements and/or user/ customer or user needs or expectations. [IEEE 610.12]
2. The degree to which a set of inherent characteristics fulfills requirements [ISO 9000]

quality assurance

Part of quality management focused on providing confidence that quality requirements will be fulfilled. [ISO 9000]

quality attribute

1. A feature or characteristic that affects an item's quality. [IEEE 610.12]
2. A set of attributes of a software product by which its quality is described and evaluated. A software quality characteristic may be refined into multiple levels of subcharacteristics. [ISO 9126]

Quality characteristics are functionality, reliability, usability, efficiency, maintainability, and portability. [ISO 9126]

quality characteristic

See quality attribute.

quality objective
Something sought, or aimed for, related to quality. [ISO 9000]

random testing
A black box test design technique where test cases are selected, possibly using a pseudo-random generation algorithm, to match an operational profile. This technique can be used for testing nonfunctional attributes such as reliability and performance.

regression testing
Testing of a previously tested program following modification to ensure that defects have not been introduced or uncovered in unchanged areas of the software, as a result of the changes made. It is performed when the software or its environment is changed.

release
1. A particular version of a configuration item that is made available for a specific purpose. For example, a test release or a production release. [URL: BCS CM Glossary]
2. See configuration.

reliability
The ability of the software product to perform its required functions under stated conditions for a specified period of time, or for a specified number of operations. [ISO 9126]

reliability testing
The process of testing to determine the reliability of a software product.

requirement
A condition or capability needed by a user to solve a problem or achieve an objective that must be met or possessed by a system or system component to satisfy a contract, standard, specification, or other formally imposed document. [IEEE 610.12]

requirements-based testing
An approach to testing in which test cases are designed based on test objectives and test conditions derived from requirements, e.g., tests that exercise specific functions or probe nonfunctional attributes such as reliability or usability.

resource utilization

The capability of the software product to use appropriate amounts and types of resources, for example the amounts of main and secondary memory used by the program and the sizes of required temporary or overflow files, when the software performs its function under stated conditions. [ISO 9126]

See also efficiency.

resource utilization testing

The process of testing to determine the resource utilization of a software product.

See also efficiency testing.

result

The consequence/outcome of the execution of a test. It includes outputs to screens, changes to data, reports and communication messages sent out.

See also actual result, expected result.

retesting

Testing that runs test cases that failed the last time they were run, in order to verify the success of corrective actions.

See also regression testing.

review

An evaluation of a product or project status to ascertain discrepancies from planned results and to recommend improvements. Examples include management review, informal review, technical review, inspection, and walkthrough. [IEEE 1028]

reviewable (testable)

An indicated state of the work product or document to be reviewed or tested, it being complete enough to enable a review or test of it.

risk

A factor that could result in future negative consequences; usually expressed as impact and likelihood.

risk-based testing

Testing oriented towards exploring and providing information about product risks.

robustness

The degree to which a component or system can function correctly in the presence of invalid inputs or stressful environmental conditions. [IEEE 610.12]

See also error tolerance, fault tolerance.

robustness testing

Testing to determine the robustness of the software product.

See also negative testing.

role

Description of specific skills in software development.

safety critical system

A system whose failure may endanger human life or lead to large losses.

safety testing

The process of testing to determine the safety of a software product.

severity

The degree of impact that a defect has on the development or operation of a component or system. [IEEE 610.12]

severity class

Classification of failures according to the impact on the user, for example degree of hindrance in using the product.

(simple) condition coverage

See condition coverage.

simulator

A device, computer program, or system used during testing, which behaves or operates like a given system when provided with a set of controlled inputs. [IEEE 610.12], [RTCA-DO 178B]

See also emulator.

site acceptance testing

Acceptance testing by users/customers at their site, to determine whether or not a component or system satisfies the user/customer needs and fits within the business processes, normally including hardware as well as software.

smoke test

A subset of all defined/planned test cases that cover the main functionality of a component or system, that ascertains that the most crucial functions of a program work, but not bothering with finer details.

Note: A daily build and smoke test is among industry best practices.
See also intake test.

software development model

Framework of software development

software item

Identifiable (partial) result of the software development process.

software quality

The totality of functionality and features of a software product that bear on its ability to satisfy stated or implied needs. [ISO 9126]

See also quality.

specification

A document that specifies, ideally in a complete, precise, and verifiable manner, the requirements, design, behavior, or other characteristics of a system or component, and, often, the procedures for determining whether these provisions have been satisfied. [IEEE 610.12]

state diagram

A diagram that depicts the states that a system or component can assume, and shows the events or circumstances that cause and/or result from a change from one state to another. [IEEE 610.12]

state transition testing

A black box test design technique in which test cases are designed to execute valid and invalid state transitions.

See also N-switch testing.

statement (source statement)

A entity in a programming language which is typically the smallest indivisible unit of execution.

statement coverage

The percentage of all statements that have been exercised by a test suite.

static analysis

Analysis of software artifacts, e.g., requirements or code, carried out without execution of these software artifacts.

static analyzer

A tool that carries out static analysis.

static testing

Testing of a component or system at requirements or implementation level without execution of any software, e.g., reviews or static code analysis.

See also static analysis.

stress testing

Testing conducted to evaluate a system or component at or beyond the limits of its specified requirements. [IEEE 610.12]

See also load testing.

structural testing / structure-based techniques

See white box testing.

stub

A skeletal or special-purpose implementation of a software component, used to develop or test a component that calls or is otherwise dependent on it. It replaces a called component. [IEEE 610.12]

syntax testing

A black box test design technique in which test cases are designed based upon the definition of the input domain and/or output domain.

system integration testing

Testing the integration of systems and packages; testing interfaces to external organizations (e.g., Electronic Data Interchange, Internet).

system testing

The process of testing an integrated system to verify that it meets specified requirements. [Hetzel 88]

technical review

A peer group discussion activity that focuses on achieving consensus on the technical approach to be taken. [Gilb 96], [IEEE 1028]

See also peer review.

test

1. A set of one or more test cases. [IEEE 829]
2. A set of one or more test procedures. [IEEE 829]
3. A set of one or more test cases and procedures. [IEEE 829]

test automation

The use of software to perform or support test activities, e.g., test management, test design, test execution, and results checking.

test basis

All documents from which the requirements of a component or system can be inferred. The documentation on which the test cases are based. If a document can be amended only by way of formal amendment procedure, then the test basis is called a frozen test basis. [Pol 02]

test bed

See test environment and test harness.

test case

A set of input values, execution preconditions, expected results, and execution postconditions developed for a particular objective or test condition, such as to exercise a particular program path or to verify compliance with a specific requirement. [IEEE 610.12]

test case explosion

Expression for the exponentially increasing work for an exhaustive test with increasing numbers of parameters.

test case specification

A document specifying a set of test cases (objective, inputs, test actions, expected results, and execution preconditions) for a test item. [IEEE 829]

test comparator

A test tool to perform automated test comparison.

test coverage

See coverage.

test cycle

1. Execution of the test process against a single identifiable release of the test object.
2. Execution of a series of test cases.

3. Execution of the fundamental test process for exactly one version of the test object, at which end there are orders for failure repair or change to the developer.

test data
Data that exists (for example, in a database) before a test is executed, and that affects or is affected by the component or system under test.

test driver
See driver.

test effort
The necessary resources for the test process.

test environment
An environment containing hardware, instrumentation, simulators, software tools, and other support elements needed to conduct a test. [IEEE 610.12]

test evaluation
Analysis of the test protocol or test log in order to determine if failures have occurred.

test evaluation report
A document produced at the end of the test process summarizing all testing activities and results. It also contains an evaluation of the test process and lessons learned.

test execution
The process of running a test by the component or system under test, producing actual result(s).

test harness
A test environment that comprises of stubs and drivers needed to conduct a test.

test infrastructure
The organizational artifacts needed to perform testing, consisting of test environments, test tools, office environment, and procedures. [Pol 02]

test item
The individual element to be tested. There usually is one test object and many test items.
See also test object.

test level

A group of test activities that are organized and managed together. A test level is linked to the responsibilities in a project. Examples of test levels are component test, integration test, system test, and acceptance test. [Pol 02]

test log

A chronological record of relevant details about the execution of tests. [IEEE 829]

test logging

The process of recording information about tests executed into a test log.

test management

The planning, estimating, monitoring, and control of test activities, typically carried out by a test manager.

test method

See test technique.

test metric

A quantitative measure of a test case, test run, or test cycle including measurement instructions.

test object

The component or system to be tested.
See also test item.

test objective

A reason or purpose for designing and executing a test.

test oracle

A source to determine expected results to compare with the actual result of the software under test.

Note: An oracle may be the existing system (for a benchmark), a user manual, or an individual's specialized knowledge, but should not be the code. [Adrion 82]

test phase

A distinct set of test activities collected into a manageable phase of a project, e.g., the execution activities of a test level. [Gerrard 02]

test plan

A document describing the scope, approach, resources, and schedule of intended test activities. It identifies, amongst others test items, the features to be tested, the testing tasks, who will do each task, degree of tester independence, the test environment, the test design techniques, and entry and exit criteria to be used, and the rationale for their choice, and any risks requiring contingency planning. It is a record of the test planning process. (After [IEEE 829])

test planning
The activity of establishing or updating a test plan.

test procedure specification
A document specifying a sequence of actions for the execution of a test. Also known as test script or manual test script. [IEEE 829]

test process
1. The fundamental test process comprises test planning and control, test analysis and design, test implementation and execution, evaluation of test exit criteria and reporting, and test closure activities.
2. The fundamental test process comprises planning, specification, execution, recording and checking for completion, and test closure activities. [BS 7925-2]

test report
See test summary report.

test result
All documents developed during the course of a test run (mostly the test log and its evaluation).
See also result.

test robot
A tool to control the execution of tests, the comparison of actual results to expected results, the setting up of test preconditions, and other test control and reporting functions in order to automate the execution of test cases.

test run
Execution of a set of test cases on a specific version of the test object.

test scenario
See test procedure specification.

test schedule
A schedule that identifies all tasks required for a successful testing effort, a schedule of all test activities, and their corresponding resource requirements.

test script

Commonly used to refer to a test procedure specification, especially an automated one.

test status report

See test summary report.

test strategy

A high-level document defining the test levels to be performed and the testing within those levels for a program (one or more projects).

test suite

A set of several test cases for a component or system under test, where the post condition of one test case is often used as the precondition for the next one.

test summary report

A document summarizing testing activities and results. It also contains an evaluation of the corresponding test against exit criteria. [IEEE 829]

test technique

1. Test case design technique: method used to derive or select test cases.
2. Test execution technique: method used to perform the actual test execution, e.g., manual, capture/playback tool, etc.

testability

The capability of the software product to enable modified software to be tested. [ISO 9126]

See also maintainability.

tester

A skilled professional who is involved in the testing of a component or system.

test-first programming

Software development process where test cases are developed before the code is developed. Other names are test-first design, test-first development, test-driven design or test-driven development.

testing

The process consisting of all life cycle activities, both static and dynamic, concerned with planning, preparation, and evaluation of software products and related work products to determine that they satisfy specified requirements, to demonstrate that they are fit for purpose and to detect defects.

testware

Artifacts produced during the test process required to plan, design, and execute tests, such as documentation, scripts, inputs, expected outcomes, set-up and clear-up procedures, files, databases, environment, and any additional software or utilities used in testing. [Fewster 99]

tuning

Determining what parts of a program are being executed the most, and making changes to improve its performance under certain conditions. A tool that instruments a program to obtain execution frequencies of statements is a tool with this feature.

unit testing

See component testing.

unreachable code

Code that cannot be reached and therefore is impossible to execute.

use case

A sequence of transactions in a dialogue between a user and the system with a tangible result.

use case testing

A black box test design technique in which test cases are designed to execute user scenarios.

user acceptance testing

See acceptance testing.

validation

1. Confirmation by examination and through provision of objective evidence that the requirements for a specific intended use or application have been fulfilled. [ISO 9000]
2. Validation confirms that the product, as provided, will fulfill its intended use. In other words, validation ensures that "you built the right thing." [CMMI 02]
3. Determination of the correctness of the products of software development with respect to the user or customer needs and requirements. ([BS 7925-1] with additions)

verification

1. Confirmation by examination and through the provision of objective evidence that specified requirements have been fulfilled. [ISO 9000]
2. The process of evaluating a system or component to determine whether the products of the given development phase satisfies the conditions imposed at the start of that phase. [IEEE 610.12]
3. Verification confirms that work products properly reflect the requirements specified for them. In other words, verification ensures that "you built it right". [CMMI 02]

version

1. An initial release or re-release of a computer software configuration item, associated with a complete compilation or recompilation of the computer software configuration item. [IEEE 610.12]
2. An initial release or complete re-release of a document, as opposed to a revision resulting from issuing change pages to a previous release.

V-model

A framework to describe the software development life cycle activities from requirements specification to maintenance. The V-model illustrates how testing activities can be integrated into each phase of the software development life cycle.

volume testing

Testing where the system is subjected to large volumes of data.

See also resource utilization testing.

walkthrough

A step-by-step presentation by the author of a document in order to gather information and to establish a common understanding of its content. [Freedman 90], [IEEE 1028]

See also peer review.

white box test design technique

Documented procedure to derive and select test cases based on an analysis of the internal structure of a component or system.

white box testing

Testing based on an analysis of the internal structure of the component or system.

Literature

[Adrion 82] Adrion, W.; Branstad, M.; Cherniabsky, J.: "Validation, Verification and Testing of Computer Software", Computing Surveys, Vol. 14, No 2, June 1982, pp. 159-192.

[Bach 04] Bach, J.: "Exploratory Testing", in [van Veenendaal 04], pp. 209-222.

[Bashir 99] Bashir, I.; Paul, R.A.: "Object-oriented integration testing", Automated Software Engineering, Vol. 8, 1999, pp. 187-202.

[Beck 00] Beck, K.: Extreme Programming, Addison-Wesley, 2000.

[Beedle 01] Beedle, M.; Schwaber, K.: Agile Software Development with Scrum, Prentice Hall, 2001.

[Beizer 90] Beizer, B.: Software Testing Techniques, Van Nostrand Reinhold, 1990.

[Beizer 95] Beizer, B.: Black-Box Testing, John Wiley & Sons, 1995.

[Binder 99] Binder, R.V.: Testing Object-Oriented Systems, Addison-Wesley, 1999.

[Black 02] Black, R.: Managing the Testing Process: Practical Tools and Techniques for Managing Hardware and Software Testing, 2nd ed., John Wiley & Sons, 2002.

[Black 03] Black, R.: Critical Testing Processes, Addison-Wesley, 2003.

[Boehm 73] Boehm, B. W.: "Software and Its Impact: A Quantitative Assessment", Datamation, Vol 19, No. 5, 1973, pp. 48-59.

[Boehm 79] Boehm, B. W.: "Guidelines for Verifying and Validation Software Requirements and Design Specifications", Proceedings of Euro IFIP 1979, pp. 711-719.

[Boehm 81] Boehm, B. W.: Software Engineering Economics, Prentice Hall, 1981.

[Boehm 86] Boehm, B. W.: "A Spiral Model of Software Development and Enhancement", ACM SIGSOFT, August 1986, pp. 14-24.

[Bourne 97] Bourne, K. C.: Testing Client/Server Systems, McGraw-Hill, 1997.

[Bush 90] Bush, M.: "Software Quality: The use of formal inspections at the Jet Propulsion Laboratory", Proceedings of the 12th ICSE, IEEE 1990, pp. 196-199.

[Chow 78] Chow, T.: "Testing Software Design Modeled by Finite-State Machines", IEEE Transactions on Software Engineering, Vol. 4, No 3, May 1978, pp. 178-187.

[Clarke et al. 85] Clarke, L.A.; Podgurski, A.; Richardson, D.J.; Zeil, S.J.: "A Comparison of Data Flow Path Selection Criteria", Proceedings of the 8th International Conference on Software Engineering, August 1985, pp. 244-251.

[CMMI 02] Capability Maturity Model Integration, Version 1.1, CMMI for Systems Engineering, Software Engineering, Integrated Product and Process Development, and Supplier Sourcing (CMMISE/SW/IPPD/SS, V1.1), Staged Representation, CMU/SEI-2002-TR-012, 2002.

[DeMarco 93] DeMarco, T.: "Why Does Software Cost So Much?", IEEE Software, March 1993, pp. 89-90.

[Fagan 76] Fagan, M. E.: "Design and Code Inspections to Reduce Errors in Program Development", IBM Systems Journal, Vol. 15, No. 3, 1976, pp. 182-211.

[Fenton 91] Fenton, N. E.: Software Metrics, Chapman&Hall, 1991.

[Fewster 99] Fewster, M., Graham, D.: Software Test Automation,

Effective use of test execution tools, Addison-Wesley, 1999.

[Freedman 90] Freedman, D. P., Weinberg, G. M.: Handbook of Walk-throughs, Inspections, and Technical Reviews: Evaluating Programs, Projects, and Products, 3rd ed., Dorset House, 1990.

[Gerrard 02] Gerrard, P.; Thompson, N.: Risk-Based E-Business Testing, Artech House, 2002.

[Gilb 96] Gilb, T., Graham, D.: Software Inspections, Addison-Wesley, 1996.

[Gilb 05] Gilb, T.: Competitive Engineering: A Handbook for Systems & Software Engineering Management using Planguage, Butterworth-Heinemann, Elsevier, 2005.

[Hetzel 88] Hetzel, W. C.: The Complete Guide to Software Testing, 2nd ed., John Wiley & Sons, 1988.

[Howden 75] Howden, W.E.: "Methodology for the Generation of Program Test Data", IEEE Transactions on Computers, Vol. 24, No. 5, May 1975, pp. 554-560.

[Jacobson 99] Jacobson, I., Booch, G., Rumbaugh, J.: The Unified Software Development Process, Addison-Wesley, 1999.

[Koomen 99] Koomen, T., Pol, M.: Test Process Improvement: A Practical Step-by-Step Guide to Structured Testing, Addison-Wesley, 1999.

[Kung 95] Kung, D.; Gao, J.; Hsia, P.: "On Regression testing of Object-Oriented Programs", Journal of Systems and Software, Vol. 32, No. 1, Jan 1995, pp. 21-40.

[Link 03] Link, J.: Unit Testing in Java: How Tests Drive the Code, Morgan Kaufmann, 2003.

[Martin 91] Martin, J.: Rapid Application Development. Macmillan, 1991.

[McCabe 76] McCabe, T. J.: "A Complexity Measure", IEEE Transactions on Software Engineering, Vol. SE-2, No. 4, 1976, pp. 308-320.

[Musa 87] Musa, J.: Software Reliability Engineering, McGraw-Hill, 1998.

[Myers 79] Myers, G.: The Art of Software Testing, John Wiley & Sons, 1979.

[Pol 98] Pol, M.; van Veenendaal, E.: Structured Testing of Information Systems – an Introduction to Tmap, Kluver, 1998.

[Pol 02] Pol, M.; Teunissen, R.; van Veenendaal, E.: Software Testing, A guide to the TMap Approach, Addison-Wesley, 2002.

[Rothermel 94] Rothermel, G; Harrold, M.-J.: "Selection Regression Test for Object-Oriented Software", Proceedings of the International Conference on Software Maintenance, 1994, pp. 14-25.

[Royce 70] Royce, W. W.: "Managing the development of large software systems", IEEE WESCON, Aug. 1970, pp. 1-9 (reprinted in Proceedings of the 9th ICSE, 1987, Monterey, CA., pp. 328-338).

[Spillner 00] Spillner, A.: "From V-model to W-model – Establishing the Whole Test Process", Proceedings Conquest 2000 – Workshop on "Testing Nonfunctional Software Requirements", Sept. 2000, Nuremberg, pp. 221-231.

[Stapleton 02] Stapleton, J. (ed.): DSDM: Business Focused Development (Agile Software Development Series), Addison-Wesley, 2002.

[van Veenendaal 04] van Veenendaal, E. (ed.): The Testing Practitioner, UTN Publishers, 2004.

[Winter 98] Winter, M.: Managing Object-Oriented Integration and Regression Testing, Proceeding of the 6'th euroSTAR 98, Munich, 1998, pp. 189-200.

Further recommended literature

Buwalda, H., Jansson, D., Pinkster, I.: Integrated Test Design and Automation, Using the TestFrame Methods, Addison-Wesley, 2002.

Dustin, E., Rashka, J., Paul, J.: Automated Software Testing, Introduction, Management and Performance, Addison-Wesley, 1999.

Jorgensen, Paul C.: Software Testing – A Craftman's Approach, 2nd ed., CRC Press, 2002.

Kaner C., Falk, J., Nguyen, H. Q.: Testing Computer Software, 2nd ed., John Wiley & Sons, 1999.

Kit, E.: Testing in the Real World, Addison-Wesley, 1995.

Ould, M. A., Unwin, C., (ed.): Testing in Software Development, Cambridge University Press, 1986.

Perry, W. E., Effective Methods for Software Testing, John Wiley & Sons, 2000.

Roper, M.: Software Testing, McGraw-Hill, 1994.

Royer, T. C.: Software Testing Management, Prentice Hall, 1993.

Whittaker, J.: How to Break Software, Addison-Wesley, 2003.

Standards

[BS 7925-1] British Standard BS 7925-1, Software Testing, Part 1: Vocabulary, 1998.

[BS 7925-2] British Standard BS 7925-2, Software Testing, Part 2: Software Component Testing, 1998. This standard was basis for the British Computer Society ISEB certification and the earlier version of the ISTQB certification. It will be revised.

[EN 50128] EN 50128: 2001, Railway applications – Communication, signaling and processing systems – Software for railway control and protection systems, European Committee for Electrotechnical Standardization.

[IEEE 610.12] IEEE Std 610.12-1990, IEEE Standard Glossary of Software Engineering Terminology.

[IEEE 730] IEEE Std 730-2002, IEEE Standard for Software Quality Assurance Plans.

[IEEE 828] IEEE Std 828-1998, IEEE Standard for Software Configuration Management Plans.

[IEEE 829] IEEE Std 829-1998, IEEE Standard for Software Test Documentation (under revision, new edition probably in 2006).

[IEEE 830] IEEE Std 830-1998, Recommended Practice for Software Requirements Specifications.

[IEEE 982] IEEE Std 982.2-2003, IEEE Standard Dictionary of Measures of the Software Aspects of Dependability.

[IEEE 1008] IEEE Std 1008-1987: IEEE Standard for Software Unit Testing.

[IEEE 1012] IEEE Std 1012-1998: IEEE Standard for Software Verification and Validation.

[IEEE 1028] IEEE Std 1028-1996: IEEE Standard for Software Reviews.

[IEEE 1044] IEEE Std 1044-1993: IEEE Standard Classification for Software Anomalies.

[IEEE 1219] IEEE Std 1219-1998: IEEE Standard for Software Maintenance.

[IEEE/IEC 12207] IEEE/EIA Std 12207-1996: Information Technology – Software life cycle processes.

[ISO 8402] ISO 8402:1994, Quality management and quality assurance – Vocabulary.

[ISO 9000] ISO 9000:2000, Quality management systems – Fundamentals and vocabulary describes the fundamentals of a QMS and specifies the terminology for a QMS. It was developed on the basis of previous standards: ISO 8402:1994 Quality management and quality assurance – Vocabulary, and lS0 9000-1:1994 Quality management and quality assurance standards – Part 1: Guidelines for selection and use.

[ISO 9126] ISO/IEC 9126-1:2001, Software Engineering – Product quality – Part 1: Quality model, Quality characteristics and subcharacteristics.

[ISO 9241] ISO 9241-1:1997, Ergonomic requirements for office work with visual display terminals (VDTs) – Part 1: General introduction (The standard consists of totally 17 parts [URL: ISO]).

[ISO 14598] ISO/IEC 14598-1:1996, Information Technology – Software Product Evaluation – Part 1: General Overview.

[RTCA-DO 178B] RTCA-DO Std 178B, Radio Technical Commission for Aeronautics, Software Considerations in Airborne Systems and Equipment Certification, RTCA Inc., 1992.

WWW-pages[73]

[URL: BCS] *http://www.bcs.org*
British Computer Society.

[URL: BCS CM Glossary] *http://www.bcs-cmsg.org.uk/glossary.htm*
British Computer Society Configuration Management Glossary.

[URL: FDA] *http://www.fda.gov/cdrh/*
U.S. Food and Drug Administration.

[URL: FMEA] *http://de.wikipedia.org/wiki/FMEA*
Failure Mode and Effects Analysis (Fehlermöglichkeits- und Einflussanalyse).

[URL: HTML] *http://www.w3.org/MarkUp/*
HyperText Markup Language Homepage of the World Wide Web Consortium (W3C).

[URL: imbus 98] *http://www.imbus.de/download/papers/dl_whitepapers.html*
"How to Automate Testing of Graphical User Interfaces", imbus AG.

[URL: imbus-downloads] *http://www.imbus.de/download/papers/dl_whitepapers. html*
Useful articles for downloads.

---

73. The referenced URLs were checked on 12 January 2006. However, it cannot be guaranteed that the URLs remain valid.

[URL: ISEB] *http://www.iseb.org.uk*
Information Systems Examinations Board (ISEB).

[URL: ISTQB] *http://www.istqb.org*
International Software Testing Qualifications Board (ISTQB).

[URL: NIST Report]
http://www.mel.nist.gov/msid/sima/sw_testing_rpt.pdf
"The Economic Impacts of Inadequate Infrastructure for Software Testing", National Institute of Standards & Technology, USA, May 2002.

[URL: RBS] *http://www.rexblackconsulting.com/Pages/Library.htm*
Homepage of RBCS (Rex Black).

[URL: Schaefer] *http://home.c2i.net/schaefer/testinglinks.html*
Homepage of Hans Schaefer.

[URL: TestBench] *http://www.imbus.de/engl/produkte/testbench.shtml*
imbus TestBench.

[URL: Tool-list] *http://www.imbus.de/engl/tool-list.shtml*
Test tool list.

[URL: UML] *http://www.uml.org*
UML-Page of the Object Management Group (OMG).

[URL: V-model XT] *http://www.kbst.bund.de/doc,-304105/Federal-Government-Co-ordinati.htm*
(or *http://www.v-modell-xt.de* in German)

[URL: XML] *http://www.w3.org/XML*
Extensible Markup Language – Homepage of the W3C.

[URL: xunit] *http://www.junit.org*
Component testing framework for Java.
See also *http://opensourcetesting.org*
Open Source Tools for Software Testing Professionals.

Further useful WWW-pages

[URL: BCS SIGIST] *http://www.testingstandards.co.uk*
The British Special Interest Group for Software Testing Standards Working Party.

[URL: IEEE] *http://standards.ieee.org*
Information about IEEE Standards.

[URL: ISO] *http://www.iso.org*
   The International Organization for Standardization.

[URL: SEPT] *http://www.12207.com/index.html*
   Supplying Software Engineering Standards Information to the World.

[URL: SWEBOK] *http://www.swebok.org/ironman/pdf/SWEBOK_
   Guide_2004.pdf*
   Guide to the Software Engineering Body of Knowledge.

Index